Centre

A. Philip Randolph
and the Struggle
for Civil Rights

THE NEW BLACK STUDIES SERIES

Edited by Darlene Clark Hine
and Dwight A. McBride

*A list of books in the series appears
at the end of this book.*

A. Philip Randolph and the Struggle for Civil Rights

CORNELIUS L. BYNUM

UNIVERSITY OF ILLINOIS PRESS

Urbana, Chicago, and Springfield

Library of Congress Cataloging-in-Publication Data
Bynum, Cornelius L.
A. Philip Randolph and the struggle for civil rights /
Cornelius L. Bynum.
 p.   cm. — (New Black studies series)
Includes bibliographical references and index.
ISBN 978-0-252-03575-3 (cloth : alk. paper) —
ISBN 978-0-252-07764-7 (pbk. : alk. paper)
1. Randolph, A. Philip (Asa Philip), 1889–1979. 2. Civil rights
workers—United States—Biography. 3. Civil rights movements—
United States—History—20th century. 4. African Americans—
Civil rights—History—20th century. 5. United States—Race
relations. I. Title.
E185.97.R27B97   2011
323.092—dc22   2010024822
[B]

Contents

Acknowledgments   vii

Introduction   ix

Part 1. Building Black Identity at the Turn of the Century

1. A. Philip Randolph, Racial Identity, and Family Relations:
   Tracing the Development of a Racial Self-Concept   3

2. Religious Faith and Black Empowerment:
   The AME Church and Randolph's Racial Identity
   and View of Social Justice   24

Part 2. Constructing Class Consciousness in the Jazz Age

3. Black Radicalism in Harlem: Randolph's Racial and
   Political Consciousness   47

4. Crossing the Color Line: Randolph's Transition from
   Race to Class Consciousness   63

Part 3. The Rise of the New Crowd Negroes

5. A New Crowd, A New Negro: The *Messenger* and
   New Negro Ideology in the 1920s   85

6. Black and White Unite: Randolph and the Divide
   between Class Theory and the Race Problem   101

Part 4. Blending Race and Class

7. Ridin' the Rails: Randolph and the Brotherhood of
   Sleeping Car Porters' Struggle for Union Recognition   119

8. Where Class Consciousness Falls Short: Randolph and
   the Brotherhood's Standing in the House of Labor   136

9. Marching Toward Fair Employment: Randolph,
   the Race/Class Connection, and the March on
   Washington Movement   157

   Epilogue: A. Philip Randolph's Reconciliation of
   Race and Class in African American Protest Politics   185

   Notes   201

   Bibliography   227

   Index   237

   Illustrations follow page 82

Acknowledgments

I would have never completed this project without the assistance, guidance, and support of several different people. The dissertation that yielded this book was directed with great patience by Olivier Zunz, Commonwealth Professor of History at the University of Virginia. His guidance and demanding attention to detail were central to the development of the core ideas at the heart of this project. In the intervening years he has continued to provide invaluable advice and support. My colleagues in the History Department at Purdue University have been equally important in the development of this book. In big and small ways, they have been instrumental in my development as a scholar and writer. In particular, I would like to thank my department head, R. Douglas Hurt, and Randy Roberts, Susan Curtis, Robert May, Frank Lambert, and Nancy Gabin, each of whom read my work and provided critical feedback that greatly improved the final product.

I would also like to acknowledge the invaluable assistance and professionalism of the library staff at the Schomburg Center for Research in Black Culture, the Newberry Library, and the Library of Congress Manuscripts Division. In particular, I would like to thank Andre Elizee and Steven Fullwood for their willingness to guide me through the Schomburg collections. There are any number of vital documents that I would have overlooked or completely missed without their thoughtful suggestions and encouragement. The staff at the Newberry was equally gracious in guiding me through the Pullman Company collection. And the staff at the Library of Congress efficiently steered me though the National Association for the Advancement of Colored People and the Brotherhood of Sleeping Car Porters collections.

In each case, the librarians that I encountered were cheerful and helpful and made some of the more tedious moments in my research a bit more pleasant.

Lastly, I would like to thank my wife, Mia. I cannot express what your love, support, and encouragement have meant to me. From the moment we met in graduate school, you have been a close confidant, steadfast friend, and companion, and there is simply no way for me to express my gratitude for all that you have done to support and encourage me.

Introduction

When nearly a quarter of a million people, black and white, gathered on the National Mall in late August 1963, they brought to life the signature moment of A. Philip Randolph's long career. Having threatened such a demonstration in 1941 to protest employment discrimination during the Second World War, Randolph was happy to see his idea for a march on Washington resurrected as a mass demonstration of support for President John F. Kennedy's proposed civil rights bill. Indeed, in the aftermath of the civil rights campaign in Birmingham, Alabama, where high-compression water hoses and police dogs shocked the conscience of the nation, the time seemed ripe to push for such legislation. As the crowd gathered and made its way from the Washington Monument to the steps of the Lincoln Memorial, chants of "pass that bill!" ushered forth, and the protest anthem "We Shall Overcome" gave voice to the undeniable spirit of common purpose that suffused the day.

However, few of those that participated in the march were aware of the building behind-the-scenes drama that threatened to mar the demonstration. John Lewis of the Student Nonviolent Coordinating Committee (SNCC) planned to deliver a speech criticizing the Kennedy administration for its lack of civil rights enforcement in the South and calling the president's proposed civil rights bill "too little and too late." In the months and weeks leading up to the march, organizers had worked tirelessly to allay government concerns about rabble rousing and potential violence. For some, Lewis's remarks threatened to stir up the frustrations that brought so many to the nation's capital. When Bayard Rustin, one of the principal orchestrators of the march, asked him to change his remarks, Lewis adamantly refused. The opening speeches were well underway when A. Philip Randolph approached Lewis and his SNCC colleagues about the unresolved conflict. Randolph, too, asked Lewis to change his speech. The seventy-five-year-old veteran activist explained that "he had waited his whole life for this opportunity" and did not want to see it ruined by controversy. This personal appeal from the venerable civil rights stalwart shook Lewis's resolve. As the first speakers made their way to and from the podium, Lewis, Rustin, and Courtland Cox, another executive member of SNCC, huddled together in Lincoln's shadow and rewrote Lewis's speech.[1]

Both march participants and historians of the era typically view the 1963 March on Washington as a triumphant moment for the civil rights movement. It was an equally triumphant moment for A. Philip Randolph. Throughout his career he had sought out mechanisms for illustrating the wide gulf between the principles of freedom and justice and the unfulfilled aspirations of the disempowered and disfranchised. His search led him to profound conclusions about the nature of genuine social justice, the interrelated character of issues of race and class, the effectiveness of interest group politics for racial minorities, and mass direct action. Though spearheaded primarily by others who set out to galvanize support for Kennedy's civil rights bill,[2] the 1963 march ultimately drew on Randolph's ideas in each of these areas to move the nation toward fulfilling its democratic promises for all. For Randolph, who remained a vocal advocate for civil rights up to his death in May 1979, the March on Washington was a culminating achievement that succinctly employed all the various aspects of his social, political, and economic thinking. As such, it was a fitting capstone to a life devoted to social justice.

In the years between the end of the First World War and the Supreme Court's 1954 *Brown v. Board of Education* decision, A. Philip Randolph organized the nation's first all-black trade union, forced the American labor movement to take a hard look at its racial policies and practices, and secured two separate executive orders—one banning workplace discrimination in war industry jobs and the other desegregating the U.S. armed forces. Over the course of Randolph's long career as a socialist, journal editor, labor organizer, and civil rights activist, the theories he formulated became the primary basis of the civil rights protest movement of the 1950s and 1960s. His views on social justice, race and class, racial minorities and interest group politics, and mass direct action largely grew out of his overall life experiences. This study endeavors to understand how the forces that shaped Randolph's life also shaped his conception of race, class, and African Americans' struggle for equal justice.

When Randolph arrived in Harlem in 1911, it marked the beginning of a remarkable personal journey that influenced key events of the interwar years and beyond. In scrutinizing his novel understanding of the intersection of race and class, two movements that have often been at odds with each other, I attempt to present an analytical intellectual history that uses biography to illuminate the origins and evolution of central aspects of Randolph's thought and activism; I examine his contributions to the problems of race, class, civil rights, and the labor movement by connecting his unfolding ideas to specific influences and experiences in his life. Most decidedly not a straightforward biography, this book examines the development of Randolph's social and political thinking to create a new and different intellectual portrait of one of the most important figures in twentieth-century American social history.

In undertaking this examination, I have chosen to concentrate on Randolph's early life and career and elected not to include any detailed treatment of his activism in the 1950s and 1960s. I view his 1950s and 1960s civil rights activism as largely illustrative of his social, political, and economic thinking rather than formative to its development. It was in the interwar years—the 1920s, 1930s, and 1940s—where the sharp contours of his ideas about social justice, race and class, interest group politics, and direct action took shape. The 1963 March on Washington is certainly an important component of Randolph's career, but for the purposes of my study it serves best as the quintessential example of how his social and political thinking fundamentally shaped African Americans' civil rights struggle.

Also, I have chosen to engage the issue of gender in terms of manhood and masculinity because this was the discourse that Randolph deployed in demanding social, political, and economic justice for African Americans. From his writings in the *Messenger* through his defense of the porters' right to bargain collectively and beyond, he adopted a civic rhetoric of manhood that harkened back to Thomas Jefferson and the Declaration of Independence. In this respect, he and prominent West Indian radicals like Hubert Harrison, Richard B. Moore, and Cyril Briggs helped to shape aspects of the Pan-African sentiment that emerged in Harlem in the 1920s. On occasion Randolph did indeed make special cases for or appeals to women, but these instances were not formative moments in his intellectual evolution. Rather, it was the language of manhood and masculinity that was prominent in Randolph's thinking about and articulation of genuine social justice.

My examination of Randolph engages many of the key themes outlined in several recent books on civil rights, citizenship, and African Americans and radical politics. Randolph's role in organizing the Brotherhood of Sleeping Car Porters is well known. But by emphasizing his understanding of the porters' union as a template for effecting economic and social change for black workers, my study overlaps such books as Thomas J. Sugrue's *Sweet Land of Liberty: The Forgotten Struggle for Civil Rights in the North* that broaden the discussion of African Americans' civil rights struggle beyond the Jim Crow South. It also complements conclusions outlined in Beth Tompkin Bates's *Pullman Porters and the Rise of Protest Politics in Black America, 1925–1945,* which examines the porters' role in the advent of mass politics and collective action as key components of African Americans' protest strategy. Randolph's view of economic opportunity as a consequential element for full inclusion in American society fits with new understandings of citizenship presented in such books as Nancy MacLean's *Freedom Is Not Enough: The Opening of the American Workplace,* Meg Jacobs's *Pocketbook Politics: Economic Citizenship in Twentieth-Century America,* and Lizabeth Cohen's *Consumers' Republic: The Politics of Mass Consumption in Postwar America.* Finally, my discussion of Randolph and socialism complements Jeffrey Perry's *Hubert Harrison: The Voice of Harlem Radicalism, 1883–1918* and Joyce Moore Turner's *Caribbean Crusaders and the Harlem Renaissance.* Both scholars probe intersections between race, class, and radical politics among black intellectuals in the early twentieth century.

Randolph's pursuit of equal justice for African Americans led him to conclude that this required that all citizens, regardless of race, be afforded fair access to the economic, civic, social, and political benefits of modern society. Since all races and classes had contributed to humanity's collective development, Randolph argued, all were equally entitled to benefit from civilization's progress. In his view, genuine social justice required the apportionment of full citizenship rights, not by race or class, but rather by the degree to which individuals were willing to perform the civic duties of a faithful citizen. Unlike most socialist critics of industrial capitalism who focused primarily on the organization and ownership of society's productive capacity, Randolph increasingly insisted upon the institution of a managed system as a means of ensuring equal economic, civic, and political participation.

Underlying this notion of genuine social justice was a concept of an open, participatory democracy that is central to understanding Randolph's evolving view of the relationship between the state and its citizens. Beginning in the late 1920s with efforts to enlist federal agencies in support of Pullman porters and their fight for union recognition, Randolph began to outline a definition of citizenship rooted in the premise that all Americans, regardless of race, were entitled to certain basic rights that the government could act to protect but could not nullify. This view influenced aspects of his threatened

1941 march on Washington and was a key philosophical justification for his campaign against Jim Crow in the military in the 1950s. It also influenced his staunch anti-communism. He came to believe deeply that African Americans could achieve equality, freedom, and dignity only within the framework of an open, participatory democracy and viewed communist tactics of infiltration as a threat to this principle. As Randolph devised a vision of social justice that blended essential features of civic, social, and political rights with economic opportunity, he also worked out a notion of citizenship rooted in the open participation of all.

Randolph's view of genuine social justice also reflected an egalitarian outlook that further distinguished his critique of the American system from that of mainstream socialism. Even though he was sometimes a harsh critic of organized religion, Randolph still argued emphatically that "if the children of God are equal before Him, segregation of God's children on account of race, color, religion, national origin, or ancestry, is not only artificial but constitutes a rejection of the idea of the fatherhood of God and is, thus, sacrilegious."[3] As such assertions became more central to his arguments against the social, political, and economic constrictions that relegated African Americans to second-class status, Randolph gave stronger voice to an egalitarian claim for equality that differed markedly from the conventional labor theory of value. Underscoring such ideas as the universal brotherhood of man and fatherhood of God, Randolph bolstered his conception of genuine social justice by investing it with religious and moral sanction. In forcefully asserting man's common humanity, he located this religious and moral appeal in a broader egalitarianism that gave an added dimension to his conception of social justice.

Randolph's framing of genuine social justice in egalitarian terms did not in any way distract him from recognizing the specific ways that race and class issues worked together to affect the lives of African Americans. Not only did African Americans face the basic class concerns that troubled all workers in the Depression era and beyond, but Randolph saw firsthand in organizing the porters' union that race still trumped class in corporate boardrooms and on the shop floor. He came to understand that racial discrimination operated as an additional obstacle that severely limited the effectiveness of strict class theory in addressing the needs and concerns of black workers. In fact, he would come to argue with increasing passion that race and class were inextricably linked for black workers. Even as the Brotherhood of Sleeping Car Porters stood on the brink of victory in its fight for union recognition, Randolph began to articulate a broader political agenda that encouraged black workers to simultaneously pursue their general economic or class interests as well as their specific racial needs.

This dual race and class consciousness that became a more central feature of his point of view in the 1930s reflected Randolph's evolving conviction that there could be no social justice for African Americans without basic economic justice. This view partly explains his continued connection to the Socialist Party even as the racial realities of organizing black workers undercut key tenets of the party's strict class appeals. He was convinced that wholesale reform of industrial capitalism would be necessary if African Americans were ever to secure genuine social justice. But as the Brotherhood's struggle for union recognition made increasingly clear, race complicated class concerns for African Americans in special ways. Randolph looked to fashion a blended strategy of race and class consciousness precisely to address this dynamic. His growing belief that social justice and economic opportunity went hand in hand ultimately comprised the basis of his determination to reconcile race and class. It was putting this notion into practical action that compelled him to take up the fair employment issue that led to the creation of the Fair Employment Practice Committee in 1941.

Inherent to Randolph's view of the link between race and class was a sense that civil rights lacked meaningful social substance without real economic opportunity. From the mid-1930s on, he persistently argued that though equality was central to democracy, freedom, and justice, African Americans were destined to remain second-class citizens unless granted economic and educational equality as well.[4] This emphasis on the economic basis of black freedom and equality further supported his contention that it was vitally important for African Americans to recognize and act on both their specific racial needs and general class interests. In building the porters' union, Randolph not only paid attention to how better labor organization might improve the specific conditions under which Pullman porters and maids worked, but he was equally concerned with using the Brotherhood as a platform for building a purposeful coalition between black and white workers behind progressive reform. From the late 1920s and 1930s through the 1960s, Randolph consistently worked to bridge the divide between African American civil rights and the American labor movement.[5]

One of the consequences of the Pullman porters' long and drawn-out struggle for recognition was Randolph's growing understanding of the potential of pressure politics for improving African Americans' lives. The demographic transformations that affected the political landscapes of cities like New York and Chicago as a result of black migration north became even more significant as Roosevelt's New Deal coalition created new political opportunities for African Americans, labor unions, and progressive reformers. For Randolph and the porters, this was an especially important development. Through the middle and late 1930s, Congress routinely ignored or overlooked the needs of African Americans in drafting labor legislation that dramatically improved the position of unions in these years. Although he continued to lobby sympathetic congressmen on the need to include African Americans under these new laws, Randolph came to understand that African Americans fundamentally lacked the political muscle needed in the war of competing interests that shaped and passed bills in Congress.

It was in pursuing favorable executive orders that addressed African Americans' needs rather than ineffective legislative lobbying that Randolph put his deepening understanding of interest group politics to good use. Even though he continued to appear before congressional committees and to meet with select members of Congress throughout the 1930s and 1940s, Randolph recognized that it was in the executive branch that he could concentrate what political leverage African Americans did possess to best effect. This strategy was even more useful in the postwar political climate when southern Democrats began to leave the Democratic Party and African American political strength outside the Jim Crow South grew. Both the threatened 1941 march on Washington and Randolph's subsequent civil disobedience campaign against Jim Crow in the military served to mobilize African Americans and generate sufficient political pressure for social change. Both campaigns reflected Randolph's deepening understanding of how minority groups could successfully maneuver in the context of American interest group politics and set the stage for the 1963 March on Washington.

Randolph's understanding of interest group politics also shaped his view of mass direct action as an effective tactic for changing the nation's racial status quo. As Congress passed new laws regulating collective bargaining in the late 1920s and 1930s that still left most black workers unprotected, Randolph became more determined to devise a strategy for pressuring the federal government into extending social and economic rights to African Americans. As the porters' struggle had made abundantly clear, neither corporations nor labor unions nor federal agencies were going to deal with black workers fairly without being compelled by some significant force. He began to look to programs of independent black organization and actions to generate the kind of force necessary to make government officials adhere to principles of freedom and justice. This understanding of the formula of mass organization and pressure politics shaped his March on Washington initiative and became a central feature of his strategy of mass direct action.

Equally important to Randolph's notion of mass direct action was his conception of nonviolent civil disobedience. Although he had at different times in his career endorsed the violent overthrow of oppression, Randolph began to explore ways in which African Americans could use civil disobedience as a mass action strategy in pushing for full citizenship rights. He understood that through such noncompliance African Americans could not only forcefully demonstrate their discontent with racial discrimination and segregation but also draw specific attention to the ways that discrimination and segregation fundamentally undercut core tenets of American democracy. He argued that the widespread institution of Jim Crow so violated American principles of equality and justice that African Americans were obligated to challenge such laws through nonviolent noncompliance. This particular strain of mass direct action marked the course of black protest activity through the civil rights movement of the 1960s.

Together chapters 1 and 2 analyze key factors that helped to shape Randolph's early racial identity. Both his early home life and his upbringing in the African Methodist Episcopal (AME) Church in Jacksonville, Florida, shaped basic aspects of his personality, character, and worldview. It is critical to understand their formative influences to appreciate fully Randolph's subsequent contributions to the civil rights and labor movements. Specifically, chapter 1 examines the direct impact each member of Randolph's immediate family had on his early race consciousness and underscores the predominant influence his family had on his sense of himself and his place in the world. Chapter 2 picks up on this examination by looking at the influence of the AME Church and its liberation theology on Randolph's racial views and understanding of social justice. The church and the liberation gospel that shaped its very founding helped to guide Randolph's subsequent ideas about social justice that blended egalitarian messages about racial self-worth and industrial reform and shaped core elements of his subsequent civil rights and labor activism.

Chapters 3 and 4 focus on Randolph's transition to Harlem and introduction to class theories. In detailing his move north, chapter 3 situates Randolph in a cohort of black radicals in Harlem that deeply influenced the community in the years leading up to World War I. Accurately locating Randolph in this radical milieu is important for outlining the critical ways that his positions on such issues as social justice came to differ from other notable Harlem intellectuals in the later 1910s and 1920s. Chapter 4 examines Randolph's introduction to class theory and entrance into the Socialist Party. Looking at his brief period of study at City College of New York, his involvement in Socialist Party politics in 1920s New York, and his effort to bridge factional lines within the party helps to illustrate exactly how Randolph thought to apply class-based solutions to problems of race.

Chapters 5 and 6 examine how Randolph used the articles and editorials published in the *Messenger* in an effort to translate African Americans' growing postwar discontent with the racial status quo into momentum for a broader revision of industrial capitalism. Chapter 5 details how through the pages of the *Messenger* Randolph worked to cast the New Negro racial militancy of the Harlem Renaissance in a broader class-conscious frame and highlight the ways that class solidarity vitally served the mutual interests of black and white workers. Chapter 6 concentrates on Randolph's deepening conviction that racial discrimination had economic roots. Between the end of World War I and the founding of the Brotherhood of Sleeping Car Porters, he used the *Messenger* to promote an elaborate class-conscious philosophy centered on labor solidarity, the mutual economic interests of black and white workers, and industrial unionism to channel African American racial militancy toward the growing labor militancy of the period.

Chapters 7, 8, and 9 point to a fundamental shift in Randolph's understanding of the efficacy of strict class-consciousness in addressing the problems of racism and discrimination. Chapter 7 chronicles the initial organization of the porters' union to demonstrate how the challenges it faced in securing union recognition transformed Randolph's thinking about straightforward class-consciousness and the problems of race. Chapter 8 continues this line of inquiry by examining the various steps Randolph and the Brotherhood took to address porters' workplace grievances. As clear-cut racial discrimination fundamentally undercut simple class-based solutions to the porters' problems, Randolph began to fashion a new understanding of the importance of a dual awareness of race and class. Chapter 9 looks at Randolph's promotion of fair employment and the advent of the Fair Employment Practice Committee (FEPC) as part of the vital link between African Americans' civil and political rights and economic needs that constituted the basis of his dual race and class consciousness. The conception of social justice at the root of his views about fair employment and the tactics used to force the creation of the FEPC ultimately laid the foundation for core features of the civil rights movement that was to come.

The primary sources for this book are largely drawn from Randolph's published writings in the *Messenger* and *Black Worker,* two of the journals that he edited, and unpublished materials housed at the Schomburg Center for Research in Black Culture in New York City and the Library of Congress, in Washington, D.C. These collections include Randolph's own papers and those of fellow Harlem radicals Frank R. Crosswaith and Richard B. Moore. Each of these collections contains extensive correspondence on socialism and radical politics, labor organization, and civil rights as well as organizational records and copies of speeches, editorials, and press releases the three men wrote addressing all manner of questions on race, racial discrimination, and African Americans' fight for full citizenship. Together they paint a detailed picture of Randolph's intellectual life, especially in the 1920s and 1930s, as well as his various organizing and protest activities.

Additionally, I used more institutional sources from the Brotherhood of Sleeping Car Porters Collection held at the Library of Congress and Pullman Company records from the Newberry Library in Chicago. These collections contain materials that outline Randolph and the porters' strategies for challenging racial discrimination and company and union resistance to recognizing black workers' claims. They contain court records, transcripts of administrative hearings, legal briefs, and correspondence between Randolph, Brotherhood officials, Pullman executives, union leaders, and federal agencies that detail the inner workings of the Brotherhood of Sleeping Car Porters and their struggle for union recognition. Collectively these sources bolster and effectively balance the largely personal reflections of the Randolph, Crosswaith, and Moore collections and objectively substantiate my conclusions about Randolph's evolving views about race, class, and the economic components of racial discrimination.

Randolph's understanding of interest group politics and mass action were significant developments in the evolution of his social and political thinking. Both drew directly on his ideas that genuine social justice required fair access to civil and economic rights and that race and class posed unique challenges for black workers. But his understanding of interest group politics and mass action also set new parameters for black political activism going forward. Even though subsequent efforts to challenge racial discrimination in other facets of American life refined all of these ideas somewhat, the basic premise of Randolph's understanding of these key constructs remained largely unchanged. His ideas undoubtedly shaped the philosophical, tactical, and strategic foundations of African Americans' civil rights struggle, and the 1963

March on Washington stands as the quintessential example of their impact. While it was the stirring oratory of Martin Luther King Jr. that aroused the nation in August 1963, it was Randolph's pioneering understanding of social justice, race and class, interest group politics, and mass action that made the moment possible. Indeed, it is difficult to comprehend the full measure of America's social and political development in the years between World War I and King's assassination in 1968 without fully grasping Randolph's social, political, and economic ideas.

PART 1

Building Black Identity
at the Turn of the Century

1

A. Philip Randolph, Racial Identity, and Family Relations

Tracing the Development of a Racial Self-Concept

Asa Philip Randolph remembered everything about his childhood. He remembered that his hometown of Jacksonville, Florida, was a racially divided city where African Americans still managed to thrive.[1] He remembered that east of Florida Avenue was the Oakland neighborhood where the city's leading African Americans lived and he first attended school. He remembered that on the corner of Jefferson and West Ashley was the Finkelstein building that initially housed a grocery store but eventually became the Hotel de Dreme, one of the city's most notorious bordellos. And he remembered the Richmond Hotel on Broad Street where in later years jazz luminaries like Cab Calloway, Billie Holiday, and Ella Fitzgerald would stay. But most of all, he remembered the great fire of 1901 that destroyed significant portions of Jacksonville's African American community.[2]

Randolph's parents and brother, the most important influences in his early life, also made lasting impressions on him. The second of James William and Elizabeth Robinson Randolph's two sons, Asa Randolph remembered his father as a dignified man who lacked even "the slightest air of arrogance or aloofness" and his mother as a tall and slender woman with a light complexion and long, wavy black hair.[3] He described his brother James as a thoughtful but rambunctious child who never backed down from an argument even when it was "moving toward the brink of a fight."[4] In their own unique ways, Randolph's father, mother, and brother all taught him important lessons that he carried throughout his life. His parents both worked diligently to create a home "passionately devoted" to race that served as a bulwark against white supremacy, while his brother's "determined and strong willed character" further encouraged Randolph to develop the resiliency needed to survive in the Jim Crow South.[5]

Born on April 15, 1889, Asa Randolph came of age during the years when Jim Crow and racial violence came to dominate most aspects of African American life in the South.[6] To avoid the worst aspects of the discrimination and violence that became even more brutal through the 1890s, his family generally withdrew into the relative security of home and church life. Asa's childhood, therefore, was primarily characterized by "prayer, poverty, and pride." Both his parents generally valued ideas over material possessions and looked to race pride, education, and religious instruction to buffer their children from the harshest features of the southern reign of terror.[7] Asa recalled that even when he was a small child, the family's conversations generally centered on discussions of race and African American history, the small family library, and the publications of the AME Church. As a result, even as customary segregation and discrimination gained legal sanction,[8] self-respect, race pride, education, and religious faith became the core values that anchored his early life.

From the very "earliest periods" of his recollections, self-esteem and race pride were central characteristics of Asa's upbringing. One of his earliest memories focused on the vivid stories his father told him and his brother about Harriet Tubman, Frederick Douglass, Nat Turner, and the other "Negro leaders who fought for liberty and justice right in the fires of slavery." Even as these stories painted a clear picture of the racial obstacles African Americans faced, they nurtured Asa's sense of self and race by casting the act of standing against racial oppression in heroic terms. It was through such family interactions that he first began to develop a deep racial awareness.[9]

James Randolph also routinely discussed with his children news items relating to African Americans that appeared in Jacksonville's local newspapers or the AME Church journals, the *Christian Recorder* and the *A.M.E. Church Review*. Often these family conversations about current events, typically held at the dinner table or around the fireplace in the evenings, centered on the basic tension between Booker T. Washington and W. E. B. Du Bois regarding the best means of racial uplift.[10] Though the elder Randolph readily acknowledged a certain practicality in Washington's program of industrial education, he nonetheless firmly believed that Du Bois's philosophy was the "sounder one."[11] A father who "never missed an opportunity" to impress upon his sons that they were as good as any white boys, James Sr. no doubt found Washington's apparent concessions to white supremacy questionable.[12] If the color line was the problem of the twentieth century, James Randolph, like Du Bois, believed that its long-term solution rested in African American culture, education, and organization.

Asa remembered such family debates partly because they further energized his parents' determination to shape his education. He understood that neither of his parents had much formal schooling, and this, in turn, fueled a special "passion" on their part to see that their children received the best education available. Even as a young child, Asa recognized that his father was determined to turn him and his brother into diligent readers. The elder Randolph required both Asa and James Jr. to spend some portion of every day reading. This particular stipulation, Asa pointed out years later, most certainly made his childhood home a "reading household." Even though the family's "fragmentary" library contained only the Bible and a few books by naturalist and evangelist Henry Drummond, Asa explained that his father frequently conducted tutorials where he had the boys read aloud while he corrected their diction. In this way, Asa noted, his father emphasized not only the importance of reading with comprehension but also that the reading of a paragraph "sound with proper resonance and light and shade."[13]

As Asa and his brother grew older and began exploring their own intellectual pursuits, their father continued to shape their thinking. Noting that the "dominant climate" of his childhood was one of ideas, Asa observed that he and his brother read Herbert Spencer, Robert Ingersoll, and Thomas Paine at early ages and spent countless evenings engaged in the "intellectual gymnastics" of proving the existence of God. Steeped in the methodology of scientific empiricism, he recollected that these debates were often "interminable" because they could never ascertain any "absolute, logical proof on the affirmative or negative." Asa remembered that his father participated actively in these verbal jousts, often pointing out that the search for God could not be conducted solely through the "instruments of reason and logic." Instead, the elder Randolph insisted that the answers that Asa and his brother sought could only be found with "the force of Christian faith."[14] Even as he encouraged intellectual independence in his children, James Randolph still hoped to guide their development.

He was equally determined to affect his sons' racial awareness and self-esteem. Recognizing his father as a man "dedicated" to racial progress, Asa noticed that the elder Randolph "never failed to emphasize" as a "historic fact" that all of the characters of the Bible—Christ, God, Moses, Peter—were not white as commonly depicted but "colored or swarthy." Even as he corrected their reading of the Scriptures, James Sr. was equally focused on correcting his children's perceptions of African Americans' place in history and the world. Though never quite clear on the extent to which his father understood the "economic, political, social, and psychological" implications of depicting God as white, Asa nonetheless believed that these conversations with his father engendered "a deep sense of solace and belonging and inner faith in the future."[15]

The focus on reading and family discussions that so vividly filled Asa's reminiscences also fit with his parents' broader plan to supplement their children's education. But as Asa explained later, this "entertainment of conversation" also became the central mechanism for teaching him and his brother about the critical issues that confronted African Americans at the end of the nineteenth century.[16] Throughout his childhood and adolescence, reading and discussing the *A.M.E. Review* and the *Christian Recorder* were staple forms of family interaction in the Randolph household. Both church periodicals, in fact, came to affect Asa's early racial and political consciousness in significant ways. As the AME Church extended its influence in the South in the aftermath of the Civil War,[17] both the *Review* and the *Recorder* devoted greater attention to the problems of racial violence and discrimination. The *Recorder*, however, was particularly significant in shaping Asa's evolving racial and political views. After the Civil War, it featured secular issues more prominently than the *Review* and placed special emphasis on fostering a national consciousness among African Americans.[18] As such, the *Recorder* was not only a source of information about church activities and other issues concerning African Americans but also stood second only to the Bible as a tool for teaching the Randolph children about the world in which they lived.[19]

These family conversations about *Recorder* articles and editorials frequently involved historical discussions of black achievement.[20] As the *Recorder* focused more and more on the intensifying racial violence of the 1890s and African Americans' response to it, Asa appreciated that these history lessons became a critical counterbalance to the propaganda of white supremacy.[21] Keenly interested in his father's interests and opinions, Asa listened eagerly when James Randolph recounted the ancient histories of Egypt and Ethiopia and their past glories. He remembered clearly that his father savored such moments, insisting that one day Ethiopia would once again "stretch forth her hand to God." The elder Randolph also relished any opportunity to tell his sons about the days during Reconstruction when black Republicans served in Congress and state legislatures throughout the South.[22] Even as a young child, Asa marked the wide discrepancies between his father's accounts of African and African

American history and the accounts of southern Redeemers. He recalled that this revelation led to his eventual realization that his father, though "not apparently anti-white," was "definitely pro-Negro and [supported] the darker races."[23] Soaking up the rich racial heritage imparted by these stories and ultimately recognizing his father's unmistakable race consciousness led Asa to a new awareness of his own developing racial identity. More importantly, perhaps, Asa emphasized that the profound contradictions between the racial oppression outlined in the *Recorder* and his father's accounts of Africa's ancient past left him convinced that there was no legitimate cause for systematically denying African Americans equal protection under the law.

African American history was an especially important component of James Randolph's "fireplace kindergarten." Asa and his brother were particularly affected by accounts of people who opposed racial oppression during slavery. As he recollected later, even though the stories of African Americans holding political office during Reconstruction were exciting, Richard Allen was the "first black hero" in whom he and his brother took a serious interest.[24] Allen not only founded the AME Church but was a central figure in the nineteenth-century Negro convention movement that played a critical role in the shaping of militant abolitionism. In addition, stories of Toussaint L'Ouverture, the African slave who led a "devastatingly successful" slave revolt in Haiti in 1792 that ended slavery and resulted in the creation of an independent black state, were compelling. Sojourner Truth also figured prominently in Asa's memories of these childhood history lessons. Acknowledging her as an "illiterate, but not ignorant" woman whose "eloquent plea" for black freedom set the nation afire, he stressed that his father's depiction of her crusade made a "dramatic" impression on him.[25] In relating such stories about prominent African Americans and their courage to oppose racial oppression, James Randolph helped to construct a broad historical perspective on African Americans' struggle for equality that positively affected his sons' racial and individual self-esteem.

Emphasizing self-respect, race pride, education, and religious faith, Asa's upbringing nurtured a profound racial worldview that stood in direct contrast to key features of white supremacy. Though driven mostly by his father's deep racial sensibilities, Asa's mother and brother also made unique contributions to his intellectual and personal development and greatly affected his racial awareness. As a result, even as race relations in the South deteriorated in the face of Jim Crow's spread, the lessons, values, and experiences of Asa's childhood engendered a fuller understanding of Africa's contributions to the world and African Americans' struggle against racial discrimination that underlined his subsequent belief in equal justice. Indeed, despite becoming one of the country's foremost African American socialists in the years to come, the race consciousness and self-esteem inculcated by his parents in these early years continued to shape Asa's view of the world throughout his life.

James William Randolph was born in Monticello, Florida, in 1864. Many details of his early life are unclear because he seldom spoke of his parents except to explain that they were both dead and that his father had been a slave. He did have at least one sister, who also eventually moved to Jacksonville with her son, Willie. Though Asa had no proof as to whether or not his father had also been a slave, he believed that James Randolph exhibited "none of the marks of physical abuse, cruelty, and hardship" normally associated with slavery. Asa instead depicted his father as a sparingly built man who always projected a sense of polish and refinement. With a long, high nose, thin lips, and silvery, silken hair, James Randolph "seemed to etch the artist rather than the preacher" even when dressed in his frock coat, clerical collar, and vestments of his ministry. Much like his sister, a woman Asa described as quiet, lovely, and refined, the elder Randolph exhibited an air of "delicacy and sensitivity" that his youngest son always considered ill-suited to the life of an itinerant preacher.[26]

In both Crescent City and Jacksonville, Florida, where the Randolph family moved in 1891, Asa noted that his father was generally well liked and respected. In fact, to his knowledge, his father was never involved in any kind of altercation or conflict with any of their neighbors. Everyone was friendly toward James Sr. because he was kind and neighborly. If one of their neighbors was in trouble or needed help, Asa pointed out that he or she was likely to show up at the Randolph house looking for his father. Not only was James Randolph faithful to the Christian directive to love thy neighbor as thyself, but as a preacher he also set high moral standards for himself and his family. In fact, Asa described his father as "essentially a Calvinist." Even though there was "nothing inherently immoral" about drinking alcohol in moderation, Asa recalled that he never once witnessed his father drink an alcoholic beverage or allow a deck of cards in the house. Honest and straightforward with everyone with whom he dealt, Reverend Randolph steadfastly condemned strong drink, lewd women, and gambling.[27]

Such moral standards not only governed the family's interaction with the surrounding community but also served as a measure of protection against much of the racial violence that characterized the South at the turn of the century. As the lynchings of the 1890s gave way to race riots in the early 1900s, African Americans watched as the violence and terror that permeated black life in the rural South spread as they sought to escape sharecropping through migration to cities in the North and South.[28] Yet, the escalating racial violence of the period had little effect on the Randolph family. Even in the Deep South where local officials often helped to orchestrate racial violence against African Americans, the Randolphs exhibited little fear of local law enforcement because they never did anything to draw the attention of the sheriff. Asa explained that "the police who patrolled the community on horseback never entered our yard or turned at our gate" because they never had reason to. In this regard, the quiet and sober life that James and Elizabeth Randolph created for their family mostly hid their home from the South's lynch law.[29]

In addition to the moral example that he set for his sons, Reverend Randolph's upright lifestyle also contributed to his position as a community leader among Jacksonville's black population. Ordained into the ministry in 1884, James Randolph pastored several churches as a circuit preacher for the AME Church and founded New Hope AME Church on Davis and Eighth streets in Jacksonville.[30] Though devout in his Christian beliefs, the elder Randolph was equally dedicated to maintaining a home "pervaded" by an "atmosphere of independence, self-assertion, and fearlessness." When rumors began to circulate that local whites intended to lynch a black prisoner in the Duvall County jail, he gathered together some of the men of the community to stand guard at the jail. He collected his rifle and "bull dog" pistol that he kept in a bedroom drawer, and throughout the afternoon and early evening, he prepared for a possible confrontation later that night. As the men he had recruited began to gather at the house, James Randolph gave his rifle to his wife with instructions to safeguard the house and children. Elizabeth Randolph "promptly" put out the house lamps, took a seat near the window overlooking the front porch, and stood vigil throughout the night with the rifle across her lap. The next morning when James Randolph returned home, Asa described overhearing his father explain to his mother that a mob did show up to take the prisoner but backed down when armed "Negroes dared them to approach the jail." Even though worry and fear coursed through him the entire night, Asa nonetheless noted what a "wonderful feeling" it was "to know that mother could protect the home when father was away."[31]

The events surrounding his father's role in this jailhouse standoff were a seminal moment in Asa's young life. Although it is not exactly clear how much detail his parents shared with him and his brother about that night, Asa clearly remembered not only that this incident left him "greatly concerned," but that it was also very "exciting and dramatic." The next morning when he quizzed his mother about her actions the night before and why she did not fire the rifle, she casually responded that there was no reason to because "nothing happened." His father was equally circumspect about that evening's events. Yet, despite such efforts to downplay the urgency and danger associated with facing down a lynch mob, Asa and his brother developed the clear and lasting impression of their father as "a peaceful man who believed in the non-violent philosophy of Jesus Christ" but who "evidently considered action with some of the neighbors in this crisis a community responsibility." Though his father may have been a preacher, Asa noticed that when it came to lynching African Americans, his father clearly "had that feeling of resentment against this form of persecution of the Negro." Even as the Randolphs withheld details of that night's events from their children, Asa nonetheless learned a very real lesson about the importance of a forceful, organized, and collective response to racial intimidation in protecting black lives. As he grew older, both his parents worked to reinforce this idea.[32]

Through accounts of Africa's history, African Americans' struggle to overthrow slavery and racial oppression, and such personal acts of courage, the elder Randolph made an indelible impression on his younger son's developing racial identity. Though the central themes of white supremacy generally emphasized African Americans' racial inferiority, James Randolph's fireside stories and brave opposition to racial intimidation fundamentally undercut such contentions for Asa and his brother. Both grew up with a distinctly positive racial self-image rooted in a deep appreciation of their racial heritage and their parents' unbent spirit in the face of racial violence. James Randolph had an equally powerful impact on Asa's personal character.

Although Asa jokingly referred to his father as a "proletarian preacher" because most of "his time was taken up as a worker rather than as a preacher," some of his fondest memories from childhood were of the frequent trips he took with his father to visit the churches to which he was assigned.[33] Quite often these trips involved traveling some distance. Asa and his father frequently traveled by steamboat down the St. James River from Jacksonville to the "rickety" wharfs of the small villages that lined the river. On such occasions they were sometimes met by a church member with an ox cart to carry them the rest of the way. More often than not, however, they had to walk the distance from the river to the cabin of the church deacon or trustee with whom they were to stay. For Asa, these journeys "trudging" along the "stumpy, zigzag, and intermittently muddy" backwoods roads of north Florida with his father were treasured moments. "Quite often," he explained, "there was no one on the road but father and I, and we would listen to the noises and music and deep, mystic silence of the jungle woods." On particularly hot days they would stop to rest under a shady tree and talk about his mother and brother.[34]

Once they reached their destination, they were "greeted with a warmth of welcomes and affection from old and young who gathered around to shake hands, embrace, and kiss us." After settling into the room where they were to spend the night, a room that generally had a ceiling through which they could see the stars at night and a pallet of colorful homemade quilts spread on the floor, Asa and his father reconvened with the rest of the church group in the cabin's main room. At this point, the gathered church members would recite a list of the dead and sick and ask Reverend Randolph to pray for them. Dinner followed these prayer requests, and everyone gathered around the table to bless the food and eat. Following dinner, the children would escape to the front yard to play while the adults continued to talk. Asa remembered that these play sessions were usually "short-lived," because "Saturday night was bath night, and then there was Sunday school the following morning." So once the tub and basin had done their duty for the evening, everyone retired for the night. As he noted, "even the dogs stopped barking in the country earlier than the more sophisticated city canine."[35]

The next morning usually began with breakfast and Sunday school. Asa always enjoyed attending Sunday school on these trips with his father because the little one-room churches that they visited allowed him to hear the questions and answers of all the teachers and students. Naturally, he was a good Sunday school student because he "heard scripture lessons read practically every day and night of the year" and, as a result, was "compelled" to absorb at least some of them. After Sunday school the other children usually got to go home. Asa admitted that he greatly "envied" their reprieve, for his "lot was always to remain at church with father and mother when at home and with father when away from home for morning service." As the pastor's son, he was expected to sit in the "highly churchly location" known as the "Amen corner" with the church trustees and steward board. "Although I grew weary sitting on the hard wooden benches," Asa resigned himself to his fate because he understood that "there was no escape." Morning services always began when James Randolph stepped up to the pulpit. Though there usually was no choir or musical accompaniment, there was no lack of singing in the country churches that Reverend Randolph pastored, because he and the church officers would always lead the congregation in song.[36]

James Randolph was a "devout, evangelical, shouting type of preacher" who always began his sermons from a written outline but, Asa explained, always ended with an extemporaneous "emotional outburst which evoked numerous 'Amens,' 'preach it Reverend,' and various unintelligible exclamations" from the congregation. As a circuit preacher, a minister charged with leading two or more congregations, Reverend Randolph usually planned his church travels to coincide with Communion Sundays when, Asa noted, witness testimony was "as a rule, hysterically, if not dramatically," given by church members. Though no one was "expected" to take Communion except those who had "lived close to God and not backslidden from Grace," from his vantage point at the front of the church, Asa always knew those "hypocrites who put on a pious face and partook of His blood and body in order to get or maintain status among the loyal members who were known to be pure in heart." At the close of the service, the church trustees turned over the money collected as church offering. According to Asa, his father seldom brought home paper money from his weekend visits unless it was nearing the time of the church's Annual Conference. At such times, James Randolph was expected to raise a dollar from each member of his congregations. The otherwise meager weekly collection of nickels, dimes, and quarters seldom added up to more than three dollars. Sometimes church members who had no money to give instead brought potatoes, smoked ham, or other food items. Asa remembered that, as a rule, the two or three churches that made up his father's circuit "hardly ever" provided more than ten dollars a month in income. In fact, Asa noted, it quite often added up to much less though his father "always came home with potatoes, some part of a hog and, perhaps, some vegetables."[37]

To supplement the meager income generated by his preaching, the elder Randolph also worked out of his home as a tailor. He had one of the only shops in the community that did cleaning, dyeing, pressing, and repairs; it also had a largely white clientele.[38] Although he also had black customers as well, Asa remembered that "those who failed to pay for work done were chiefly Negroes," and his soft-hearted father would take "almost any hard luck story" from customers who could not pay. As a general rule, James Randolph generated business for his shop by canvassing the community in the morning to solicit work and doing repairs in the afternoon. Because the shop was in the home, it was essentially a family enterprise in which everyone but Asa's brother James participated. Elizabeth Randolph was "quite capable of running the shop alone" and did so on those occasions when her husband's ministry took him away from home. Asa pitched in by cleaning and pressing suits but was not trusted with dyeing because it involved mixing dyes and boiling clothes until they were properly dyed; only experience could teach when a garment was adequately boiled. Despite the family's entrepreneurial spirit and "fairly good" returns on occasion, the business never generated "sufficient prosperity at any time to provide a surplus above expenses" that might permit the family to save or achieve a higher standard of living.[39]

This lack of income compelled James Randolph, the household's primary breadwinner, to seek out other means of supporting the family. Asa recollected that his father occasionally ventured into the meat market business for brief periods despite Elizabeth Randolph's misgivings about such undertakings. Although little start-up capital was seemingly necessary for such an enterprise, an important factor considering that James Randolph was "never able to accumulate any savings," he never operated his business for more than a month or so at a time. Even with the in-kind payments of meat that he frequently received from the rural churches he served, Asa noted that his father lacked sufficient capital to stock his business properly. Even as a child, Asa recalled worrying about a "meat market with very little meat." James Sr. also refused to keep the market open for longer periods because he was afraid of getting into debt beyond his ability to repay.

As the sharecropping system that dominated southern agriculture in the late nineteenth century came to depend on spiraling cycles of debt to entrap tenant farmers, James Randolph's concerns about debt in part reflected a very real understanding of one key economic mechanism for exploiting African Americans in the South.[40] The elder Randolph also tried his hand at selling firewood to supplement the family's income. With the idea of duplicating the success of his father-in-law who ran a marginally profitable wood yard in Baldwin, Florida, James Sr. decided to rent a horse and cart and hire a man to help him sell wood in the neighborhood. Unfortunately, his chronic lack of capital prevented him from purchasing sufficient quantities of wood to negotiate a low enough wholesale price to make a retail profit.

The failure of these various business ventures led Asa to some very early conclusions about his father's business acumen. Despite Reverend Randolph's zeal to provide for his family, it was quite clear to his younger son that he was "much too big and generous-hearted" to succeed as a businessman. Asa understood that with both the meat market and wood yard, his father too frequently extended credit to his customers and then "vainly" waited for them to pay the bill. Though such generosity served his religious convictions, Asa pointed out that it was flawed as a practice of good business. "It is almost axiomatic," he reflected later, "that one without credit can hardly afford to give it."[41] Despite such criticism of his father's business judgment, Asa nonetheless respected his flexibility and determination in trying to provide for the family.

One consequence of James Randolph's entrepreneurial missteps was that Asa and his brother James learned to assess material wealth in different ways. "While our table fare was humble," Asa noted, "I can never remember being without some kind of food in the home, and brother James and I were always served without stint or limit." Even though Reverend Randolph's generosity may have cost the family some of life's material comforts, it never deprived Asa of life's necessities; they may have been poor, but James Randolph "was a good provider" who "gave everything that he had to his family." This understanding complemented other values that James and Elizabeth Randolph set out to teach their children. Though he and his brother occasionally disobeyed their parents and sometimes "handled the truth a bit loosely," Asa pointed out that they were really "incapable of being dishonest." The most "basic reason" for their essential integrity, he reasoned, was the lack of emphasis his parents placed on material things, "including money," as a measure of wealth. Although like all children they enjoyed toys and other gifts, Asa and his brother learned to value character more. A great admirer of the disciple Paul, James Randolph stressed how Paul met challenges with courage and fortitude and always finished his course; as a man of strong racial convictions, James Sr. sought to steep his children in the concept that what mattered more than race were merit, quality, and worth. In recalculating the value of material wealth for his sons around such traits, Asa explained that his father was a "major influence" on his life.[42]

Just as his emphasis on African and African American history and opposition to racial intimidation shaped key features of A. Philip Randolph's racial identity, James Randolph's efforts to provide for his family fundamentally affected central aspects of his son's personal character. Though his various business ventures never resulted in much improvement in the family's standard of living, the determination and flexibility he exhibited even in the face of repeated failure embodied the resolve and courage that African Americans needed to survive in the South during this period. As the principal role model for his sons, James Randolph attempted to provide for his family in ways that exemplified the need for persistently pursuing a task even in the face of major setbacks.[43] His example of perseverance is an important backdrop for understanding A. Philip Randolph's later tenacity in organizing the Brotherhood of Sleeping Car Porters and his determination to secure equal justice for African Americans.

Born in Monticello, Florida, in 1872, Elizabeth Randolph was one of six children of James and Mary Robinson who, though descendants of Virginia slaves, were both free before the Civil War. Of the Robinsons' four daughters, Elizabeth most resembled her mother in both appearance and personality. She was tall and slender, with a light complexion and long, wavy black hair. Although all four sisters were religious, Randolph identified his mother as the only one who was both "religious and churchly" like his maternal grand-mother. In fact, he remembered that as a child he felt his mother, father, and grandmother were "saintly . . . true believers," but his grandfather, aunts, and uncles were generally "unchurchly," if not sinful. All of them used profanity, and neither Asa nor his brother could see any of their aunts or uncles "in the role of an angel in Heaven."[44]

Elizabeth Robinson met her future husband in church while the Robinson family was living in Monticello. At the time, Reverend Randolph was teach-ing Sunday school in the local AME Church and working as a tailor in the community. When the Robinsons moved to Baldwin, Florida, in the mid-1880s and joined Campbell AME Chapel, Mary Robinson pushed the small congregation to appoint James Randolph as the church's new pastor. Not particularly satisfied with the quality of its ministry, church elders agreed and hired Randolph. As the church's new pastor, James Randolph was responsible for preaching on the first and third Sunday of each month, leading prayer meetings on Wednesday evenings, and teaching Sunday school each Sunday morning. As a bachelor and family friend new to the Baldwin community, he frequently visited the Robinsons in his free time and was warmly welcomed into the household as a member of the family. In 1885, James Randolph mar-ried Elizabeth Robinson, one of his brightest Sunday school students. Eliza-beth gave birth to the couple's first son, James William Randolph Jr., in 1887 and their second son, Asa Philip Randolph, two years later.[45]

The portrait painted of Elizabeth Randolph by her younger son is complex. Asa described her as a woman of "regal bearing and stride" who possessed strong likes and dislikes and insisted that her children always look people "straight in the eyes." He emphasized that "her general character and reaction to ideas, people, and movements were affirmative or negative, never neutral." This sort of personal and intellectual stringency seemed to manifest itself most clearly in her interaction with her children. Asa noted that although his father actively participated in his children's discussions, they were always careful never to conduct debates on the existence of God in his mother's presence. She was "emotionally set against any such discussion." Asa believed that his mother possessed a sharp and incisive mind, but her education was "too limited to enable her to understand that this discussion was a form of intellectual entertainment." For such a devoutly religious woman, discussions questioning God's existence, even as a form of entertainment, were offensive. Yet Randolph also maintained that his mother wholeheartedly endorsed his father's determination to teach him and James Jr. about African and African American history. Her view was that such instruction not only nurtured self-esteem but also fit with her fundamental belief that her children should take pride in their racial heritage and always stand up for themselves.[46]

Elizabeth Randolph was frequently depicted as a "strict disciplinarian" who was firm with her children but never stern or brutal, and Asa was quick to point out that his mother always "gave bounteously of her whole being to her family." Nonetheless, in his overall sketch of her, Randolph routinely stressed her disciplinarian nature. On numerous occasions he remarked that she "was unbending and inflexible when it came to chastisement with the rod if, as, and when" she deemed it necessary. Asa reminisced that her judgment, in keeping with a personality that tended toward the extremes, was generally swift and severe. As children, he explained, he and his brother always looked forward to family visits in the hope that guests "might divert a bit of maternal wrath and chastisement." However, he and his brother were often disappointed in this regard because none of their mother's sisters "would presume to question mother's use of the rod" lest they too "came under her benevolent fire." Without a doubt, both Asa and his brother understood quite clearly that their mother was not inclined to "spare the rod."[47]

Elizabeth Randolph's interactions outside the Randolph household were no less complicated than her relationship with her children. On the one hand, she clearly impressed her son as a capable, loving parent. Despite her strictness, Asa insisted that "she was dedicated to her family" and especially "lived for her children." He emphasized that she had a "radiant smile" that illuminated her entire appearance and gave a "sort of delightful light and shade to her beauty." But even he seemed struck by the fact that she never attempted to make many friends outside the family. In fact, aside from family visits by her sisters, Asa could not recall many women ever "congregating in the home or even making friendly visits." Even though he maintained that she was quite close with their neighbors and a few members of the family's church, his mother "never called on them and they seldom called on her." This circumstance seemed to have puzzled Asa because, despite her strict parenting style, he remembered her as a quite "lovely and lovable person" who was "always gracious to new acquaintances."[48]

Asa seemed to have concluded that in general his mother was "friendly but not intimate." This characterization even applied to her relationships with her husband and children. Though his mother undoubtedly was devoted to her husband, Asa admitted that his parents' marriage was not distinguished by "great romantic warmth expressed in public embraces and kisses." Neither did Asa's description of his mother's parenting style conjure up images of a woman who showered hugs and kisses on her children. Instead, she seemed

to have expressed her feelings for her family mostly through constant attention to her children's care and upbringing and sincere, if not enthusiastic,
support of her husband's ministry and business undertakings.[49]

This view of Elizabeth Randolph certainly fits with the significant role that
she played in running the Randolph household. Asa acknowledged that even
as children he and his brother were "not unaware" of the fact that their mother
"was the quiet, relentless power" that kept their father moving. In addition to
helping manage the family's tailoring shop, Elizabeth also occasionally took
in laundry to help supplement the family income.[50] Though her work was
generally "daintily and immaculately done," her sometimes frail health and
the low wages paid for such work prevented her from expanding her business.
She also helped her husband manage his church ministry. Asa remembered
watching as she helped his father count out the "dollar money," the annual
tax of a dollar per member required of each church, in preparation for the
AME Church's Annual Conference to ensure that her husband could meet his
quota when his name and circuit were called. A consistent record of meeting
these financial expectations was an important factor for advancement in the
church. For Reverend Randolph, whose soft-heartedness often overrode his
determination to collect payments from customers, Elizabeth Randolph was
undoubtedly an important spur prodding him to push his congregations to
pay their annual tithes.

Elizabeth Randolph also demanded absolute honestly from Asa and his
brother. If Asa or James Jr. brought home anything unusual—money or clothing, for instance—their mother "severely cross-examined" them as to its
origins and ordered them to return it unless their explanation proved satis-
factory. In such instances, Asa explained that she often told them "in tones
and words" that could not be misunderstood that "we didn't need anything
we didn't have and we shouldn't want that which we didn't need." Though
neither he nor his brother wholly agreed with this philosophy, Asa conceded
that he could not recall "ever craving for material possessions even though
our playmates had them, and we could have enjoyed them and, perhaps,
sooner or later, got them."[51] Even so, in this regard the attention that Elizabeth placed on distinguishing between needs and wants not only paralleled
her husband's emphasis on ideas over material wealth but also stressed the
importance of remaining free of personal debt or obligation.

Moreover, whereas James Randolph's impact on his children's development
is most clearly seen in their strong racial identity and keen awareness of discrimination, Elizabeth Randolph fundamentally influenced their spirit and
sense of self. Although his mother was not known as person who "engaged

in any knock-down and drag-out row with anyone," Asa stressed that she unequivocally demonstrated that she was "not one to be trampled upon by anyone." A "fearless" and "high-strung" woman, Elizabeth Randolph made it "unmistakably clear" that she despised cowardice. Although James Randolph proclaimed the "moral and spiritual power of nonviolence" and generally counseled peace in the face of conflict, Elizabeth Randolph insisted that her sons always stand up for themselves. She did not encourage them to seek out confrontations, but she absolutely demanded that they "fight anybody who fought us." Asa knew that if he or his brother "went home with blackened eyes and reported that we were in a fight," they were likely to be "whipped again by our mother unless we convinced her that we fought back." This was surely a dangerous parenting strategy for African Americans in the Jim Crow South, but Elizabeth Randolph was determined to teach her children to face life's challenges with unyielding courage. Perhaps more than any other member of the Randolph family, she was responsible for her son's clear recollection that "there was no sense of fear of anything in our home."[52]

Elizabeth Randolph's insistence that her sons not allow themselves to be bullied or intimidated was as formative an influence on Asa's personality as any of James Randolph's lessons about African American history. Even though his father's stories about Africa and notable African Americans provided a critical psychological barrier against the onslaughts of white supremacy, Elizabeth gave hard and pointed lessons about the personal tenacity that African Americans needed to survive Jim Crow with some measure of dignity and self-respect. Though she was perhaps somewhat harsh in her methods, the resolve to challenge both personal and racial intimidation and oppression that she set out to instill in Asa and his brother was really no different from the underlying subtext that wove together James Randolph's personal standoff against a lynch mob and his stories about Fredrick Douglass, Harriet Tubman, and their struggles against slavery into powerful testimonies of racial courage.

More like his mother in temperament than his father, Asa's brother James was never one to back down from an argument. Asa knew that despite all of their father's admonitions about the Christian principle of turning the other cheek, his brother, whom he affectionately called "Brother James," was "hotheaded" and "high-strung" like their mother. Even in play, Asa saw that his brother had a "reckless and fearless spirit." James's daring was a source of constant concern for his younger brother because, as Asa confessed, "he and I were inseparable and I was never sure he would return home as he had left."[53] An adventurous boy, James clearly took seriously his mother's lessons about facing life's challenges straight on, and he seldom passed on opportunities to prove his courage.

However, he too was deeply affected by the intellectual environment their father fostered in the Randolph home. Older by two years than Asa, the younger James Randolph was indeed a bright child who early on displayed an unusual interest in and aptitude for metaphysics, philosophy, and theology. Even as a youngster, Asa boasted, his brother was not only quite familiar with the works of Thomas Aquinas but "never failed to list the five arguments and proofs for God's existence." In high school, moreover, Brother James began exploring Herbert Spencer's views on the known and unknown and "hugely enjoyed elaborating upon the successive extension of the boundaries of the known by pure and applied science and the reduction of the field of the unknown in the areas of nature."[54] Despite the more spirited demeanor that James Jr. exhibited, as a child he was just as influenced by James Sr.'s love of learning as he was by Elizabeth Randolph's fieriness. And throughout childhood and adolescence, he was a clear and ever-present role model for combining their parents' disparate, and sometimes competing, values for the younger Asa.

James and Asa's play world was fairly typical in spite of their mother's strict household rules. Although they sometimes sneaked out of the yard to play when they had been explicitly forbidden to do so, their mother's "hypercritical attitude" toward strange children generally confined most of their play life to inside or on the street in front of the house. As children, they spent most of their free time playing children's games like mumble peg or testing each other's strength. "We were not only at play in the form of cooperation, such as when we played on the same team in a baseball game," Asa recalled, but also in "competitive play" like running, jumping, wrestling, boxing, and playing checkers and marbles. More assertive than Asa, James usually won these brotherly contests except when it came to boxing or baseball. In these instances the determination that Asa exhibited later in organizing the porters' union came to the fore. Marbles consumed much of their play time. Brother James always wanted to play in the "big" sidewalk games because the "competition was sharp." In general, however, the players in these sidewalk games were the "roughneck" sort with whom "fighting was a sort of way of life." Asa noticed that these games "invariably wound up in free-for-alls" as some dispute always broke out over the interpretation of the rules or whether or not someone had cheated. He described frequently having to jump into these "scrapes" too because he "had to stick with James." Such memories make clear that throughout their childhood adventures and misadventures Asa and his brother shared "a sort of unconscious realization" of the significant bond they shared.[55]

Though James was not nearly as influential on Asa's development as their parents, the deep relationship between the brothers reinforced in significant ways many of the values James and Elizabeth Randolph hoped to instill in their children. Generally more timid than James and more eager to avoid altercations when possible, Asa appreciated that he was nonetheless affected by his brother's "determined and strong willed" character.[56] In this area where Elizabeth Randolph demanded such traits from her sons, Brother James provided Asa with an immediate example of such qualities. Asa relayed one instance when, selling the local newspapers—the *Jacksonville Times Union* and the *Evening Metropolis*—he, his brother, and other black paperboys challenged the newspapers' discriminatory practices in distributing their dailies. He explained that although everyone picked up their newspapers from the same place, the normal practice was to make the black paperboys wait at the end of the line while the white paperboys got their papers first. Getting served first meant getting the best corners from which to hawk the newspapers. Dissatisfied with being served last and thus left with the corners the white paperboys did not want, Asa and the other black paperboys followed James's lead in breaking out of line and demanding their newspapers on a first come, first served basis. Because the distributors "couldn't afford to hold up the line," Asa maintained, he, his brother, and the other black paperboys got their newspapers and "broke down that form of discrimination."[57] Given their mother's strong insistence that her sons always stand up for themselves, it is not surprising to find Asa and his brother in the middle of such a protest.

In school, James Jr. was even more of a mentor to Asa. Both boys went to Oakland Elementary School, a public institution on Jacksonville's east side. But when the boys got older, the Randolphs decided to transfer them to Edward Waters College, a trade school run by the AME Church.[58] Elizabeth Randolph in particular felt that her sons were getting into too many playground altercations with the rougher sort of children that attended Oakland Elementary. However, in both schools Asa and James always took the same classes despite the two-year difference in their ages. Not surprisingly, despite his parents' insistence that he and his brother diligently attend to their studies, Asa struggled to keep pace with his school work. It was only with the patient tutoring of Brother James, gifted in mathematics and Latin, that Asa managed to succeed in classes that were otherwise too advanced for him. Indeed, he pointed out that until he reached high school, his brother "was really my teacher." By the time they reached high school and began attending Cookman Institute, though, Asa began to flourish academically with little help from James.[59]

Although their parents provided a household that nurtured self-esteem, racial pride, and courage as basic family standards, James Jr. was in many ways Asa's most important teacher. Despite the sometimes severe methods of instruction their mother employed to get her points across, James was the ever-present foil by which the younger Asa routinely tested himself. Whether at play, at work, or at school, throughout their childhood and adolescence Asa watched closely as his brother brought to life the central values their parents taught them. Notwithstanding the immeasurable regard Asa possessed for his parents and their influence on him, as he grew older and began to explore his world more independently, it seems clear that to a large degree it was his brother James whom he tried to emulate most.

In his own way Asa was as adventurous as his brother. When he was fourteen, he got a job working as a water boy for a railroad line.[60] Although he had several after-school jobs prior to this and the fact that his mother especially opposed his taking this job, Asa determined that he had lived "a sort of se-cluded life" without any "real hardship" and wanted to find out firsthand what life in the South generally offered African Americans. In reflecting back on this experience, Asa described his duties on the railroad as a "combination job." When he was not carrying water to the other workers, Asa had to help shovel dirt off flat cars that was used to level the terrain for new cross ties and rails. What struck him most about this experience was that while he and the other African Americans "were at their job the trainman, who was a white man, sat with a gun across his lap." Though not prisoners, Asa emphasized that he and the other black workers were "conscious" of what that gun meant for them: they were to pay attention to the job at hand and ignore thoughts of strikes and better wages. Even though he could earn as much as three dollars a week, good wages for an African American of any age in the South during this period, Randolph stayed on the job for only two weeks.[61]

This particular work experiment was another formative moment in Asa's childhood. The racial oppression and exploitation represented here by the white trainman's shotgun not only pervaded his early job history, which included stints as a grocery store clerk, a porter for the Chemical Drug Company, and a factory worker in a fertilizer factory for seventy-five cents a day, but they were fundamentally at odds with central elements of the values his parents taught and his brother modeled.[62] To be sure, on the eve of his graduation from Cookman Institute in 1907, Asa was intently aware of two very different but connected visions of the world: on the one hand, his family encouraged him to be a race-conscious, self-reliant, courageous, and intelligent young man in part to counterbalance the ravages of white supremacy; on the other hand, however, his first real forays outside the protection of the Randolph household unequivocally demonstrated the kind of jeopardy he courted in exhibiting such traits.

Undoubtedly, the values that permeated the Randolph house, his relationships with his parents and brother, and personal encounters with racial oppression in these early years fundamentally shaped A. Philip Randolph's racial identity. Although Jim Crow firmly proscribed the lives and opportunities available to African Americans especially in the South, the emphasis on racial and individual pride, opposition to racial oppression, and education that pervaded most aspects of Asa's upbringing not only undercut the core tenets of white supremacy but also became the basis of his life-long push for equal justice for African Americans. In seeking to understand Randolph's motivations and decisions in coordinating and conducting his subsequent protest organizations and campaigns, the home life, values, relationships, and experiences of his childhood provide vital insights into the origin and evolution of his racial consciousness.

Even as he became more intrigued by class theory in later years, these early family conversations about African and African American history and the contributions of people of color to human civilization continued to affect A. Philip Randolph's later conception of social justice. In the years to come he and others would challenge racial discrimination by arguing that every race of people was entitled to partake of society's political, economic, and social advancements because all had contributed to civilization's progress. In so doing, he clearly echoed many of the underlying sentiments of his father's fireside lectures on the history and achievements of the race. As his determination to fashion a program for demanding social justice for African Americans intensified in the 1920s, 1930s, and beyond, it is indeed vital to re-examine these formative conversations about the scope and scale of Africa's place in the world and in human history as important to Randolph's belief that African Americans were as deserving as any other group to participate fully in the American system. Even as class concerns became more important to Randolph's thinking about social justice, the racial consciousness spurred by these childhood lessons remained a critical part of his determination to improve the lives of black workers.

Likewise, the connection between Randolph's childhood memories of his father's standoff with a white lynch mob and his later conception of mass action is extremely important. To a large degree, his threatened march on Washington in 1941 emerged out of a deep conviction that whites would respect black demands for equal justice only when compelled to do so. Just as his father and other black men from Jacksonville stared down whites intent upon lynching a black prisoner, Randolph devoted a good deal of his later life and career to devising forceful strategies for challenging white supremacy and racial violence. Accordingly, in the 1930s and 1940s he focused on developing mass action tactics as vital moral and political tools for African Americans to use in pursuing the cause of equal justice. In a fundamental way, therefore, it seems clear that his early memories of his father's role in the armed defense of black life was a seminal lesson. Very early in his life Randolph came to understand how, in the absence of compelling force—be it a gun or political pressure—African American rights quickly succumbed to the inflamed passions of whites.

Elizabeth Randolph, too, had a direct impact on Randolph's later career and activism. Her insistence that her sons not allow themselves to be pushed around by neighborhood bullies helps to explain one source of Randolph's remarkable resolve in organizing the Brotherhood of Sleeping Car Porters in the 1920s and 1930s. In organizing this union and spearheading its fight for recognition as a bona fide labor union, Randolph had numerous opportunities to walk away from the porters' cause. On many occasions, in fact, the Pullman Company offered to pay him to step down from the union's leadership. Yet even though he often went without pay for extended periods in the union's early years, Randolph doggedly refused to yield the porters' fight. In locating the source of his determination to push forward with the porters' demands, it seems clear that Elizabeth Randolph's unambiguous insistence that Randolph and his brother always stand up for themselves as children was no small factor.

Even as Randolph's life and career took him further and further away from his modest but safe childhood home in Jacksonville, he nonetheless carried the lessons and values learned from his parents close at hand throughout his life. Though he would become one of the nation's foremost black Socialists in the years to come, race pride, self-sufficiency, and opposition to racism—core traits inculcated by his parents—remained as central features of his protest strategy. Consequently, in an examination of Randolph's subsequent understanding of social justice, mass action, and the importance of independent black organization and action as key elements for challenging Jim Crow, the direct link between his upbringing and his racial consciousness cannot be overstated.

2

Religious Faith and
Black Empowerment

*The AME Church and
Randolph's Racial Identity
and View of Social Justice*

As a child, Asa Randolph distinctly remembered being quite dismayed that not all African Americans were members of the AME Church, an institution revered in the Randolph household for its longstanding and firm opposition to racial oppression.[1] Like thousands of other African Americans who joined the AME Church in the years after the Civil War, he and his family viewed church affiliation not only as a profession of religious faith but as an equally important assertion of personal and racial independence.[2] "In fact," Asa explained, in recalling his upbringing in his father's church, both he and his family believed that the main significance of the church's "strength and symbolism" was "as much racial as religious."[3] The church, in turn, deliberately fostered such connections by emphasizing mutual aid and self-help strategies, civil rights, race pride, education, and opposition to racism as central features of its basic ministry.[4] From its inception, but especially during and after Reconstruction, the church fashioned a unique gospel of liberation that not only placed overturning white supremacy on par with saving souls but stressed basic principles that closely matched the Randolph family's core beliefs and values.

Thus, in addition to a home and family life that set the basic parameters of his racial consciousness at an early age, Asa's upbringing in the church and his understanding of its mission in both religious and racial terms expanded the context of his racial awareness. Explaining that "there was no institution except our home which was as close to us as the church," he pointed out that his father's frequent lectures on the AME Church and its history led both

Randolph boys to view the church less in terms of religious instruction than as a steadfast and enduring beacon for racial uplift. Religion, too, became less about salvation than faithfully persevering in the face of relentless racial persecution. Church quatrains such as the following one about Richard Allen and the church's founding certainly contributed to this early shift in his perceptions of the church:

> Before I'd be a slave
> I'd be buried in my grave
> And go home to my God
> And be free.[5]

As it became clear to Asa that his father was as "steeped" in the church as an institution of racial advancement as he was in his belief in Christianity, Asa's interest in the church became even more focused on its racial, political, and organizational significance for African Americans.

The roots of African Methodism extend back to the latter years of the eighteenth century when Richard Allen and Absalom Jones led other African Americans out of St. George's Methodist Episcopal Church in Philadelphia to protest racial segregation in the church. Though African Americans, both slave and free, had worshipped at St. George's freely for years and had been welcomed, white congregants became increasingly concerned and sought to establish a policy of segregation as the number of African American communicants grew in conjunction with the city's expanding black population. These events significantly influenced Asa's view of the church and its mission. As children, he and his brother spent countless evenings listening to their father detail the story of how, when confronted by white church leaders during Sunday morning prayers in the spring of 1787, Allen and Jones refused to be escorted to the church's balcony and proceeded to lead their fellow African Americans out of the church. Both Allen and Jones determined to form churches where African Americans would not be subjected to such discrimination.[6] For Asa and hundreds of thousands of African Americans who would join the AME Church in the postwar and Reconstruction years, such dramatic accounts of Allen and Jones's resolute resistance to discrimination and determination to form churches for African Americans in Philadelphia free of racial persecution made the issue of race a central feature of their religious conversion and instruction.[7]

In these first days, however, the group led by Allen and Jones initially organized itself as an ethical and beneficial association called the Free African Society. Meeting in members' homes or in the local schoolhouse run by

Quakers to educate the city's black population, the group primarily focused on promoting orderly and sober living standards among its members rather than any specific religious liturgy. Mainly representing the city's free black population, the Free African Society undertook oversight responsibilities for its members, attacking practices like cohabitation that were closely associated with slavery.[8] Under the leadership of Allen and Jones, the Free African Society also functioned as a mutual aid society that provided sickness and poverty relief as well as death benefits to families of deceased members.[9] Despite its relative success in caring for the sick and destitute among Philadelphia's free black population, in the closing years of the eighteenth century both Allen and Jones became convinced that the group's future depended on a stronger religious connection. The question of whether the new congregation should become Protestant Episcopal or remain Methodist created a split between society members that resulted in the founding of the AME Church.[10]

Although both Allen and Jones believed that Methodism best suited the needs of African Americans in Philadelphia, most of the Free African Society's membership remained bitter toward the Methodist Church for the way they had been treated at St. George's. The bulk of the membership favored joining the Episcopal Church. Jones agreed and took steps toward securing a church facility for this faction. Purchasing a plot of land just east of the seventh ward, the center of Philadelphia's black community, Jones witnessed the dedication of the nation's first African American church, First African Church of St. Thomas, in the summer of 1794. Jones eventually became the first black rector in the Episcopal Church. Meanwhile, Allen and his contingent withdrew from the Free African Society and founded their own church, Bethel Methodist Church. In 1796 Allen and his congregation moved into their first permanent sanctuary and proceeded to grow from a single church into a large denomination spawning new churches throughout the city and the free states. With the establishment of an independent episcopacy in 1816, the small congregation that founded Bethel Methodist Church took on the hierarchical structure with bishops appointed to different sections of the country that formed the African Methodist Episcopal Church. Richard Allen became the AME Church's first bishop.

For Asa and his family, the origin of the AME Church was a significant point of racial pride. Even as a child, he understood the implications of standing firm against racial oppression in the midst of slavery. As his father's frequent accounts of Richard Allen and the church's longstanding determination to oppose discrimination reinforced a view of the church as a great moral and spiritual force, Asa also began to see more clearly the connection between religious faith and racial and political militancy. Increasingly, he came to understand religious conversion as an assertive statement of racial independence, not merely a commitment of faith.[11] As it did for other African Americans who joined the AME Church in the postwar period, this substantial blending of race and religion in the institution of the church had a formative impact on his budding racial identity. By promoting self-help and self-defense strategies, race pride, civil rights, and opposition to racism through such outlets as the *Christian Recorder* and other church publications, the AME Church helped to transform African Americans' struggle for freedom from a political protest into a moral calling.[12] For Asa in particular, this commingling of race and religion is key to understanding the link between the racial ideology of his childhood and his subsequent ideas about social justice.

Through such journals as the *Recorder* the AME Church deliberately worked to refine and forcefully articulate a specific liberation theology that challenged the fundamental moral underpinnings of white supremacy and unequivocally affirmed the equality of all people. From the very outset, Elisha Weaver, the *Recorder*'s first editor, questioned the moral and legal legitimacy of white supremacy. Writing in 1865 under the masthead "God our Father, Man our Brother, and Christ our Redeemer," he asserted that all could not help but know that racial discrimination was "diametrically opposed to the letter and spirit of the Declaration of Independence as well as the expressed command of God."[13] In a later editorial drawing a parallel between the "Pharaoh of old that fought against God and would not let his people go" and the unreconstructed South, Weaver set out to illustrate vividly the basic incongruity between racial oppression and Christianity. He warned that other "Tyrants" throughout history had followed in the footsteps of ancient Egypt and "oppressed, without cause, the weak" convinced, perhaps, "like the American rebels" that their position of dominance was divinely ordained. But, he continued, God's laws "never for a moment cease to operate," and like Pharaoh, "its violators must, sooner or later, pay the penalty which only increases in severity by delay."[14]

Weaver's argument in these early commentaries that racial oppression in general and white supremacy specifically ran counter to the dictates of Christian faith set a longstanding editorial tone for the *Recorder* that marked it as a primary outlet for disseminating the church's uniquely race-conscious religion.[15] Though some have argued that the black church was primarily a compensatory institution preoccupied with otherworldly relief from racial oppression, and others have pointed to it as a dynamic political agent of social change, this deliberate effort to incorporate a civil rights agenda into a coherent liberation theology afforded the AME Church the means to preserve and promote African American self-respect as well as forthrightly attack racial discrimination.[16] Operating from the premise that God was the father of all, the church purposefully fashioned a system of beliefs determined to expose the fundamental depths of racism and plainly demonstrate the moral and religious falsity of discrimination.[17] The *Christian Recorder* was particularly important in outlining the church's religious and moral opposition to racial oppression and, as such, deeply affected Asa's racial worldview. As the militant tone set by Weaver became characteristic of the *Recorder* throughout the nineteenth century, its editorial stance complemented many of the life lessons Asa learned at home.

Asa's racial worldview was also greatly affected by W. E. B. Du Bois's *The Souls of Black Folk,* a compelling narrative published in 1903 that Asa read as a youth. Whereas James Randolph often used the Bible as well as the *Recorder* to teach lessons about race and racism, Du Bois made a powerful moral argument in support of black equality that explained the comprehensive ways in which African Americans' civil and social rights were inextricably linked. The deeply spiritual tone Du Bois adopted in detailing the connections between African American civil and political rights was strikingly similar to the tenor of the *Recorder*'s religious tack in opposing racial discrimination. His rendering of the plight of African Americans forcefully supported the church's deliberate intention of exposing the myth of white supremacy. Coupled with the values imparted by James and Elizabeth Randolph, this potent nexus of moral and religious opposition to black oppression had a profound impact on Asa's evolving racial identity.

Throughout the nineteenth century, the *Christian Recorder* intentionally cultivated within the AME Church the kind of racial worldview passionately presented in Du Bois's essays. Benjamin Tucker Tanner, who assumed editorship of the *Recorder* in the 1870s, picked up the thread of militant commentary first set forth by Weaver with relentless attacks on racism, segregation, and discrimination. He harshly criticized the 1876 Democratic Party platform that repeatedly denied African Americans' "common humanity" with whites as "absolutely unchristian and infidel." Such a view, Tanner maintained, represented a fundamental "denial of the Scripture which declares God made of one blood all nations of men."[18] In this case, Tanner's critique of the racist rhetoric of southern Democrats is an important example of the church's determination to affirm the humanity of African Americans by appropriating core Christian beliefs to advance a nonracist viewpoint. Like

James Randolph, who had always stressed to his sons that they were as good as any white boys, Tanner laid claim to a common lineage with whites and, by extension, a common right to full citizenship. The underlying precept of Tanner's point, that African Americans were equal heirs to God's grace and equally entitled to full citizenship, further elaborated the church's position linking Christian faith with social and political equality.

This connection between religious faith and racial militancy that stands at the heart of the AME Church's distinct liberation theology also gave rise to a particularly racial view of the church's overall purpose. Increasingly both church leaders and members came to view the church as responsible for serving a specific racial mission while attending to African Americans' basic spiritual needs. The church, as Tanner outlined in 1877, was "called especially to minister to a whole race."[19] Even though discrimination may have impelled African Americans to create their own organizations and institutions, Tanner and others insisted that God had set before the AME Church the special religious and missionary task of challenging racial oppression.[20] For Asa, this particular view of the church's special calling fundamentally cast it as a critical medium for claiming both citizenship rights and individual salvation. Tanner again articulated this very point, arguing in the post-Reconstruction years that the "work of the hour" for the church and its membership was to fight for freedom and prove the Negro's equality. The hope of every church member, he acknowledged, was that "the organization he represents shall under God" put the question of the Negro's worth to rest once and for all.[21] Such commentaries clearly served to define the advancement of social justice for African Americans as a central duty for the church and its membership.

The goal of racial advancement also shaped the church's exegetical perspective. While antebellum Protestant missions to southern plantations focused on slaves' Christian duty to obey masters, the AME Church deliberately emphasized those Scriptures that offered hope to the downtrodden and inspired African Americans to actively resist racial oppression.[22] In 1877, Tanner turned to the Book of Isaiah to encourage African Americans concerned about the future of Reconstruction, insisting that "when the enemy shall come in like a flood, the Spirit of the Lord shall lift up a standard against him." Recasting the notion of "liberty" as Christ in the resurrection narrative, Tanner went on to proclaim that the "spirit of liberty" emerged from its tomb and "struck the shackles from the limbs of four million, and bade the whole race of ours to stand forth in God's sunlight, free."[23] In this instance, Tanner set out to bolster African Americans' spirits as Republicans and Democrats fashioned the Compromise of 1877, and he also made two critical points central to the AME Church's special liberation theology. First, by exchanging liberty for Christ, he turned the resurrection narrative into a moral justification of African Americans' quest for full citizenship. Second, in posing liberty as God's intended condition for African Americans, he used this narrative to imply that anything less than African Americans' full commitment to securing equal rights was a betrayal of God's will.

This racial interpretation of the resurrection narrative represented the explicitly race-conscious theology promoted by the AME Church that so affected Reverend Randolph, his wife, and their children. Ordained into the ministry in 1884 when Bishop Henry McNeal Turner dominated the social and religious climate of African American communities in the South, James Randolph incorporated both Turner's political militancy and the church's racial radicalism into both his sermons and parenting. He made sure that his sons knew of and understood Turner's significance to both the AME Church and African Americans generally. Whenever the church held its Annual Conference in Jacksonville, the elder Randolph made a point of taking his sons with him to introduce them to the different church leaders in attendance. On one such occasion, he introduced them to Bishop Turner. Thinking back on this moment years later, Asa remembered Turner as an "imposing figure" with distinct features, freckles, and stern eyes. The lasting impression this meeting made on him was certainly enhanced by the "impassioned" speech Turner gave to open the conference. As Turner discussed the challenges of building new independent black churches in the Old South and improving the lives of African Americans, Asa recalled that he "pulled two revolvers out of his pocket and placed them on the pulpit" to emphasize how, as an "angry Negro man of God," he had overcome the dangers of carrying the Gospel to the four corners of the South.[24]

This conference experience had a powerful effect on Asa's racial awareness. Perhaps more than any other single experience in these formative years, Turner's speech solidly cemented for him the link between racial militancy and religious faith. Turner's fiery conviction and clear endorsement of black self-defense not only shaped the consciousness of a generation of African Methodists but also complemented the sermonizing Asa routinely heard both at home and from his father's pulpit. As Asa subsequently affirmed, Turner's determination to improve the spiritual and material lives of African Americans in the South made "an indelible impression on me."[25] For Asa, Turner's personal demeanor and church work forcefully embodied the defiant resistance to racism that characterized so many of his early influences. Like his father's gathering of men in the community to face down a white lynch mob, or his mother's insistence that he always stand up for himself, or his brother's determination to challenge discrimination even as a child, Turner's armed evangelizing helped to make clear the value of appropriate force in response to racial oppression. Though Asa would eschew physical violence in developing his own ideas about social justice, these formative examples of opposition to discrimination led him to view both mass action and civil disobedience as vital but nonviolent corollaries for opposing racism.[26]

Even as leaders like Henry McNeal Turner continued to preach salvation and equal rights in the postwar years, others focused the AME Church's racial and religious dialogue on African American self-esteem. To this end, the *Recorder* encouraged African Americans to reject the term "Negro" on the grounds that it had "the smell of the horrors of the Middle Passage about it." This interest in shaping African American racial self-esteem took on greater significance as Reconstruction came to an end and church leaders took greater note of the relationship between a positive racial psyche and African Americans' capacity to resist discrimination. In 1878, Tanner editorialized that African Americans should "spurn" the term "Negro" as a denial of their racial heritage. He pointed out that like the people of Western Europe, the descendants of "African tribes must be accorded the common privilege of naming themselves" rather than being "doomed to wear the name imposed by the pirates who ravished their coasts." In summarizing the prevailing opinion of the church's leadership, Tanner explained to *Recorder* readers that as people of African descent "we might in particular be Basses, or Yeys, or Deys, or Mandingoes; but to answer to the call Negro, we would never."[27]

The underlying sentiment of these editorials, that African Americans should acknowledge and take pride in their racial heritage, reinforced many of the lessons that James and Elizabeth Randolph taught their children. In fact, in teaching Asa and James Jr. about Africa and African American history, James Sr. frequently echoed directly the *Recorder's* militant racial attitude. As Asa recalled later, throughout his childhood his father routinely referred to African Americans as "black, Afro-Americans, and colored people" because he believed that "these names designated the race to which we belonged the original home of which was Africa." Such militancy, when coupled with James Randolph's deliberately racial interpretation of the Scriptures, created a home environment where race was central, and Asa developed a lasting impression of his father as something of a black nationalist.[28]

The racial attitude that so thoroughly permeated the Randolph household was as much a part of the AME Church's general racial ethos as it was the result of James and Elizabeth Randolph's personal points of view.[29] Especially as

Reconstruction ended, the church set out to translate the racially militant theology preached from its pulpits into practical solutions for African Americans living in ever more hostile southern communities. Asserting that "the gods help those who first help themselves," Benjamin Tanner routinely emphasized the need for greater racial self-sufficiency. Throughout his editorial tenure, he argued that African Americans must be prepared "to keep ourselves and help each other, asking only even-handed justice of the white man."[30] In this vein, racial self-improvement became an even more vital moral imperative. Stressing that "the one pertinent question" facing his readers was not "were you born ignorant," but rather "have you had opportunities to learn," Tanner maintained that African Americans were "responsible to God" as well as the race for pursuing self-improvement through education.[31]

Even as it encouraged African Americans "to organize societies in every state in the Union" for the "looking after, protection, and elevation of the race and its interests," the *Recorder* continued to demand equal justice for African Americans.[32] Although some, including renowned church figures such as Henry McNeal Turner, began to advocate black emigration back to Africa, Tanner and others continued to maintain that African Americans should settle for nothing less than "the fullest possible granting of our rights" as American citizens. Just as self-sufficiency and self-improvement became basic moral and racial obligations, the *Recorder* counseled that God held out the hope of both spiritual redemption and political salvation for those of faith. As Tanner proclaimed to his readers, though some may "get hopeless and retire from the contest" and others may "run away to Africa and elsewhere," he was resolved to stand with "the vast majority" of the race who intended "to stand still and see the salvation of God" bring about a second, more complete emancipation. Any other course was untenable in his view, for if African Americans "could keep heart and work and pray under slavery," then they could "surely do the same thing now" as free men and women.[33]

The emphasis that Turner, Tanner, and the *Recorder* put on shaping the racial worldview of the church affected Asa deeply. The unique blend of faith, race, and militant politics that constituted the central features of the AME Church's gospel of liberation fundamentally shifted his core religious and racial sensibilities to a more secular point of view. Even though he enjoyed attending his father's churches and the church in general remained an important aspect of his life and experience throughout his childhood, Asa later confessed that he began to evince a "marked intellectual sophistication in relation to religion" as a young adult. He became increasingly critical of literal interpretations of the Bible and came to appreciate the church more for its racial significance than for its religious doctrines. In his view, the founding of the AME Church was not so much a "revolt against a pattern of theology," but rather a "revolt against a pattern of religious hypocrisy" in the form of "racialism."[34] He thus came to revere the church more as an agent of social and political protest than as a mere vehicle of spiritual salvation. This in part explains why he resisted any formal religious affiliation after leaving Jacksonville in 1911 and did not actually rejoin a church until 1958, when he was sixty-nine years old.[35]

Even as the AME Church's race-conscious religion helped to shape Asa's early racial awareness, the explicit social and political aspects of its liberation theology provided a link to a broader socio-religious movement known as the social gospel that would significantly affect his subsequent understanding of class. As the nation began to experience the first effects of industrialization following the Civil War, an influential group of Protestant theologians began to challenge the conservative Christianity of the Gilded Age by emphasizing the centrality of Christian principles to all facets of life. Horace Bushnell, Henry Ward Beecher, Washington Gladden, Walter Rauschenbusch, and other progressive ministers of the period began to abandon the Calvinist doctrines of election and reprobation in favor of a more humanistic theology that interpreted Christ's teachings as social, ethical, and deeply concerned with this world rather than strictly the metaphysical.[36] In their view, God's plan of salvation involved redemption of humanity as a whole, not just the individual. Also, by stressing Christ's essential humanity, their "new theology" closed the distance between sinful man and a perfect God and offered new hope for what might be achieved in this world if society would simply follow Christ's moral example. It was this heightened concern for the conditions of this world that connected the nascent social gospel to the AME Church and the deep racial sensibilities of Asa's early life.

The notion that God's grace not only applied to a spiritual afterlife but could also transform present society was a significant theological breakthrough for progressive Protestants of the postwar period. It meant that individuals could now seek their own redemption rather than rely solely on the judgment of an enigmatic God. This new role for man's ethical conduct in determining individual salvation also made it more difficult to explain and justify social inequality and injustice. Poverty was no longer simply the consequence of divine retribution for sin, but rather a social ill that the church was morally obligated to address. For these forerunners of the social gospel who believed that Christ preached of a terrestrial, social kingdom as well as spiritual one, redemption became an inclusive earthly doctrine promoting the brotherhood of man and involving the application of ethical standards to all social relationships and institutions.[37] As the nineteenth century came to a close, this new sense that individuals could be agents of their own salvation and that the work of God required due attention to the general conditions of contemporary society paved the way for the full development of the social gospel.

Despite ignoring issues of race and racism, the social gospel's concern for the conditions of this world resonated with the AME Church's long-standing regard for African Americans' sacred and secular well-being. In many respects, the very origins of the AME Church were rooted in a basic understanding of the ways in which racism and discrimination undercut African American spiritual life; from its inception the church had placed the day-to-day needs of its members at the heart of its basic ministry. In like fashion, the social gospel now challenged industrial capitalism's distribution of wealth as part of its general mission to foster both spiritual salvation as well as an ethical society. Even though most of the progressive Protestants who ushered in this new religious perspective ignored the ravages of racial discrimination, their deepening disquiet over the plight of the urban poor nonetheless extended the bounds of Christian concern and created a new social consciousness especially suited to the AME Church's core mission.

The humanitarian emphasis of the new theology of the postwar era received a significant boost in the 1880s from a growing number of young Protestant ministers who began applying European historical scholarship to the Bible. They insisted that religious doctrines stand up to the standards of an increasingly empirical worldview and, therefore, began to minimize the miraculous in the Scriptures in favor of a more ethical study of Christ. As a result, growing numbers of progressive Protestants came to view God and the universe less in terms of transcendence than immanence and came to expect that longstanding religious doctrines pass muster under the scrutiny of nineteenth-century morality.[38] Coupled with the concurrent development of a knowable God, this "social" Christianity not only made it possible for postwar Protestants to focus on the conditions of this world but also established new requirements for social action by the church. Like the AME Church, then, which viewed social service as an integral part of its church work, more and more white Protestants, swayed by the twin influences of the new theology and social Christianity, entered the twentieth century charged and ready to apply Christian principles to all aspects of modern industrial life.

Although the innovations of Bushnell, Beecher, Gladden, Rauschenbusch, and others worked to neutralize the conservatism of the Gilded Age, the social gospel did not achieve full form until its reinterpretations of the Scriptures on social questions resulted in modifications of theology and produced specific social reforms. This began to happen in the 1880s when budding social gospelers began to challenge the underlying rationale of classical economic theory, condemn the robber barons' business practices, attack the growing problems of urban life, and regard the intensifying conflict between labor and capital as the fundamental moral crisis of the industrial age. It was these early assaults on the ill effects of industrial capitalism that marked the beginning of an intertwining of religious and social thought that gave the social gospel clear shape.[39] As the social gospel continued to inform efforts like the settlement house movement of Jane Addams and Graham Taylor, the first instructor of Christian sociology at the Chicago Theological Seminary, it infused a sense of moral urgency into social investigation.[40] More than just applying Christian principles to social problems, the social gospel produced progressive social reform that went beyond simple philanthropic efforts to alleviate the strains of urban industrial life to critically reassessing the fundamental structure of industrial society.

Even though the social gospel refocused Christian concern on the mundane rather than the miraculous, the AME Church worked from the beginning to translate its religious doctrines into a concrete program of social and political advancement for African Americans. It promoted race pride, self-help, self-defense, and opposition to racism as necessary survival strategies for African Americans, especially in the South, while simultaneously incorporating such distinctly racial values into the very fabric of its religious calling.[41] For Asa, though, the linkage between race and religion created by the church took on new shape in the context of the social gospel's increasingly harsh appraisal of industrial capitalism. He and other African Americans came to see in its stinging indictment of urban industrial society a whole new way of explaining the hardships that African Americans faced. Although race continued to influence his understanding of the challenges of being black, the social gospel's reassessment of the problems of poverty, vice, and urban overcrowding began to make more and more sense to him.

In the last years of the nineteenth century, early advocates of the social gospel began to subject the assumptions of classical economic theory to searching scrutiny on the basis that unrestricted competition was an arrogant contradiction of Christian ethics. Though the basic precept of laissez-faire economics—the strong survive by devouring the weak—continued to shape the business practices of the day, social gospelers sharpened their criticism of the ability of raw individualism to produce socially beneficial results. They questioned the appropriateness of self-interest as an engine of economic growth and insisted instead that economic questions could not be adequately considered outside the context of Christian morality. Rather than blindly following the tenet of supply and demand, economist Richard T. Ely, along with Gladden and others, invoked Christian principles as the proper counterbalance to naked individualism and the ruthless tendencies of economic forces.[42] Even if such forces were immutable, these social gospel theorists asserted, they were still subject to moral considerations.

In challenging the social value of classical economic theory, the social gospel also called into question the business practices it precipitated. Social gospelers were appalled by the commonly practiced and accepted dishonesties of industrial conglomerates, and they viewed corporate avarice as both individually and collectively corrosive. Because the business practices of such leading individuals significantly affected the shape of industrial society, Ely, Gladden, and others argued that the business elite had a distinct moral duty to temper their profit seeking in favor of the common good. The church, too, had to reevaluate its emphasis on spirituality over morality in teaching its members the ethical basics of Christianity. By ignoring the social consequences of greed and unchecked self-interest, the church not only allowed individuals to drift toward spiritual damnation but also betrayed the broader social aspects of its mission.[43] Highlighting the perils of wealth and indifference to social need, expanding slums, the problems of tenement housing, and the impact of all these conditions on the church's ability to teach ethical and religious character, social gospel proponents maintained that the church had a fundamental obligation to address such issues as part of its mandate to redeem society as a whole. Perhaps more than any other single development, it was this understanding that focused the attention of the social gospel on industrial labor relations.

The shift in emphasis from spirituality to morality that moved religion out of the sanctuary and into the daily lives of church members also shaped social gospelers' charge that industrialists who engaged in unfair or cruel business practices that undermined working families sinned against God. They insisted that it was Christianity's moral duty to define and regulate the industrial relationship between workers and employers to ensure justice and fair play and protect workers from exploitation. Whereas the conservative Christianity of the past associated idleness with sin, Gladden and others now recognized workers' right to strike, arguing instead that if workers chose to stand aside rather than accept an offered wage, they had every right to do so. Gladden maintained that the key to peaceful labor relations was for employers to measure profits and workers to measure wages by the dictates of the golden rule: capital should act as the conscientious steward of workers' well-being, and labor should be honest and hardworking.[44] The proper organization of industry, then, was a cooperative arrangement between capital and labor that protected private property while simultaneously providing the means for workers to join the capitalist class. Though neither Gladden nor other progressive Protestants were prepared to endorse socialism at that moment, their zeal to reorganize industrial relationships around cooperation rather than competition validated even more radical critiques of industrial capitalism.

For Asa, the negative assessments of industrial society precipitated by the social gospel deeply influenced his subsequent conceptions of social justice. Though many of the values intrinsic to the central teachings of the AME Church had a decisive impact on his racial, social, and political awareness throughout his life, he and other African American radicals in Harlem in the 1910s and 1920s found new support for their campaign for equal justice in the principles of social Christianity.[45] They began to insist that genuine social justice required equal access for all to the social, economic, and political levers of an open, participatory democracy and that all races of men were equally entitled to benefit from the fruits of modern society.[46] Especially as progressive reformers inspired by the social gospel began to advocate for and institute sweeping social changes, more and more Asa and his fellow Harlem radicals equated the practical application of social Christianity with socialism. Even as some in the AME Church began to reevaluate the significance of the social gospel for African Americans and interpret its mandate to heal the whole person as a moral duty to address racism's harmful effects, Asa in particular found himself drawn to a more radical critique of industrial society rooted in class.

The impact of socialism on Asa's conception of social justice was profound. Though the values of his childhood that centered on race continued to affect his overall understanding of the plight of African Americans, class critiques of industrial capitalism began to make more sense to both him and the associates that gathered around his journal, the *Messenger*.[47] W. A. Domingo, a Jamaican-born Harlemite who wrote for the *Messenger* in its first years, explained socialism to *Messenger* readers as an "economic doctrine" that set out to adapt the "pure Christianity preached by Jesus and practiced by the early Christians" to modern industrial society. He argued that like Christ, who sought and offered solace to all who were "weary and heavy laden," in industrial society, only "the scarlet banner of international socialism" offered any sort of relief to "millions of oppressed people."[48] This link between social religion and socialism upon which Domingo expounded connected directly with the liberation theology of the black church and became even more concrete for Asa in the late 1920s and 1930s.[49] Although his determination to improve the lives and livelihoods of black workers was to some degree shaped by the racial focus of his upbringing, the social gospel's emphasis on fair labor relations was an important factor in his subsequent views of social and economic justice.

Even as class theories reshaped Asa's understanding of discrimination, the potent social and political subtext of the AME Church's racial religion made him more responsive to such ideas. At the turn of the nineteenth century, race-conscious AME Church leaders such as Reverdy C. Ransom and R. R. Wright Jr. worked to incorporate the precepts of the social gospel into the church's broad social mission. This not only resulted in specific efforts to adapt progressive reforms to the needs of African Americans but was also one of the avenues by which African Americans were introduced to comprehensive critiques of industrial capitalism.[50] For Asa, who as a young man had already begun to evince a more intellectual than spiritual regard for the church, this integration of nascent progressivism and the church's social ministry only deepened his appreciation of the church's substantial ability to shape African American expectations for equal justice.[51] It was this early appreciation of the church's racially militant potential that, when subsequently exposed to Ransom's incredibly active social outreach program in Harlem, appealed directly to Asa's budding radicalism.

A product of Wilberforce University, an institution founded by the Methodist Episcopal Church in 1856 and taken over by the AME Church in the early 1860s, Ransom strongly believed in the importance of education in overcoming the impact of racism. He maintained that in an increasingly complex society the clergy in particular had to be fully prepared to minister to the needs of their communities. Enrolling in the department of theology in 1881 and returning in 1883 after a one-year hiatus wherein he attended Oberlin College, Ransom's education closely followed the advent of new scientific theories that had already begun to put religious dogma on the defensive. Especially as the theory of evolution further exposed the disconnection between the church and the modern world, Ransom became more convinced of the value of education in integrating such science into a meaningful faith and ministry. In many ways, it was this personal need to reconcile tensions between science and religion that initially opened Ransom to the social gospel. His interest in the social applications of religion deepened after his graduation in 1886 when his ministerial travels put him in direct contact with social gospel preachers and practitioners like Washington Gladden, Jane Addams, and Graham Taylor.[52]

In 1893 Ransom attended the Parliament of Religions, a global religious conference convened in connection with Chicago's World Columbian Exposition, and heard Gladden's stirring keynote address actively encouraging the church to seek equitable solutions to labor conflicts. Like many others, Gladden believed that in the aftermath of the Haymarket Square riot of 1886 and the shocking events surrounding the 1892 Homestead Strike, labor unrest posed perhaps the greatest single threat to the nation. For Ransom, however, the importance Gladden placed on justice and fairness for society's most alienated and ostracized was particularly relevant to African Americans. Even though the problems of discrimination never garnered much attention from Gladden or his progressive audience, his depiction of a just society inspired Ransom to emphasize the special problems of discrimination in the job market. Just as Gladden saw a moral duty for the church to fairly oversee industrial relations between labor and capital, Ransom understood that the unique constraints imposed on African American workers by racism and discrimination necessitated special intervention from the AME Church. Even as he came to share the underlying class sympathies of the social gospel, Ransom's thought and ministry were nonetheless shaped by a religious, social, and historical perspective ultimately defined by race.[53]

In addition to bringing class issues to his attention and strengthening his connection to the social gospel, the Parliament of Religions was also important for Ransom because it put him in contact with Jane Addams and Graham Taylor, pioneers of the Chicago settlement house movement and important role models for the practical application of social Christianity. Their use of social science methodology in addressing urban poverty demonstrated practical ways of translating theology into sociology and introduced Ransom to new tools for confronting problems made more complicated by racial discrimination.[54] Appointed pastor of Chicago's Bethel AME Church in 1896, Ransom arrived in the city at a time when its growing African American population was increasingly confined to slum districts. Yet, he discovered that neither Hull House nor Chicago Commons, the settlement founded by Graham Taylor in 1894, was prepared to deal with the devastating effects of racial discrimination in employment or housing. The utterly desperate conditions that African Americans faced combined with the sheer disregard of white progressives motivated Ransom to adapt Addams and Taylor's settlement house model to the entwined problems of poverty and racism facing African Americans migrating to the city.

In 1900, he founded Institutional Church and Social Settlement (ICSS) to provide educational and recreational services to the growing African American community on Chicago's South Side. Although ICSS was open to anyone in need, Ransom believed that its primary purpose was to provide basic assistance in adjusting to urban living to the tidal wave of African Americans flooding into the city in this period. Insisting that the church should "live what it believes" rather than just being "content with hearing sermons," Institutional Church was open seven days a week to provide spiritual guidance and support to the community as well as continuing education classes, a kindergarten, business courses, industrial training, cooking and sewing classes, visiting nurses, a dispensary, and free baths to black South Siders.[55] In providing such services, Ransom purposefully envisioned ICSS as a community-based, self-help organization founded by African Americans specifically to help African Americans. He hoped that, like Hull House and other settlements throughout the city that helped working-class immigrants adjust to industrial society, Institutional Church's comprehensive spiritual and social program would result in similar progress for African Americans. Indeed, he hoped Institutional Church would become "an inspiration and help not only to our connection but to the entire race."[56] In many ways, this combined emphasis on racial self-sufficiency and progressive reforms sparked by social science defined new parameters for the AME Church's longstanding social ministry.

Institutional Church and its programs also set out to involve Chicago's small African American middle and professional classes in the care and uplift of the city's growing African American population.[57] Ransom, a contemporary of W. E. B. Du Bois and fellow member of the Niagara Movement, was certainly aware of the emerging and increasingly sharp criticism Du Bois leveled at middle-class and professional blacks. Though church leaders like Tanner had as early as the 1870s raised questions about whether the time had come for "our men of means to undertake to do for the colored people what white men of means do for white people," in the 1890s Du Bois began using empirical sociological research—the tools of the social gospel—to challenge racial stereotypes and urge the African American middle and professional classes to participate in helping poor migrants entering northern cities.[58] For Ransom, who was supremely interested in the application of social science techniques to this very problem, such criticism functioned as a call to action in shaping the founding of ICSS and further highlighted the usefulness of social science in analyzing and addressing the special problems of race.

For Asa, though, Ransom's social ministry gave concrete shape to the core ideas articulated by the *Christian Recorder* and deeply affected his sense of race, community, and class. In the same years that Ransom was blending the AME Church's liberation theology with the social gospel, Asa was becoming less and less enamored with the church's spiritual features. Instead, he found himself increasingly drawn to the strong emphasis it placed on opposing racism and discrimination and its unique potential to galvanize African Americans against racial oppression.[59] This view of the church was more clearly etched for Asa after his move to Harlem in 1911, where Ransom and his brand of social ministry had already influenced the community deeply. Ransom, who was appointed pastor of Bethel AME Church in Harlem in 1907, brought with him many of the concepts that shaped Institutional Church's social programs.[60] More important for Asa, perhaps, Ransom also brought with him a clear sympathy for class theory and a deep understanding of the plight of African American workers. These features all came together during his tenure at Bethel to create a vibrant social outreach program especially focused on African American youth and young adults that also helped to create deeper class sensibilities in the community. For Asa in particular, participation in Bethel's young adult programs was vital to both his early acclimation to the city and introduction to class theory.[61]

The religious experiences of Asa's childhood affected his intellectual development just as deeply as they did his moral character. With its intense focus on opposition to racism and social uplift, the AME Church's distinctive theology both broadened his racial perceptions and made the social gospel and its class-conscious undertones more accessible. As the spiritual features of the church's mission faded into the background of his awareness, Asa's interest in class-based critiques of industrial capitalism increased. With prominent African Americans such as Reverdy Ransom and R. R. Wright Jr. recasting the social gospel in racial terms, Asa began to reconsider the complex ways in which race and class issues complicated questions of social justice for African Americans. In this regard, the church became the main link connecting key features of his early racial identity to his subsequent ideas about class consciousness among African Americans. Yet, even as class became a central component of Asa's social awareness, the racial sensibilities inculcated by his childhood and early religious education continued to influence his path. Despite his subsequent interest in socialism, central aspects of the protest strategy that he would later formulate developed out of his upbringing in the AME Church.

During the same years in which Ransom began redirecting the social gospel, the AME Church expanded dramatically in the ex-Confederate states.

Even though there were no African Methodist churches in the South prior to 1865, the AME Church had approximately three million southern congregants by the end of the nineteenth century.[62] This incredible growth in membership resulted from the determined efforts of early African Methodist missionaries to bring southern freedmen into the church structure. Following the lead of men like James Lynch, James Hall, and William Gaines, some of the first African Methodist missionaries to travel through the South organizing new churches, Henry McNeal Turner aspired to create independent AME churches in the region to facilitate the development of mutually supportive African American communities.[63] In so doing, he helped to build a vibrant and race-conscious institution in the South that was especially important to Asa's subsequent intellectual and political growth.

Turner joined the AME Church in 1858 after hearing the story of Richard Allen and the church's founding from Willis Revels, pastor of St. James Church in New Orleans. Revels explained to Turner that the AME Church was like the regular Methodist Episcopal (ME) Church South in that it was a connectional organization. But, unlike in the ME Church South, in the AME Church African Americans could serve as deacons, elders, and bishops. This particular feature was extremely appealing to Turner and the thousands of other African Americans who joined AME churches after the Civil War.[64] As soon as he could after joining the church, Turner moved to Baltimore and spent the next few years ministering to successively larger and more prestigious AME congregations. His success in Baltimore eventually led to his ordination as a deacon and later as a church elder by the Baltimore Conference. In June 1863, Turner left the regular pastorate of the church to serve as a chaplain in the Union Army. It was this military service that sent him into the Carolinas, Georgia, and Florida and marked the beginning of his AME church building.

As the Union Army began to occupy more and more territory toward the close of the war, Turner's concern for the religious affiliation of African Americans in the South grew. Like other African Methodist missionaries in the South, he emphatically believed that the freedmen made important declarations of their new autonomy in forming independent black organizations. For Turner and other black missionaries, religious affiliation became an especially crucial surrogate for testing the freedom of the former slaves. In addition to the AME Church, the Colored Methodist Episcopal (CME) Church and the African Methodist Episcopal Zion (AMEZ) Church also sent missionaries into the South in the 1860s. Turner was stationed in North Carolina in 1865, where his efforts to win new congregations for the AME Church were largely frustrated by the early success of James Hood, a key missionary for the AMEZ Church in the state. Hood had arrived at least a year ahead of Turner, and his active evangelizing quickly won over African Americans in North Carolina. Shortly after being transferred from his Union Army post in North Carolina to the Freedman's Bureau in Georgia in December 1865, Turner resigned his commission to focus on building the church there.

Turner's determination to free African Americans in the South from the influence of white churches like the ME Church South both reflected and created deep tensions between black and white Methodists in the South as well as between some African Americans and the AME Church. Organized in 1845 as a result of growing sectional conflict over slavery, the ME Church South engaged in missionary work with southern African Americans with the intent of supporting the racial status quo.[65] Consequently, many white southern Methodists opposed the spread of the AME Church in the region. As Turner and other African American missionaries succeeded in organizing new churches in the Reconstruction years, southern whites increasingly perceived the spread of African Methodism as a threat. They clearly understood the troubling implications for the South's racial hierarchy of the creation of independent black churches prepared to preach a race-conscious theology. Likewise, some newly freed African Americans felt threatened by the growth of the AME Church in the South. Many feared that they would lose positions of influence if their congregations affiliated with the AME Church. To a large degree, their concerns were justified because many of them were not ordained by the church to preach and, therefore, could not expect to continue leading AME congregations.[66]

Despite these obstacles, however, energetic evangelists like Turner were very effective in spreading African Methodism across the South. In the twenty-five years between the end of the Civil War and the 1890 census, the first government survey to collect data on congregations by race, African Methodist missionaries succeeded in establishing churches in every ex-Confederate state. This fact is even more remarkable considering that African Methodism was officially banned in each of these states following the 1820s slave revolt led by Denmark Vesey. In addition to the more than 300,000 southern African Americans who had joined the AME Church by 1890, Turner and his fellow missionaries helped to establish more than 3,000 churches in the region with property valued at more than three million dollars. Turner was just as active in organizing African Methodists in Florida, Randolph's home state, as he was in Georgia. He convened the first Annual Conference of the church in Florida in 1867 and traveled the state extensively recruiting new members and building a local itinerancy. As a result, the AME Church in Florida grew rapidly, numbering more than 150 churches and approximately 20,000 members by 1890.[67]

Asa's recollections of Bishop Turner were vivid and certainly contributed to his perceptions of the church as a vehicle for mobilizing African Americans against racial discrimination. Throughout his childhood he frequently heard stories of Turner's missionary exploits and had several opportunities to meet him while attending Annual Conferences with his father. During one church conference, Asa heard Turner outline details of his confrontation with the Georgia legislature over the seating of African American delegates. He recalled that Turner, who had been elected to the state House of Representatives in 1868 but was denied his seat on account of race, said that no African American should "raise a musket to defend a country" that denied his manhood or lift even a finger in its defense unless it "acknowledges that you are men and invests you with the rights pertaining to manhood."[68] Coupled with his father's sermonizing and frequent lectures on church history, exposure to church leaders like Turner accounts for Asa's evolving regard for the AME Church as more of a social and political institution than a strictly religious one.

As the church continued to grow in the South and preach a potent race-conscious religious doctrine, Asa's view of African Methodism came to center on its radical potential more than its spiritual content. As his recognition of the dynamic social impact of the church deepened, the connections he began to make between the church and racial politics became more concrete. In many ways, the evolving view of the church by this son of an ardent, race-conscious Republican who preached a racially charged Gospel, used the militant editorials published in the *Christian Recorder* to teach important life lessons, and exalted church leaders like Henry McNeal Turner as role models was largely predestined. The church's liberation theology as expressed through men like James Randolph, Henry McNeal Turner, and Reverdy Ransom directly shaped Asa's subsequent ideas about social justice that combined egalitarian messages about racial self-worth and industrial reform into fundamental elements of his later civil rights and labor activism. As he continued to reconsider his religious values in the years to come, the core principles he came to associate with African Methodism—race pride, self-sufficiency, opposition to racism—would continue to shape his consciousness.

PART 2

Constructing
Class Consciousness
in the Jazz Age

3

Black Radicalism
in Harlem

*Randolph's Racial and
Political Consciousness*

Just as he remembered the Jacksonville of his childhood, Asa had equally vivid recollections of Harlem in the 1910s and 1920s. Despite his parents' strong misgivings about him leaving home, Asa moved to Harlem in 1911 and thus was on hand to witness some of the most momentous events of the period.[1] He was present in 1916 when Marcus Garvey arrived in the city and made his first public speech in Harlem. He was there in February 1919 when the all-black Fifteenth Regiment of New York's National Guard returned from World War I and marched through the streets of Manhattan to Harlem. And he was a regular attendee at the lavish Harlem soirées thrown by A'Lelia Walker, daughter of millionairess Madam C. J. Walker, where he mingled with the likes of W. E. B. Du Bois, Walter White, and Countee Cullen.[2] These events and the cultural renaissance that thrived in the early and mid-1920s were important parts of the social and political vibrancy of Harlem that so affected Asa for the rest of his life.

More important, however, Asa's move to Harlem marked the beginning of a series of profound transitions that significantly redirected the course of his life. Unlike the segregated South in which he grew up, New York in the 1910s was a much more open place, and Asa was struck by the opportunities afforded African Americans to participate in the cultural life of the city.[3] He was particularly aware of the success of the Johnson brothers, James Weldon and J. Rosamond, fellow Jacksonville natives who wrote songs for several highly acclaimed stage productions. This new sense of freedom accompanied an equally important transition in his thinking about race. His life to this point had revolved around the racial identity fostered by his father, the

AME Church, and his southern upbringing, but Asa found a well-developed radical milieu in Harlem that pushed him to engage a significantly broader political perspective centered on class.[4]

Free of his mother's rigid discipline and the suffocating constraints of Jim Crow, he began calling himself A. Philip and energetically embraced the new and seemingly wide-open intellectual, cultural, and social horizons of black Manhattan. While this name change partly reflected his new independence and adult status, it was also a telling marker in an incredibly important period of transition in Randolph's life. A remarkably sheltered child given the racial realities of the South in the 1890s, Randolph came to New York determined to pursue his own course. Though he was not nearly as assertive as his older brother James, it is easy to imagine that even a meek young man coming into full adulthood might chafe under the strict morals and rigid discipline that governed Randolph's childhood. He certainly felt confined by his parents' expectations. Even as he continued to participate in church activities and studied the Bible at home with his father, he found himself driven less by religious faith than by sociability and intellectual curiosity as he got older.[5] At twenty-two years old, Randolph clearly arrived in New York looking for ways to break away from adolescence by replacing his childhood name with a more stately and authoritative one. In one sense, then, this deliberate act of reinvention reflected the growing divide between the child Randolph was and the man he saw himself becoming; it can be reasonably viewed as an important rite of passage into manhood.

But it was also so much more. It symbolized Randolph's ultimate transition from race to class consciousness. One can imagine that as his interest in the church changed, so too did his interest in following in his father's footsteps. He instead found himself increasingly drawn to Du Bois and his clarion call for a new generation of race leaders. His migration to New York was certainly part of his growing identification with Du Bois's "talented tenth." His decision to begin calling himself A. Philip, a name perhaps intentionally selected to emulate Du Bois, reflected this new self-image. And as Du Bois, whose socialist leanings became more pronounced throughout the 1910s, became a more prominent role model for Randolph, so too did his politics.[6] After securing stable employment and settling into his new community, Randolph set about establishing himself as one of the foremost African American radical intellectuals in Harlem. The changing of his name seems a likely part of this process. In restyling himself A. Philip Randolph, he took a first step toward claiming a position of race leadership and embarked on an intellectual and philosophical journey that would lead him first to explore and then question the efficacy of class consciousness as a solution to the problems of race.

Even before he permanently resettled in New York, Randolph had a very clear sense of the greater economic and social opportunities available to African Americans in the North. While in high school he spent portions of each summer visiting relatives who lived in New York and worked in Harlem. His cousin William Thomas was an apartment building superintendent and routinely hired Randolph to work as a hall boy in the Harlem apartment building he managed. For helping residents with packages, removing trash, and sweeping the hallways Randolph earned eight to twelve dollars a month plus lodging.[7] Yet, the brighter economic fortunes that New York seemed to offer were only part of what fired his imagination about the city. As more and more African American professionals, businessmen, and intellectuals fled the Jim Crow South and settled in places like New York and Chicago, Harlem began to look increasingly like the central place for race-conscious African Americans to live.[8] For Randolph, the arrival of men like W. E. B. Du Bois and later James Weldon Johnson—noted diplomat, poet, and political figure—added an additional air of uncompromising and determined opposition to discrimination to his impression of the city.

Even as these views of Harlem continued to maintain a compelling hold on Randolph's imagination, the impetus for his eventual migration north was much more personal. After graduating from Cookman Institute in 1907, Randolph seemed to flounder a bit as he searched for a direction in life. His father wanted him to enter the ministry, and his mother wanted him to study medicine, but neither course really appealed to him. Instead, he found himself drawn to the performing arts. As a child, he had regularly participated in community and church productions and greatly enjoyed reciting poetry and singing hymns. The annual Christmas cantata put on by his family church was especially important to him. As he recalled these performances in later years, he noted that he was always "given certain parts and sang them with joy."[9] But despite this early interest in performing arts, Randolph never seriously considered acting as a career. His parents frowned on such a career choice as frivolous, and Randolph later explained that on some level he always understood that his "first ambition" was to develop some strategy or organization to challenge segregation. As this realization became more concrete, Harlem seemed like the ideal place to distinguish himself as a leader of his race.[10]

As was the case with many new arrivals to America's urban centers, Randolph's transition to life in Harlem was made substantially easier by his extended family.[11] His cousin William Thomas had left Jacksonville as a young man and eventually settled in Harlem with his wife and daughter. Cousin Willie, as Randolph and the rest of the family affectionately called him, nonetheless returned to Jacksonville every two or three years to visit his mother.

One of these visits precipitated Randolph's first trip out of the South. Although there are not many specific details about how or what decisions were made by the family regarding his visit to New York with Willie, Randolph recalled that it was Willie who first "carried me North on the Comanche." For a youngster who had never been far away from home, this journey to New York City was clearly one of the more exciting instances of his youth.[12]

However, not all of his subsequent trips to New York were as pleasant as this first visit appears to have been. In reflecting back on these experiences, Randolph remembered Willie living with his wife and daughter the first few times that he stayed with the family, but Willie's relationship with his wife deteriorated over time. Randolph recalled his cousin's wife as a "quite portly" woman who was taller than her husband, and as a "kindly and friendly" woman who catered to her husband's needs. Willie, on the other hand, "tended to the sporty side of life." He was a "sort of ham prize fighter" who became violent with his wife, especially when on one of his "periodic drinking binges." One can assume that Willie's drinking got progressively worse over the years. Given the strict Christian morals that governed the Randolph household and James Randolph's explicit condemnation of "strong drink," it is unlikely that Randolph would have been allowed to go to New York if Willie's problems with alcohol were as acute as they eventually became. Randolph himself eventually became a target of Willie's "fits of drunkenness and anger."[13]

Randolph first earned a living in Harlem by working at various odd jobs in and around New York City. Too old at twenty-two to work as a hall boy any longer, he spent a short period of time bouncing around area apartment houses working as an elevator operator for about eighteen dollars a month. It is not clear what role, if any, his cousin may have played in helping him secure any of these positions. The general impression that emerges from Randolph's recollections of these years is that his interaction with Willie decreased significantly as Willie's drinking became more pronounced and he became more violent. Randolph also briefly worked the lunch counter at the Jersey Central train station, temporarily filling in for a regular waiter who was sick. This kind of instability in employment typified his early work history in New York. It was only after he landed a job as a porter for the Consolidated Gas Company on Amsterdam Avenue in the winter of 1912, which paid ten dollars a month, that Randolph experienced anything approaching financial security.[14]

Randolph's experiences in relocating to Harlem and finding stable employment in the city were very much a part of the dynamic that propelled the mass exodus of African Americans out of the South in the first decades of the twentieth century. An increasingly severe cotton crop failure precipitated in part by the spread of the boll weevil across the Mississippi Delta in the late nineteenth century and the heightened racial intimidation associated with the spread of Jim Crow made life more difficult for many African Americans in the South. Also, more and more African Americans found themselves pulled toward the expanding social and economic opportunities created by the rapid industrialization of northern cities.[15] Unfortunately many of the expectations of those who participated in this great migration went unfulfilled. Like Randolph, who found his hopes only partly realized by his move to Harlem, African Americans discovered that the jobs typically open to them in these new industrial centers resembled the ones they left behind in the South: domestic and personal service and menial labor.[16]

Nonetheless the mass movement of African Americans to Harlem was pivotal in the African American urbanization process. In several respects, their increasing concentration in places like Harlem created the foundation for the development of modern black communities in New York and other cities.[17] Despite the existence of distinct black neighborhoods throughout Manhattan earlier, it was only after large numbers of African Americans began moving to Harlem between 1890 and 1910 that the city's black community began to develop the necessary resources to build strong independent institutions. The concentration of African Americans in Harlem created a viable consumer base to support a small but significant African American urban professional class that, in turn, helped to produce community leaders and support institutions that pushed to expand African American equality.[18] Moreover, the size and cohesion of Harlem's African American community afforded it a new measure of protection from racial violence. These changes played a significant role in the growth of a new spirit of racial pride among African Americans during and after World War I that found its clearest expression in the rise of the New Negro and the cultural outpouring of the Harlem Renaissance.[19]

By the time of Randolph's arrival in the city, these developments were well under way. In Manhattan the massive demographic shift of the great migration quickly engulfed the boundaries of the city's established black neighborhoods. In the first decades of the twentieth century, the city's African American population grew 51 percent to 91,709, leaving only Washington, D.C., with a larger urban black population overall.[20] Residents from the city's first distinctly black settlements, the Tenderloin and San Juan Hill neighborhoods, began making their way to Harlem as early as 1900. Despite roots that stretched back to some of the founding families of the colonial era and the continued residency of some of the city's elite, Harlem was primarily a working-class enclave made up of various European ethnic neighborhoods when these first African Americans arrived. The complexion of the area changed dramatically, however, as the city began to feel the full impact of the growing influx of southern black migrants.[21]

As the nineteenth century came to a close, Harlem grew in conjunction with the general development of New York City. Improved sanitation and water supplies along with a proposal to extend the city's elevated train service to the area in the 1880s helped to transform what was mostly undeveloped, open land at midcentury into the country's largest urban African American center by 1910. Initially the municipal improvements undertaken in Harlem to attract white residents led to rampant land speculation as local real estate developers raced to cultivate new properties along expected lines of service. But this optimism quickly gave way to despair as overbuilding glutted the housing market, construction delays pushed back the completion of the train system, and the anticipated demand for new homes in the area failed to materialize. By 1900, developers on Harlem's west side found themselves overburdened with new housing stock and in heated competition to attract consumer interest. The intensifying pressure to fill this vacant residential space led them to view the growing black communities spilling over the narrow boundaries of the Tenderloin and San Juan Hill neighborhoods in new ways.[22]

This need to fill Harlem's new residential space occurred at a time when Manhattan's industrial development and racial tensions began to push African Americans out of their established west side neighborhoods. In 1903 the Pennsylvania Railroad began buying up large tracts of land in the Tenderloin district to build the Pennsylvania terminal. The new construction destroyed several blocks of predominantly African American housing.[23] Also, eruptions of racial violence hastened the exodus of African Americans from the west side. Throughout the 1890s, years in which the city's African American population continued to expand, racial hostility between black and white workers simmered. Desperate for work but largely excluded from local labor unions and most industries, African Americans nonetheless put downward pressure on wages as a ready source of labor when white workers walked off their jobs.[24] Tensions escalated, and racial violence ensued as white workers became more sensitive to the economic threat that African Americans posed. Racial violence broke out in the Hell's Kitchen area in 1900. By the time it spread to the San Juan Hill area in 1905, African Americans were moving to Harlem in ever larger numbers.[25]

This inflow of African Americans to the area helped to rescue Harlem's real estate market from financial ruin. Despite some initial reluctance to accept black residents, the dire need to realize some measure of return on real estate investments opened the way for significant numbers of African Americans to move into the area. Rather than focus on new home sales, developers converted properties into rental units and began recruiting African American tenants. Offered decent housing for the first time in the city's history, African Americans flocked to Harlem in droves. As early as 1905, all of the households on One Hundred Thirty-third and One Hundred Thirty-fourth streets between Lenox Avenue and Seventh Avenue were occupied by African Americans. Within a few years, Harlem's black population was estimated at approximately fifty thousand, establishing it as the new center of black Manhattan and the nation's largest African American neighborhood.[26]

A. Philip Randolph was very much a part of the dynamic that propelled the great migration forward. But personal considerations were equally important in his decision to leave Jacksonville. A great admirer of Du Bois and his thoughtful critique of Booker T. Washington's advocacy of industrial education, Randolph viewed himself as a member of Du Bois's "talented tenth" and believed New York was the best place to distinguish himself. Upon arriving in the city, Randolph sought out the educational, social, and cultural resources to achieve this goal.[27] It was this compelling drive to distinguish himself as a race leader that led him to enroll at City College of New York and participate in the various community and group activities that would profoundly reshape his thinking about the causes of and solutions to the problem of racial discrimination.

As a backdrop, Harlem was uniquely situated for nurturing the transformation of Randolph's racial outlook. The steady influx of African Americans in the prewar years created a special environment where emerging radicals like Randolph began to engage each other as well as an older generation of African Americans like Du Bois and James Weldon Johnson.[28] The resulting interaction was critical in the continuing development of black radicalism in Harlem. Even though African Americans in other northern cities also flirted with socialism and communism in the 1910s and 1920s, "most of the socialist and communist activities during the period," Randolph noted, had their "loci in the black and white intelligentsia" that was most vibrant in New York.[29] In addition to developing relationships with key state and national Socialist Party figures such as Morris Hillquit and Eugene Debs, Randolph also established several important connections with black radicals in Harlem in his first years in the city. Shortly after his arrival, he met Hubert Harrison, whom many regarded as the "pioneer Afro-American advocate of socialism" prior to Socialist Party organizing activity in Harlem.[30] He and Frank R. Crosswaith, an active member of the Socialist Party who tirelessly promoted class consciousness among African Americans as a general organizer for the International Ladies Garment Workers Union under David Dubinsky, became close colleagues in the years leading up to World War I. He and Chandler Owen, a Columbia University graduate student, partnered together to found the *Messenger* in 1917. And both Cyril Briggs, the West Indian Marxist who wrote editorials for the *Amsterdam News* and later began his own radical publication called the *Crusader,* and Richard B. Moore, co-founder with Briggs of the militant African Blood Brotherhood, were also important early acquaintances.[31] Randolph's relationship with each of these individuals was vital to his intellectual development because of their substantial impact on his awakening class consciousness as well as Harlem's radical landscape.

In addition to forming a unique backdrop for the development of Randolph's nascent radicalism, Harlem's emergence created a viable readership for the various journals that he and his associates published in these years. The subsequent development of a significantly more militant racial attitude associated with the growing ghetto and the cultural outpouring of the Harlem Renaissance helped to legitimize his evolving criticism of industrial capitalism among African Americans in substantial ways.[32] As African Americans continued to move into northern cities throughout the war years, many of these new urban residents began to think about their increasingly independent and self-sufficient communities as new vehicles for demanding greater inclusion into the social landscape of these cities. These "New Negroes" focused their attention on cultivating the growing political and economic strength of their communities into effective demands for recognition of their right to participate in urban society on a more equal basis.[33] As these New Negroes increasingly insisted on their fair share of political representation, patronage, and municipal resources, the basic themes of organization and social justice that would constitute the heart of Randolph's critique of industrial capitalism encountered a considerably more sympathetic audience. Even though most African Americans never lost faith in the basic tenets of capitalism, the radical critique that Randolph and others began to espouse during World War I and beyond fit with the New Negro phenomenon of the period.

Radicals such as Randolph and his close associate Frank R. Crosswaith were very much aware of the important connections between this evolving New Negro attitude and the class consciousness they set out to foster among

African Americans after World War I. From the end of the war through the Depression years, they steadfastly maintained that New Negroes should persistently demand social and political equality and sought to connect the rising tide of African Americans' racial militancy to postwar labor radicalism. The basic contours of this view took shape in the *Messenger*, where essays such as Randolph's "A New Crowd—A New Negro," published in the May–June 1919 issue, demanded "complete social, economic, and political justice" and pushed African Americans to join with white radicals to build an open, color-blind, democratic society.[34] This sentiment also shaped Crosswaith's Harlem Labor Committee and Trade Union Committee for Organizing Negro Workers that worked to organize barbers, laundry workers, and elevator operators in Harlem. Both groups carried the message of race consciousness and interracial class cooperation through the early 1920s.[35] Randolph's Brotherhood of Sleeping Car Porters (BSCP) and the campaign to organize Pullman porters extended this connection into the 1930s. It was this point that Crosswaith intended to highlight in a 1938 commentary criticizing more mainstream African American journalists. Instead of "interpreting to the outside world the life and conduct of this race in terms purely sensational, comical, and religio-fanatical," he insisted that African American journalists should more keenly note that "negro working men and women today in ever encouraging numbers are learning the efficacy and importance of economic organization." He argued that the growth of union membership among African Americans was "a highly significant phenomenon" because this "vast army of New Negroes . . . are learning how to rely upon the organized might of their class and race as the way out of our present social and economic Gethsemane."[36] The connection that Crosswaith made between organizing black workers and broad-based economic and social justice for African Americans was a theme that he and Randolph consistently sounded through these years and was central to the socialist vision that they adopted in this period.[37]

Crosswaith made this point more explicitly in a 1934 speech before the Commonwealth Club, a socialist organization in San Francisco. Using this instance to explain further the need for organization among African Americans, he contended that it "ought to be plain to all who possess observing eyes that so long as injustice obtains in the world, especially on the scale such as that of which the Negro has been the peculiar victim, the day is bound to come when that injustice will stretch its treacherous hand across lines of class and nationality and so-called race." African Americans, he noted, faced a particularly critical "crossroads" where in one direction led the "beaten path of the status quo . . . lavishly strewn with the blood and bones of all workers, a path piled high with the bleached bones and charred bodies of Negroes, the path of exploitation, of war, of race prejudice, of lynching, of segregation and disfranchisement." This was the "path of capitalism with its inherent injustices and inequalities: the path of capitalist competition and human exploitation for private gain." Conversely, he explained, the other path led in the direction of "peaceful cooperation, to social and economic and political equality of all God's children who usefully serve society regardless of race, creed, or color." Because industrial capitalism promoted the kind of economic and social competition that allowed the "exploiters of labor to keep the working class divided" by race and, thus, more effectively "rob, rule, and exploit both black and white labor," Crosswaith maintained that "the logic of economic and social evolution" pointed "unerringly to socialism."[38]

At the core of Crosswaith's explanation of the choices facing African Americans was a view of "social equality" that held that "all social agencies and institutions in the world are the result of the contributions of all the so-called races." His contention, one that Randolph shared, was that because every race of man had "contributed its quota of knowledge, experience, and culture to the sum total of what we call civilization," everyone was "entitled to the use and enjoyment of all the available advantages accruing there from on a basis of equality with every other contributing group." This condition of equality, however, could not exist "under our present socio-economic setup" because "capitalism rests upon inequality." He insisted that the centralization and monopolization of land, natural resources, and the means of production in the hands of an ever smaller class and the growing propertylessness of the majority of the population made "futile and meaningless" any discussion of "equality, democracy, liberty and such other myths under the capitalist system." True democracy, liberty, fraternity, and equality, Crosswaith maintained, could only be realized when the world was free of the "monstrosity of private ownership for profit in the socially necessary means of life."[39]

The central threads of Crosswaith's argument—that African Americans could secure their particular interests only through industrial organization and that the voracious competition at capitalism's core fundamentally undermined social justice for all but the privileged few—are also key to understanding Randolph's view of socialism. Like Crosswaith, Randolph believed that industrial organization was critical to labor's effort to secure its "moral right to its share of work" and the "resulting value" it produced. In a 1942 speech to Canadian Pacific Railway workers he explained that wealth was "primarily" the result of the "combination of labor, land, capital, and management" and that workers' rights could be secured only through concerted action according to their economic interests. To illustrate his point, Randolph referred to the suffrage movement and the struggle over voting rights for women. He noted that while women were "entitled to the right to vote years and years before they secured it," their ability to exercise that right depended on the "practical and scientific functions" of "organizing their forces." Labor could do no less if it expected to overthrow the economic exploitation of industrial capitalism. To this end, he insisted, it was vitally important that workers understood the "basic principles" that underlined labor's struggle for organization.[40]

This emphasis on labor organization both grew out of and shaped Randolph's critique of industrial capitalism. In a speech to the Educational Political Conference in Chicago, Randolph explained that war, unemployment, and totalitarianism were the "unmistakable proof that our present political and economic capitalist order is unable to satisfy the needs of modern man or to keep him from disaster." In his view the "problem" of industrial capitalism was "organic" in that the system has "never been able to supply sufficient purchasing power to feed itself." Despite a higher standard of living than Europe, the wage scale for American workers "has never been high enough to consume the products that needed to be consumed in order to keep the productive plant operating." Moreover, because big business could always "take back most of labor's gains through the manipulation of prices," industrial capitalism created the conditions by which "one section of the population appropriates a part of the product which others have produced without giving any equivalent exchange." In Randolph's estimation this "technical defeat" endemic to capitalist economic systems was more than just economic injustice; it amounted to deliberate economic exploitation.

Having explained the basic flaws of industrial capitalism, Randolph then insisted that the ability to address these problems effectively depended upon whether the nation could work out a constructive understanding of the relationship between the "democracy expressed in the Declaration of Independence [and] the federal Constitution we now have and the change in our social and economic system we now need." He viewed the kind of competition inherent to capitalist systems as antithetical to open, participatory democracy. The "socio-economic-political debacle" of capitalism so threatened the nation's fundamental democratic ideals, he insisted, that "if the democratic forces of the people do not decide one way soon . . . who shall control our economic life and to what end . . . the fascist forces inherent in monopoly capitalism and in the nature of the state will decide it another way." For Randolph, the only meaningful solution to the shortcomings of capitalism was the implementation of a system of democratic socialism that would "constitute a break with the old political and economic order" and would "refuse entangling alliances with the old capitalist parties." What was needed, he argued, was a "socialized economy and a democratized society."[41]

The nexus between industrial organization and social justice at the center of both Crosswaith's and Randolph's criticisms of capitalism accurately reflected and significantly shaped the way black radicals in Harlem in the 1920s understood socialism's relevance to African Americans.[42] Following the war, Randolph, Crosswaith, and the intellectual cohort they represented spread throughout the community to proselytize about the virtues of class consciousness among African Americans.[43] Yet, their success in this cause was marginal at best. Despite a sincere belief in his message, Randolph understood that most "black audiences who came to listen to the *Messenger* editors and other black radical speakers were not so much concerned about the exposition of Marxist and socialist thought as they were in listening to the attacks by the speakers on conservative advocates." Citing the basic political, social, and economic conservatism of most African Americans as the principal "reason why there was no dynamic mass movement of black socialists and communists in America during this period," Randolph maintained that African Americans in Harlem were "primarily interested in seeing and listening to a black radical" rather than "becoming involved in such a militant movement."[44] Despite this lack of success in converting large numbers of African Americans to socialism, the message of unionization and social justice that Randolph, Crosswaith, and others continued to preach became an important component of the racially militant atmosphere created by the New Negroes and captured in the Harlem Renaissance.[45]

The available record of Randolph's early days in Harlem paint a picture of a young man fascinated by the sights and sounds of the city and involved in a wide range of activities in the community. His childhood interest in the performing arts found new outlets in the variety and vaudeville shows that were so popular in New York during this period, and he initially spent a considerable amount of his free time in the city's theaters. Though he never seriously considered acting as a profession, Randolph was "pretty well seasoned in Shakespearean lore" and, shortly after settling into his new surroundings, founded a Shakespearean society called Ye Friends of Shakespeare. This acting troupe, which included his future wife, performed scenes from *Hamlet*, *Julius Caesar*, *Othello*, the *Merchant of Venice*, and *Romeo and Juliet* in Harlem's churches and community centers. These productions helped to draw

Randolph into the social life of the community, but they also informed his evolving worldview. *Hamlet* in particular stood out in his mind. In reflecting back on this time years later, he explained that throughout his life and career he strove to abide by Polonius's admonition to Hamlet "above all to thine own self be true then thou canst be false to no man."[46]

Randolph was also actively involved in the young adult auxiliaries of several Harlem churches.[47] Even though he had shed the religiosity of the country churches in which he grew up, he still clearly viewed the church as an important source of community and eagerly participated in its social activities.[48] In addition to the Baptist Young People's Union of Mount Olivet Baptist Church and the Lyceum of Saint Mark's Methodist Church, Randolph also was particularly active in the Epworth League of Salem Methodist Episcopal Church, where Frederick Cullen, father of the noted poet Countee Cullen, served as pastor, and the Allen Christian Endeavor Society of Bethel AME Church under Reverdy Ransom. Both of these latter organizations affected Randolph's life in significant ways. In the winter of 1912–13, he and an acquaintance from the Epworth League named Ernest T. Welcome jointly formed the Brotherhood of Labor, a "glorified employment bureau" for newly arrived African American migrants from the South. Though short-lived, this endeavor was Randolph's first attempt to put his incipient class sensibilities into practice. He later recalled that he made a determined effort to "give the organization a fraternal-labor complexion."[49]

The Brotherhood of Labor was also the catalyst that fortuitously brought Randolph together with his future wife, Lucille E. Green. Randolph and Welcome opened their employment agency in a ground-floor apartment on the corner of One Hundred Thirty-fifth Street and Lenox Avenue. Around the same time, Lucille Green, a former school teacher turned hairdresser, opened a beauty salon in an apartment down the hall. It was this confluence of events that brought Randolph and Green together. At thirty-one, Green was several years older than Randolph. Their courtship was relatively short, and they married later in 1914. Over the next forty-nine years, the couple, who affectionately called each other Buddy, established a solid, loving relationship that also spilled over into Randolph's Socialist Party activities and organizing work. Unlike Randolph's mother, Elizabeth, who mostly eschewed the world outside her family, Lucille Green Randolph not only owned her own business but was also active in the social and political affairs of Harlem. A protégé of Madam C. J. Walker and friend of her daughter A'Lelia Walker, Lucille Randolph was a regular member of the Harlem glitterati that surrounded the Walkers' lavish brownstone on One Hundred Thirty-sixth Street;

she became an active member of the Socialist Party and ran for a seat in the New York State Assembly on the party's ticket in 1921. Eugene V. Debs, five-time party nominee for president, even came to Harlem to campaign with her. Even as her politics and Randolph's deepening radicalism and outspoken criticism of Harlem's elite eventually eroded the customer base of her salon, Lucille Randolph steadfastly supported her husband's class causes and trade union activities.[50]

Around the same time that the new couple started their courtship, Randolph also met Chandler Owen, a young law school student at Columbia University. Originally from North Carolina, Owen came to Columbia in 1913 after graduating from Virginia Union University in Richmond, Virginia. Initially introduced to Lucille Randolph by a mutual acquaintance at one of A'Lelia Walker's parties, Owen and the Randolphs became fast friends. In the years to come Randolph and Owen founded and co-edited the *Messenger*, a radical journal with a decidedly Marxist point of view. Randolph recalled that their relationship first blossomed as a result of reading the works of Lester Ward, Karl Marx, and other books checked out of Columbia's law library.[51] This early interaction was vitally important to Randolph's intellectual and radical development and explains why he listed Owen among those individuals who "greatly influenced" his life and career. Together with a New York University student named John Ramsey, Randolph and Owen organized a discussion group called the National Independent Political Council and held forums on political, economic, social, and religious questions. Primarily concerned with the "fight for racial and social justice," Randolph's Independent Political Council eventually attracted the attention of other like-minded African American radicals like Harrison, Briggs, and Moore.[52]

Like other radical discussion groups in Harlem, Randolph's Independent Political Council often conducted meetings at Bethel AME Church. Reverdy Ransom, who served as pastor there until 1912, also embraced socialism as a bulwark against the onslaughts of industrial capitalism.[53] He fervently believed that the raw individualism and naked competition at capitalism's core fundamentally undercut God's "ultimate goal" for mankind. He ardently supported the working class, insisting in part that socialism brought "all the people to participate in the rivalry of life upon a footing of equality."[54] The atmosphere of social engagement that Ransom created at Bethel closely matched Randolph's deepening interest in addressing the key social and political issues that confronted African Americans. The combination of Ransom's commitment to social action, his class critique of industrial capitalism, and the evolving racial consciousness of radicals like Randolph pushed socialism and its merits to the forefront of the Independent Political Council's agenda. As Randolph began to develop a stronger class consciousness in the years leading up to World War I, one can look back on his early involvement with Ransom and Bethel AME Church as an important moment.

Bethel was also a key component of Randolph's introduction to and interaction with established Harlem radicals. Even though he was aware of intellectuals like Hubert Harrison, one of Harlem's most renowned African American radicals and soapbox orators, Randolph's opportunity to get to know Harrison personally came from their shared association with Bethel.[55] Harrison held regular sessions of his Liberty League, a discussion group organized to inspire and educate African Americans in Harlem, at Bethel, and Randolph was "very impressed" with the radical nature of the group's discourse.[56] Over time Randolph came to consider Harrison a good friend, and their association placed him near the center of Harlem's radical milieu. As Richard B. Moore, a protégé of Harrison and frequent contributor to the *Messenger* in its early days, recounted, Harrison was central to the development of "a score of young, militant, and studious Afro-Americans" who began to enthusiastically embrace class theories and discuss their practical application for challenging racial discrimination. In addition to his various other community activities, Moore remembered Harrison's outdoor "university"— Harrison's nightly street corner lectures on different topics related to race and the achievements of people of color—as especially influential. Even though Harrison began to move toward a more "race first" orientation after 1917, he remained a vital figure among Harlem intellectuals, and the relationship that he and Randolph developed as a result of their mutual association with Bethel helped to move Randolph toward the center of Harlem's radical network.[57]

In addition to Harrison, several other militants and intellectuals around Harlem in these years played important roles in the various endeavors that Randolph undertook early in his career. Randolph singled out W. A. Domingo, a Jamaican-born immigrant, as a "close associate" and "brilliant" leader of the period. Domingo became a regular contributor to the *Messenger* and later went on to publish his own weekly called the *Emancipator* to "preach deliverance to the slaves." Along with Harrison, Crosswaith, George Schuyler, and a few others, Randolph placed Domingo at the forefront of those African American intellectuals who "carried the torch on behalf of black radicalism" during World War I. This group of radical intellectuals also pioneered the Harlem street corner meetings that Randolph viewed as one of the "most effective" educational tools of the time. Harrison and Domingo were especially prone to turning these street meetings into "very far-reaching discussions

about the role of black Americans in the struggle of the African people."
Randolph recalled that even some young white radicals like Jay Lovestone, a
socialist and founding member of the American Communist Party, "shared
the soapbox with us in carrying the message and the fight against imperialism in Africa." In fact, it was this campaign against imperialism that gave
Marcus Garvey his first platform in Harlem.[58] Although they would shortly
become bitter opponents as Randolph's class sensibilities became more pronounced and Garvey's race-first appeal became more popular, in these early
days there was room enough for both of them on Harlem's street corners.[59]

Randolph's early years in Harlem reflected the significance of the combined
impact of New York's open cultural landscape, Harlem's unique radical atmosphere, and the various relationships that he developed as a result of his
participation in groups such as the Allen Christian Endeavor Society on his
social consciousness. The personal and intellectual relationships that he cultivated in his first years in New York helped to significantly reshape his basic
understanding of the origins of racial discrimination. Despite his lingering
attachment to the racial worldview of his childhood, as his understanding
of class theories deepened Randolph became increasingly convinced that
racial inequality was endemic to industrial capitalism and was not simply a
byproduct of racial discrimination. His brief stay at the City College of New
York further nurtured this new trajectory in his thinking.

4

Crossing the Color Line

Randolph's Transition from Race to Class Consciousness

In some ways, campus life at the City College of New York (CCNY) in 1912–13 directly complemented aspects of the radical environment that Randolph found in Harlem. While Hubert Harrison, W.A. Domingo, and other black radicals were turning uptown street corners into open-air forums on racial discrimination, socialism, and the worldwide plight of people of color, CCNY students were organizing campus rallies to protest the spread of authoritarian governments in Europe and supporting textile strikes in Lawrence, Massachusetts (1912), and Patterson, New Jersey (1913), led by the Industrial Workers of the World (IWW).[1] The energy and vociferous support such activities generated on campus helped to familiarize Randolph with key Socialist Party figures like Eugene V. Debs and William "Big Bill" Haywood, who were both incredibly popular with CCNY students.[2] When the Intercollegiate Socialist Society, an organization dedicated to promoting the study and advocacy of socialism among college students and faculty, established a chapter at CCNY, it helped to give even more order and regularity to on-campus socialist rallies and sustain the radical nature of campus politics during Randolph's tenure.[3]

This dynamic campus activism largely complemented the radical discourse that permeated Harlem.[4] Even as Harrison, Domingo, and others railed against racial injustice and exploitation, they spoke from the same radical lexicon as student demonstrators protesting militarism and unchecked capitalism. For Randolph this overlap placed class theory in a new light. Prior to enrolling at CCNY, his dealings with class had primarily revolved around study group discussions of its efficacy for African Americans.[5] The campus activism and radical politics that so animated CCNY's student body served to elaborate further core aspects of class theory and give new shape to its practical application. Thus, despite the obvious racial and ethnic differences that separated campus life at CCNY from the black community that ultimately developed around it in Harlem, Randolph found important encouragement in both realms that promoted greater class consciousness.[6]

Randolph began taking evening classes at City College in 1912 through its Teachers' Extension Program. Organized by the school's Department of Education in 1908, the extension program provided continuing education classes to area teachers, offering a full slate of liberal arts and fine arts courses. Randolph's initial course load was weighted heavily toward the performing arts. A young man intensely interested in Shakespeare, an interest further nurtured by a CCNY course he took in English literature, Randolph initially enrolled in drama and public speaking classes to hone his acting skills and polish his elocution. He quickly turned his attention to politics and economics, however, as he was drawn more deeply into the political life of the campus and became more active in Harlem's radical circles. In fact, it was this academic transition that gave Randolph's commitment to socialism new momentum. He dropped his drama and public speaking courses to enroll in history and economics classes. This slate of new subjects focused on the distinguishing features of European civilization with specific emphasis on the aims, principles, and history of socialism in Europe and the concrete problems associated with trade unionism. These new areas of study broadened his understanding of Marx, brought him into closer contact with student activists on campus, and propelled him toward the Socialist Party.[7]

Such courses were not always a part of City College's curriculum, however. The College of the City of New York was founded in 1848 largely as a response to growing public pressure for free public education beyond the elementary level. As early as the 1830s, working-class New Yorkers as well as many of the city's businessmen began to push for reforms that would expand educational opportunities and effectively equip students with practical business skills.[8] However, the initial organization of this new municipal college, originally called the Free Academy, proceeded along very different lines. Its intention was to surpass its private counterparts by offering a curriculum that combined the practical studies and college preparation of the city's established academies with the traditional classical studies offered at the time in most American colleges. Its first students took courses in mathematics, history, classic languages, chemistry, physics, and civil engineering.[9] This basic curriculum remained in place until 1903, when CCNY underwent a comprehensive transformation that significantly changed the composition of its faculty, its student body, and the general character of the institution.

In 1895 the board of trustees voted unanimously to move the college to St. Nicholas Heights between One Hundred Thirty-eighth and One Hundred Fortieth streets, where it would have more room to expand. This physical relocation coincided with even more sweeping changes over the course of the next decade. As part of a series of administrative reforms in these years that created a more progressive executive committee, the board of trustees also hired John Huston Finley as college president in 1902. Finley, a graduate of Johns Hopkins University and protégé of progressive economist and social science pioneer Richard T. Ely, came to New York with a vision for modernizing CCNY's curriculum.[10] Emphasizing the importance of original research especially in the social sciences, a professional faculty committed to scholarly research, and individualized instruction rooted in the elective system pioneered in the 1860s by Harvard University president William Eliot, Finley overhauled the classical focus that had dominated the college's past program of study.[11] This triumvirate of administrative changes—the progressive reorganization of the board, the presidency, and the faculty—was only one component of a broader institutional transformation that took place in the years surrounding the turn of the century.[12]

As the city of New York took on the characteristics of a genuine metropolis in the late 1880s and 1890s, the pressure on City College to reorganize itself intensified. The reorganized board of trustees and some influential alumni sensitive to the reform measures reshaping other area institutions began pushing for an overhaul of CCNY's classical character.[13] They watched as other institutions began to implement a whole host of progressive reforms and grew deeply concerned that CCNY would continue to fall behind other schools of its rank if it remained the same conservative liberal arts college it had always been.[14] In addition to fundamental changes in the school's basic curriculum, they sought to expand the faculty and encourage more modern teaching methods. Despite steadfast opposition from a cohort of old-guard central administrators and faculty committed to classical instruction, new momentum for such changes developed with the move uptown to St. Nicholas Heights. These new facilities and the ample room they provided for expansion gave reformers new leverage to push for change.

The board quickly took steps to change the composition of the faculty. In 1897 it voted to promote eight longtime instructors to the rank of assistant professor, giving them pay raises and a new voice in shaping academic policy. This infusion of new faculty became the foundation of a younger, more liberal contingent of new professors who created the progressive majority needed to help transform the school. At the same time the board moved to purge old-guard adherents to classical instruction and thus further strengthen the progressive character of the faculty. When the New York state legislature voted to create a special pension fund near the turn of the century, the board quickly pressed several senior members of the faculty and central administration, including former president Alexander Webb, into retirement. This move effectively neutralized long-standing opposition to implementing the progressive curriculum and instructional style that came to characterize modern metropolitan universities.[15]

These vital administrative and pedagogical changes implemented by the board in the 1890s paralleled changes in the composition of the student body that were equally significant. Initially City College drew the bulk of its students from the city's established middle-class, native-born whites of several generations standing and the descendents of Northern and Western European immigrants. However, as the origins of the city's steady influx of immigrants shifted to Southern and Eastern Europe in the 1880s and 1890s, CCNY began to attract more students from the city's growing population of Russian Jews.[16] In fact, by the time Finley assumed the presidency in 1902, Russian Jews comprised approximately 75 percent of the total student body.[17]

For Randolph, this transformation in the student body was critical. These students significantly changed the political consciousness and urgency of campus life. They remained deeply interested and engaged in the events of Eastern Europe and immersed in the long and deep socialist traditions that fundamentally shaped immigrant communities in New York in these years.[18] Whatever Randolph learned in his classes about socialist movements or class critiques of modern economies, it was the dynamic campus atmosphere created by his classmates that taught him meaningful lessons about the practical application of class theory and radical protest.

Randolph's on-campus experience was also shaped by his interaction with Morris R. Cohen, City College's liberal professor of philosophy who was an influential mentor for some of the school's most politically active students. A forceful critic of both the philosophical pragmatism of William James and realism's preoccupation with the objectivity of the physical, Cohen used his classroom to convey the scale and scope of difficult and unresolved philosophical questions. He brought a discursive intellect to bear on class discussions that often left students with more questions than answers.[19] Describing his interaction with Cohen, Randolph explained that he could never get a definitive answer from him on any subject. Cohen's determined refusal to take a concrete stand on issues forced Randolph and his classmates to think for themselves and reason out solutions on their own. At the same time, then, that Randolph was learning about socialism in his courses and watching his classmates organize in support of workers' rights, his interaction with Cohen prompted him to take a more nuanced view of Marx, class consciousness, and African Americans' place in American society.[20]

Given his active involvement in student life and obvious regard for faculty members like Cohen, Randolph's enrollment at City College was surprisingly brief. School records list him as a member of the class of 1919, but he was actually there only between 1912 and 1914, and there is no indication that he ever graduated. Though there is some speculation that he left school for financial reasons, a more likely explanation is that his deepening interest in trade unionism drew him away from his studies.[21] Reflecting back on these years, Randolph explained that it was during this period that he "first began the job of organizing black workers." He sought and received a federal charter from the American Federation of Labor to organize New York's elevator operators. The effort ultimately failed, for the "organization was not of long standing."[22] Although he would not officially join the Socialist Party of America for several more years, Randolph's departure from CCNY marked the beginning of his final break with the exclusively racial worldview that shaped his childhood.

After leaving City College, Randolph's interest in class issues and trade unionism seemed to deepen. In 1917, he and Chandler Owen were arrested at an antiwar rally in Cleveland, Ohio, for advising African Americans not to support the war. While Randolph was speaking to the audience and Owen was distributing antiwar literature, federal agents moved in and took them into custody for violating the Espionage Act, which prohibited seditious activities. Eugene V. Debs was arrested on the same charge one year later. Debs was sentenced to ten years in prison, but at Randolph and Owen's arraignment the judge dismissed the complaint against them because he did not believe two African Americans were capable of independently producing such articulate antiwar propaganda.[23] Randolph recalled that the judge remained doubtful when told that Randolph and Owen were solely responsible for the distributed leaflets. The judge told their lawyer that he "believed that some of the leaders of the Socialist Party are using these boys."[24] This was perhaps the first and last time that the pervasive racial bias that so constrained African Americans' lives during this period worked in Randolph's favor; he and Owen were released and allowed to return to New York.

Randolph returned from this antiwar tour of the Midwest and almost immediately became part of the growing opposition among some Harlem radicals to Marcus Garvey's increasingly race-first appeal. Though Randolph was not ready to launch the "Garvey Must Go" campaign that took shape in the pages of the *Messenger* after the war, Garvey's rapidly growing popularity seriously offended Randolph's evolving class sensibilities.[25] It seems likely that his perception of this developing tension between race and class in Harlem factored in his effort to form the League of Darker Races in 1917.[26] One of the central themes of his antiwar message was that war primarily grew out of capitalism's imperial efforts to expand markets. This critique closely coincided with African Americans' efforts to raise the issue of European colonialism in Africa as a key issue at the Paris Peace Conference that followed the war.[27] In organizing the League of Darker Races, Randolph apparently intended to build greater support among African Americans in Harlem for anti-imperialism in Africa. But Randolph's growing rivalry with Garvey cannot be overlooked as a significant factor in the organization's origins either. Garvey, too, opposed imperialism in Africa but based his position on a strictly racial point of view.[28] In forming the League of Darker Races, Randolph offered Harlemites concerned about postwar Africa an alternative to Garvey that also fit with the class consciousness he had begun to embrace.[29]

With the war coming to a close, Randolph made a second attempt to draw African Americans into trade unionism. He and Owen traveled to Newport News and Portsmouth, Virginia, to organize the large number of African Americans who worked there in the shipyards. In recounting this trip, Randolph noted that they "encountered tremendous opposition" from black church leaders who were firmly "under the influence of the shipping corporations." Area churches stood solidly "against the organization of black workers in the shipyards." In Randolph's estimation, the staunch opposition of these churches explained why he and Owen never made "any appreciable and measurable" progress in unionizing black workers in Virginia.[30] They returned to New York just in time for the 1917 mayoral election where Morris Hillquit, leader of the Socialist Party in New York, ran as the party candidate. Randolph worked as Hillquit's campaign manager in Harlem and found himself pulled into a closer orbit around the New York party. Even though he was not yet an official party member, Randolph managed to turn out about 25 percent of the vote cast in Harlem for Hillquit. Hillquit ultimately lost to John F. Hylan, who ran on the Tammany Hall ticket, but the 1917 campaign marked the beginning of Randolph's longtime affiliation with the Socialist Party.[31]

Randolph joined the party the following year. Even though it had lost much of the organizational cohesion that propelled Debs's 1912 presidential campaign, Randolph still came to view it as African Americans' best political option. Increasingly convinced that the primary cause of African Americans' plight was the impact of racial discrimination on their ability to "sell their labor in the market effectively," he came to believe that the solutions to this problem rested with the unionization of black workers, the overhaul of industrial capitalism, and the Socialist Party.[32] Like his father, who organized African Americans in Jacksonville to defend themselves against racial violence, Randolph intuitively understood the need for African Americans to organize for the purpose of economic self-defense. Moreover, his brief college experience illustrated the potential power of radical politics to energize whole communities. Both his childhood experiences and his recent and deepening class consciousness, then, became a potent backdrop for Randolph's emerging view of the Socialist Party as the only real option for African Americans in national politics.

Founded in 1901, the Socialist Party of America drew together a diverse coalition of left-wing organizations that strongly opposed the rapid advance of American industrialization following the Civil War. Drawing on previous radical movements like the Grange and Populists, the party brought together a wide array of groups and political points of view. At its center, though, were "constructivist" elements led by Victor Berger in Milwaukee and Morris Hillquit in New York, revivalists from the Plains states who fused socialist theory with the open emotion of the camp meeting, the remnants of Debs's American Railway Union, and syndicalist groups in the West associated with the IWW. Initially sharing little but a general antipathy for industrial capitalism, representatives of each faction arrived at the Socialist Party's founding convention in Indianapolis with widely varying ideas of how to affect best the cooperative commonwealth.[33] Any tensions that may have emerged, however, were substantially overshadowed by the delegates' genuine belief in their eventual triumph over industrial capitalism. This abiding belief in their ultimate success is central to understanding the Socialist Party before the 1920s.[34]

The bright-eyed optimism that characterized the Socialist Party's founding convention impacted Randolph's memories nearly twenty years later. His recollections are replete with the many "delightful" party meetings he attended, where he and others passionately discussed the "baleful effects of uncontrolled capitalism upon the working class and the role of socialism in ushering in the dawn of a new day for the oppressed and disinherited toiling masses." Even the wide gulf between party conservatives like Berger and Hillquit and radical western syndicalists did not dampen Randolph's exuberance; he praised both factions with equal vigor. He commended Berger and Hillquit for "steadfastly" holding to the principle of individual liberty and the "philosophy of democracy and pluralistic sources of authority and power" and, at the same time, lauded William "Big Bill" Haywood and the IWW for challenging the process of "government by injunction." So long as there was basic agreement that industrial capitalism "did not provide for the enjoyment of basic freedoms by all the people of the country," Randolph turned a blind eye to differences within the party.[35]

In leading their respective local parties in Milwaukee and New York, Victor Berger and Morris Hillquit pursued an electoral strategy that sought to build political alliances with local trade unions to win elective offices. Both firmly believed that without clear evidence of capitalism's eminent demise, socialists should work to win over workers and ensure that they were all aware of their class interests. Berger set out to ameliorate the harsh conditions of the shop floor by pushing progressive reforms that addressed workers' daily concerns, whereas Hillquit thought to transform capitalism by gradually implementing social and economic changes through political action.[36] Berger was more supportive of the American Federation of Labor (AFL) than Hillquit, but both agreed that the Socialist Party's main objectives could be achieved most efficiently through the AFL rather than the IWW. They not only opposed dual unionism, building parallel political organizations within existing labor unions, but were also put off by the syndicalist view of industrial sabotage as an acceptable tactic for effecting change. Though he was no ardent supporter of the AFL, Hillquit in particular believed that dual unionism created a level of labor competition that would alienate the AFL and its affiliates. In general, both Hillquit and Berger shared the view that gradual improvements in work conditions and progressive reform were preferable to the unchecked hegemony of capital.[37]

For Randolph and the small group of African American socialists who had been recruited into the New York Socialist Party's Harlem district as early as 1917, this commitment to progressive reform and political mobilization was attractive. Despite Hillquit's strict emphasis on class and Berger's blatantly racist appeals to Milwaukee labor unions, Randolph and others clearly understood that there were significant, if untended, implications inherent in the party's stance for African Americans "seeking human status and full freedom."[38] Randolph's deeply held belief that the Socialist Party's emphasis on social and economic reform could be turned to the specific advantage of African Americans initially led him and others to overlook the party's indifference to issues of race. Randolph, in particular, argued that African Americans could "become a power to be feared and respected throughout this nation" only by joining the Socialist Party. He went so far as to maintain that the Socialist Party was the only political party where "no prejudice will be found anywhere." Even though some Harlem radicals became disenchanted with the party after the war, Randolph's involvement deepened. He accepted the party's nomination to run for state comptroller in 1920 and ran as the party nominee for secretary of state in 1921.[39] Even as socialists failed to meet the expectations that initially attracted Randolph and others to the party, Randolph's steadfast personal affection for Debs, who rooted his socialist appeal in a deeply moral context, helped turn his party association from a strict calculation of its utility for advancing African Americans' concerns into a lifelong affiliation.

In many ways, Eugene V. Debs personified the core spirit of the Socialist Party. As a five-time party nominee for president and leading editorial writer for nearly two decades, Debs largely embodied the Populist, Christian, Marxist, and trade union traditions that initially constituted the central elements of the Socialist Party.[40] His approach to reform blended the progressive traditions of Populism and social Christianity that sought to ensure a civic role for workers commensurate with their contributions to society with a firm belief in the efficacy of industrial unionism to secure economic and social justice. His views made him a powerful and charismatic figure and enabled him to speak to all factions of the party. Like Berger and Hillquit, he opposed dual unionism because he believed that it created internecine competition that undermined working-class political power. But he also strongly opposed the craft-oriented AFL on the grounds that the trade unionism of groups like the IWW offered a more sensible union structure; only the full economic and political solidarity of all workers could effectively protect society from corporate tyranny. His passionate and persuasive sincerity led many people to cast ballots for Socialist Party candidates in state and local elections across the country; more than nine hundred thousand voted for him in the 1912 presidential election.[41]

Randolph was certainly intensely struck by Debs's sincerity and moral conviction. He even listed Debs with his father and Chandler Owen as the individuals who "most influenced" his life and career. As his class consciousness and involvement with the Socialist Party deepened in the years following World War I, Randolph's admiration for Debs also deepened. He came to regard Debs as much for his "great spiritual" leadership as for his class critique.[42] Randolph's affection for Debs mirrored sentiments that he had for his father. James Randolph profoundly shaped his son's racial worldview and helped to illustrate how the church could galvanize African Americans to opposed racial discrimination. Debs's abiding moral commitment to economic and social justice helped to persuade Randolph that the Socialist Party, like the AME Church, could be an effective tool in pursuing economic and social justice for African Americans. Even though the party largely overlooked issues of race and Debs only addressed the subject infrequently, Randolph and other African Americans attracted to socialism could easily construe Debs's emphasis on social justice in ways that implicitly included justice for African Americans. Randolph's propensity to include race in Debs's critique of industrial capitalism helped to make class a comfortable container for the explicit racial worldview that shaped his childhood and grounded much of the black radicalism that suffused Harlem in the war years. Until the Great Depression exposed the limitation of class for fully addressing the special problem of racial discrimination, Randolph would continue to promote class consciousness and trade unionism as the paths to equal justice for African Americans.

By blending the racial worldview of his childhood with an increasingly class-conscious perspective, Randolph's membership in the Socialist Party illustrates a key parallel between Du Bois's racial ideology and Debs's producer theory of socialism that helped facilitate Randolph's transition from race to class. Du Bois's seminal work, *The Souls of Black Folk*, set out to explain the complex impact of racial discrimination on the lives of African Americans and made a strong moral claim for the righteousness of black voting rights and civic equality. In this powerful collection of essays Du Bois cast the fundamental discrepancies in America's professed ideals and its treatment of African Americans in a dramatic light.[43] Similarly, Debs appealed to the uniquely American values of economic mobility, political action, and industriousness to promote workers' rights. Like Du Bois, Debs based his appeal on moral notions of justice.[44] In both instances, Du Bois and Debs attempted to drive home their respective points by emphasizing the vast distance between America's professed values and its treatment of specific groups of people. The disparity constituted a basic attack on the values of individualism and manhood at the root of the American social psyche. The commonality of this underlying critique significantly eased Randolph's transition from the primarily race-conscious point of view of his adolescence to the class consciousness he began to exhibit in the war years.

Addressing a 1923 political rally organized by the Twenty-first Assembly District of the Socialist Party of New York, Debs delivered an impassioned speech titled "Appeal to Negro Workers" to the predominantly black audience that filled New York's Commonwealth Casino. In this address, he intentionally racialized his ideas on manhood by arguing that as long as African Americans were "willing to be the menials and servants and slaves of the white people," they were destined to be treated as such. If, however, black workers united and stood together with whites—to "rise in the majesty of your manhood and womanhood"—then they would command and receive the respect and consideration they deserved. He insisted that such interracial class coopera- tion was a solemn "duty" that African Americans owed "to yourselves and your class, to your race and to humanity."[45] In challenging his audience to reconsider its political allegiances to the "capitalist parties" of the Republi- cans and Democrats, Debs poignantly asked, "have you not within you the holy spark of freedom, the glowing aspiration to be a man?—not a slave but a MAN!"[46] Despite his continued insistence that the race question resolved itself into a class question, he believed deeply that black workers who aspired "to be men and women" needed to "stand up for just once and see how long a shadow you can cast."[47] In pitching his appeal to black workers in such terms, Debs adopted a tone and tenor that closely resembled the view of manhood and freedom that Du Bois outlined in *The Souls of Black Folk*.

This intersection between Du Bois and Debs on notions of manhood and their racial implications for African Americans served as a bridge for Ran- dolph's transition to socialism. Although he would increasingly channel his thinking into a class-conscious framework after joining the Socialist Party, he eventually reconsidered Du Bois's racial viewpoint. Randolph eventually reformulated the race and nation dialectic of Du Bois's double consciousness around allegiance to race and class as he led the Brotherhood of Sleeping Car Porters in its fight with the Pullman Company. However, as the nation prepared for World War I and he became more and more convinced that capitalism deliberately exacerbated racial tensions to sharpen competition between black and white workers, Randolph began to articulate a broad so- cialist critique of American society. Pointing specifically to the exploitative character of capitalism, he criticized America's involvement in the war. He argued that because there were always "spurious" attempts during wartime to appeal to the patriotism of labor to work for less while capitalists continued to raise prices, "white and black laborers must recognize their common in- terests in industry, in politics, in society, in peace." He explained that African

Americans and whites "should join hands not from any abstract altruistic motive, but for their mutual advantage."[48] In attributing new significance to class theories in these years, Randolph firmly established himself at the forefront of black radical politics in Harlem.

In raising issues of manhood in his appeal to African Americans, Debs also tapped into a theme that was a prominent feature of the radical discourse taking shape in Harlem among black intellectuals in the war years. The dual impact of war and revolution on questions of black identity gave rise to new conceptions of black transnationalism as such intellectuals as Du Bois, Cyril Brigg, W. A. Domingo, and others searched for the means to guarantee the political inclusion of black people in the modern world. It was in seeking to promote a kind of international black self-determination as part of the broader discourse on freedom, taking shape around the Paris Peace Conference, that radicals like Briggs cast the New Negro as an important manifestation of black freedom and self-expression.[49] Linking anti-imperialism with notions of revolutionary black nationalism, this international New Negro came to embody a new racial manhood that forcefully challenged racist assertions about black cowardice and military ineptitude and unequivocally demanded the entitlements of full citizenship in the modern world.[50] Debs's entreaty to African Americans, cast in "manhood" terms, hit many of the very same notes that Briggs and others sounded in projecting the New Negro beyond the bounds of Harlem.

As the country prepared for war, Randolph and others increasingly viewed socialism as an effective countermeasure to racial exploitation at home and abroad. Richard B. Moore, an early associate of Randolph's, underscored this point in a lecture titled "Afro-Americans and Radical Politics." Moore explained that he, Randolph, and other black radicals diligently set out to apply "socialist theory as a method of social analysis to the Afro-American situation and to that of oppressed colonial peoples in Africa, the Caribbean, and elsewhere." Randolph similarly explained that they were opposed to the war not only because "Negro soldiers were victims of discrimination and Jim Crowism in the army,"[51] but also because of a sincere belief that, at its root, the war was a simple conflict over markets and capitalist imperialism. While the underlying connection between Du Bois and Debs bridged the ideological gap between race and class for Randolph, Harlem's radical political climate during and after the war provided Randolph with a rich context for exploring his class sensibilities more fully. Indeed, Randolph's class-consciousness deepened at a time when a growing number of African Americans were beginning to focus more and more on the racial ideology of Marcus Garvey.

The well-developed network of public lectures, study groups, and periodicals that appeared in Harlem throughout this period simultaneously helped to fuel incipient black radicalism rooted in nationalistic and socialist themes as well as contextualize Randolph's move to the left.[52] In this regard, Harlem's street corners played a key role. During the war years, such black intellectuals as Harrison, Moore, Randolph, Crosswaith, and Garvey regularly used area street corners to deliver public lectures on subjects ranging from anticolonialism in Africa and the Caribbean to the merits of socialism. Moore's recollections of the scenes surrounding these public gathering points paint a vivid picture of the radical atmosphere of these years. In reflecting on the intellectual cohort of which both he and Randolph were integral parts, Moore recalled that it was "from the street corners of Harlem" that "these youthful Afro-American socialists spoke out against the wrongs inflicted upon their people and pointed to socialism as a means for the complete liberation of all oppressed mankind."[53] Randolph remembered "135th Street on Seventh Avenue and Lenox Avenue and also 125th Street" as being particularly lively."[54] Although Moore later criticized the Socialist Party because he believed that its "pure class" position failed to recognize the "real character of the Negro question," he, Randolph, and others held firm to the view that the "crude theories" of race derived from biblical references and "biological characteristics" that "declared Negro people closer to lower forms of animal life" were manufactured as a "weapon for oppressing Negro people and dividing the toiling masses."[55]

These street corner orators frequently addressed various interpretations of the "Negro Question" in public presentations on topics such as the "World Problem of Race." What were largely extemporaneous remarks in the war years became much more formal with the organization of the respective discussion groups that radicals like Randolph, Harrison, and Moore put together to examine the connections between capitalism, colonialism, and racial oppression. Moore's 1935 lecture titled "History of Negro Liberation" is a good example of this transformation. Though written years later and after he joined the Communist Party, this lecture touched on many of the same themes that he, Randolph, and others delivered off the cuff in the 1920s. In this essay, Moore traced the history of African slavery from the Atlantic slave trade through John Brown's raid on Harper's Ferry in 1859 and applied a decidedly Marxist interpretation to this history by arguing that there was a "definite relationship" between the "oppression of negroes" and the development of capitalism. He strenuously argued that "race theories are the result of class interest." In the eighteenth and nineteenth centuries, he explained, concepts of race were intentionally developed by capitalists to forestall soli-darity between white workers and black slaves. He consequently concluded that the effective "emancipation of all people enslaved under capitalism" required a fundamental "unity of workers."[56]

Between the end of the war and the Depression years, Harlem's street corners became a place of intense competition between black Marxists and Marcus Garvey and his nationalist disciples. With questions of Africa's future looming large as the war wound down, competition between radicals like Randolph and Moore and Garveyites for the attention of Harlem audiences became increasingly heated.[57] The intensity of their rhetorical (and sometimes physical) rivalry undoubtedly arose from the mass appeal of Garvey's vision of an independent African state founded on black commercial enterprise in Harlem and elsewhere.[58] In many ways, Garvey's unprecedented success in recruiting large numbers of African Americans into his Universal Negro Improvement Association compelled Randolph, Moore, and other black Marxists to specifically address the issue of race within the context of their class-based message. To this end, Moore's "Outline on the Negro Questions" included a pointed reminder that, because "this outline does not cover the Negro question in all sections of the world," it was imperative that he "not fail to bring out the relationship between the struggles of the American Negroes and those in the colonial countries" and "show how these struggles mutually intersect upon each other."[59]

The simmering tension between Randolph and Marcus Garvey became much more personal in the summer of 1922. Having been indicted in federal court on charges of mail fraud in February, Garvey raised the ire of Randolph and any number of other prominent African Americans when he tacitly admitted in July to holding a secret meeting with Edward Young Clarke, imperial wizard of the Ku Klux Klan. For Randolph and the *Messenger*, as well as more mainstream Garvey critics like Du Bois, this admission was the final straw. Arguing that Garvey's open endorsement of Klan-like groups was the logical conclusion of his race-first agenda, Randolph excoriated Garvey in editorial after editorial and designated himself the leader of the "Garvey Must Go" campaign to "drive the menace of Garveyism out of this country."[60] Unperturbed, Garvey retaliated with his own rhetorical fire in the pages of the *Negro World*, the journal of his Universal Negro Improvement Associa-tion (UNIA), warning all of dire consequences for any interference with his organization or its program.[61] Though it is not exactly clear what role Garvey's warning may have played, it was nonetheless shocking to Randolph and the *Messenger* staff when he subsequently received an anonymous package containing a human hand.[62] The sender of this ominous parcel was never identified, but the contents served as an apt, if gruesome, metaphor for how vicious the anti-Garvey campaign became.

In addition to their street corner lectures, Harrison, Randolph, Moore, and others also organized a wide variety of community study groups to examine class principles further and to refine their class-based message.[63] As with the Independent Political Council and the League of Darker Races, Randolph formed the Friends of Negro Freedom in 1920 as a vehicle for applying class solutions to the problem of racial discrimination.[64] Moore's People's Educational Forum, a study group of black socialists that regularly met on Sunday afternoons, served a similar purpose. Moore's group discussed the writings of Marx and Engels and sought to engage issues vital to African Americans with invited guests like Du Bois, anthropologist Franz Boas, and Algernon Lee, a prominent New York socialist and close associate of Morris Hillquit. In 1919, Moore also collaborated with Harrison to form the Institute for Social Study, "an independent agency of education devoted to a thorough study of the vital social problems which affect the lives and welfare of the great masses of the people."[65]

In general, these study groups focused heavily on the twin themes of anticolonialism and nationalism within a class framework. Consider the Institute for Social Study's advertisement for Harrison's 1926 lecture series titled "World Problems of Race" and for a similar 1927 series titled "Problems of Race and Imperialism" by Joseph Freeman. Touting Harrison's "breadth of knowledge and profundity of thought," the description of his lecture series claimed that the material covered was essential for "intelligent and courageous race-statesmanship." In an attached syllabus that listed "Expansion and Dominance of Europeans" and "Race Problems in America" as discussion topics, Harrison listed among his key course goals a detailed exploration of African contributions to the European "awakening" and a thorough review of the "materialistic roots" of American racial tensions and their colonial consequences for the Caribbean. Likewise, Freeman's series on "Problems of Race and Imperialism" aimed to "impart a clear understanding of the basic forces which produce race problems and imperialist conflicts." Throughout the postwar era, the radical ferment engineered by intellectuals like Harrison and Moore addressed directly the issues that propelled the various study groups that they and Randolph organized in and around Harlem.[66]

The numerous lectures, study groups, and organizations that Randolph, Moore, and others put together in these years reflected their growing determination to broaden socialism's appeal to African Americans. Increas-

ingly convinced that the Socialist Party was the only political party to offer a philosophy and economic program that seriously addressed the root
causes of racial discrimination, Randolph later explained that he and others
sought to make clear that African Americans not only needed to "fight for
the rights of our workers as black workers," but also to "fight and struggle
for the elimination of discrimination of all kinds."[67] In the pages of the *Messenger,* the monthly magazine he and Owen initially began to publish in 1917
as the official organ of the Headwaiters and Sidewaiters Society of Greater
New York, Randolph consistently argued that the predominantly working-
class status of most African Americans dictated that they join in a political
and economic alliance with white workers to pursue labor's common class
interests. To the extent that all workers sought higher wages, shorter hours,
and better working conditions, he maintained that black workers "ought to
belong to the workers' party . . . the Socialist Party."[68] Moreover, as a result
of this effort to encourage African Americans to join the party, Randolph
and Owen took it upon themselves to firmly hold New York socialists to
their class convictions. They consistently argued that "race prejudice has no
place in a labor organization."[69] Randolph went on to insist that the "primary
tenet" of the Socialist-led Workingmen's Council should "be to help all labor
without regard to race, creed, or color" in mobilizing the forces of labor for
its "final and complete emancipation."[70]

As an acknowledgment of their efforts on behalf of the party and the
soundness of their economic and social interpretations of industrial capitalism, the Rand School of Social Science offered both Randolph and Owen an
invitation to lecture on "The Economics and Sociology of the Negro Problem." Organized in 1916 by the American Socialist Society to train workers in
economics, politics, and labor union tactics, the Rand School put Randolph
in more direct contact with the leading socialist intellectuals of the day.[71] His
interaction with Max Eastman, Oswald Garrison Villard, Scott Nearing, and
Norman Thomas, all prominent members of the New York Socialist Party's
intellectual elite, gave Randolph a degree of intellectual legitimacy within the
party that helped bolster his stature among radicals of all persuasions.[72] By
the time that the party had begun to split along factional lines in response
to the war and the 1919 Bolshevik Revolution, Randolph had become the
central socialist figure in Harlem: Du Bois had resigned from the party prior
to the 1912 presidential election; Hubert Harrison, the most prominent black
socialist in Harlem in the years leading up to World War I, had abandoned
the party to push a race-conscious agenda; Cyril Briggs, Richard B. Moore,
and other members of the African Blood Brotherhood migrated into the
Communist Party after the war.

In many ways, Randolph's ascendance in this regard was a reflection of his somewhat odd position within the national Socialist Party. On one hand, he clearly identified with Hillquit and other New York intellectuals who encouraged cooperation with the AFL on the grounds that only through such collaboration could labor hope to challenge the hegemony of capital. Yet, Randolph simultaneously pushed a more radical agenda of class conflict wherein black and white workers joined forces as "a powerful lesson to the capitalist of the solidarity of labor" and consistently criticized racial discrimination in the labor movement.[73] Based on this view, one might have thought that Randolph would have more strongly challenged Hillquit and the New York Socialist Party on its support of the AFL whose leadership staunchly opposed the racial integration of its labor unions. In many ways, Randolph's explanation of this apparent contradiction—that he continued to support Hillquit and remained in the New York party because they stood "at all times and in all countries against race prejudice"—is unsatisfactory. Hillquit and the party countenanced discrimination by the AFL. More likely, Randolph remained in the party because he clearly believed that doing so was a far better political alternative for African Americans than joining either the Republican or Democratic parties.[74]

On the other hand, while it would seem that his political temperament would align him far more closely with the IWW and the Socialist Party's left wing, no clear relationship ever appears to have developed between Randolph and William Haywood. Despite its support of sabotage as an acceptable labor tactic, Randolph was effusive in his praise of the IWW as an alternative to the American Federation of Labor. Whereas he accused the AFL of being "criminally negligent . . . in either ignoring or opposing Negro workers," Randolph commended the IWW for having never "in theory or practice, since its beginning twelve years ago, barred the workers of any race or nation from membership."[75] Yet, Randolph continued to endorse a more moderate view. The conflict represented here reflects the fact that as Randolph sought to make socialism and the Socialist Party more appealing to African Americans in Harlem, he found himself in a unique position that required him to maintain a flexible relationship with all elements of the party.

It is therefore difficult to firmly define Randolph's ideological position within the Socialist Party in the years surrounding World War I. His membership in the New York Socialist Party and relationship with Morris Hillquit and other party intellectuals seems at odds with his clear affinity for the IWW and antipathy for the AFL. Moreover, Randolph's strong personal and ideological attachment to Debs, who withdrew from the IWW in 1913 because he disagreed with its endorsement of sabotage and violence, seems to conflict with his frequent praise of the party's left wing. Understanding Randolph's position in the party in these years requires a nuanced perspective on the changing dynamics of Socialist Party operations in the 1910s. Throughout these years the Socialist Party actually grew in strength at the state and local levels but witnessed a dramatic decline in organizational cohesiveness nationally.[76] This lack of national cohesion allowed Randolph to move fluidly between party factions without serious philosophical or political difficulties. Indeed, the ability to shift back and forth between party factions became an important aspect of Randolph's effort to draw African Americans into the party. By highlighting those factional characteristics that could be most easily appropriated to oppose racial discrimination, Randolph hoped to illustrate clearly the value of socialism to African Americans.

For this reason, Randolph spent a great deal of time explaining working-class racial prejudice. Consistently adopting an orthodox critique of industrial capitalism, Randolph maintained that racial discrimination was a tactic used by the "employing class . . . to engender race hatred" between black and white workers and forestall "any movement of labor that threatens the dividends of the industrial kings." He argued in the *Messenger* that black and white workers needed to recognize their "common interest in improving the condition of the wage-working class." Throughout the early 1920s, he consistently returned to the contention that as long as employers kept the "white and black dogs, on account of race prejudice, fighting over a bone," the "yellow capitalist dog" would get away with the profits.[77] Accordingly, he maintained that "the only problem then, which the colored worker should consider, as a worker, is the problem of organizing with other working men in the labor organization that best expresses the interests of the whole working class against the slavery and oppression of the whole capitalist class."[78] This proposal for addressing the plight of black workers placed Randolph squarely within the party's center and left while also further exposing the growing gap between his class theories and the ever more popular racial ideology of Garveyism.

In the years immediately following World War I, years in which Randolph's attachment to class theories grew stronger, both New Negro professionals and Marcus Garvey's Universal Negro Improvement Association helped to foster new strategies of racial self-sufficiency in black communities throughout the urban North. Both looked to cultivate the emerging economic and political strength of growing black ghettoes to assert African American equality.[79] Indeed, Garvey effectively co-opted much of the New Negro ideology of self-help and racial independence to bolster his nationalist agenda. Through the Universal Negro Improvement Association, he managed to tap into the well-ing sense of racial pride vividly expressed in the cultural outpouring of the Harlem Renaissance.[80] For his part, Randolph's intense opposition to Garvey further underscored the growing distance between his class consciousness and the ideology of racial self-sufficiency that gripped most northern African Americans of the day. As he turned increasingly to socialism to explain and solve the problems of racial discrimination, an increasing number of mainstream African Americans in Harlem began to embrace new ideologies of racial self-sufficiency.

In some ways, this explains the vehemence with which Randolph and other black Marxists in Harlem attacked Garvey and his supporters. Jealous of Garvey's influence in Harlem and the rapid growth of his Universal Negro Improvement Association elsewhere, Randolph, Moore, and others feared that Garvey's separatist appeals would undermine their recruiting efforts with both black and white workers. Consequently, Randolph became a leader of the "Garvey Must Go" campaign.[81] Like his peers in the New York Socialist Party, Randolph firmly believed that only interracial class cooperation could effectively overcome the inequitable conditions created by racial discrimination. To this end, he responded to Garvey's separatist appeals by forcefully arguing that as long as "white and black workingmen . . . still fight over race prejudice . . . rich white plutocrats [will] pick the pockets of both."[82] While most African Americans generally sought comfort in building their own communities and institutions as well as in the achievements of the race, Randolph sought to "educate Negroes so that they may understand their class interests."[83]

As the country emerged from war and Harlem witnessed the first flowering of the coming cultural renaissance, Randolph found himself in the curious position of being both accepted and somewhat isolated in Harlem. On the one hand, by the early 1920s he had become one of the most prominent African American socialists left in the Socialist Party. Du Bois, Harrison, Moore, Briggs, and others who had played active roles in bringing the Socialist Party to Harlem, had resigned from the organization and become harsh critics of the party. On the other hand, in shifting his ideological affiliation from Du Bois to Debs, Randolph separated himself in substantial ways from the evolving strategies of racial self-sufficiency that had captured the hearts and minds of African Americans everywhere. In the years to come, both circumstances would fundamentally impact his effort to transition from class theorist to trade unionist. As he turned his attention to the plight of Pullman porters and maids, the ineffectiveness of orthodox class theory to address the grievances of the Brotherhood of Sleeping Car Porters led Randolph to fashion a new middle ground between race and class.

Lucille Green Randolph, ca. 1910. Photographs and Prints Division, Schomburg Center for Research in Black Culture, The New York Public Library, Astor, Lenox, and Tilden Foundation.

A. Philip Randolph (third from right) and *Messenger* Staff. Also pictured: Wallace Thurman (first from left) and Frank R. Crosswaith (fourth from right), ca. 1920. Photographs and Prints Division, Schomburg Center for Research in Black Culture, The New York Public Library, Astor, Lenox, and Tilden Foundation.

A. Philip Randolph and officers of the Brotherhood of Sleeping Car Porters, ca. 1930. Photographs and Prints Division, Schomburg Center for Research in Black Culture, The New York Public Library, Astor, Lenox, and Tilden Foundation.

Early Brotherhood of Sleeping Car Porters meeting, ca. 1925. A. Philip Randolph is center and Frank R. Crosswaith stands to his immediate left. Photographs and Prints Division, Schomburg Center for Research in Black Culture, The New York Public Library, Astor, Lenox, and Tilden Foundation.

A. Philip Randolph meeting with Edwin P. Marrow, chairman of the Railroad Mediation Board, ca. 1928. Photographs and Prints Division, Schomburg Center for Research in Black Culture, The New York Public Library, Astor, Lenox, and Tilden Foundation.

A. Philip Randolph, presidential address at the Second National Negro Congress, Philadelphia, 1937. Photographs and Prints Division, Schomburg Center for Research in Black Culture, The New York Public Library, Astor, Lenox, and Tilden Foundation.

A. Philip Randolph, president of the National Negro Congress, 1937. Photographs and Prints Division, Schomburg Center for Research in Black Culture, The New York Public Library, Astor, Lenox, and Tilden Foundation.

A. Philip Randolph, president of the Brotherhood of Sleeping Car Porters and head of the National Council for a Permanent FEPC, ca. 1945. Photographs and Prints Division, Schomburg Center for Research in Black Culture, The New York Public Library, Astor, Lenox, and Tilden Foundation.

A. Philip Randolph, Eleanor Roosevelt, and Fiorello La Guardia at a 1946 Madison Square Garden rally to save the Fair Employment Practice Commission. Photographs and Prints Division, Schomburg Center for Research in Black Culture, The New York Public Library, Astor, Lenox, and Tilden Foundation.

A. Philip Randolph picketing against Jim Crow in the Armed Services, ca. 1950. Photographs and Prints Division, Schomburg Center for Research in Black Culture, The New York Public Library, Astor, Lenox, and Tilden Foundation.

PART 3

The Rise of the New Crowd Negroes

5

A New Crowd,
A New Negro

The Messenger *and*
New Negro Ideology
in the 1920s

Harlem during World War I was a place of incredible energy. The community was growing rapidly as the mass migration of southern blacks continued apace; Marcus Garvey's stirring message of race pride rang from street corners and convention halls throughout the community; and black journalists and essayists of all political stripes published page upon page of commentary on the plight of black people the world over. It was in this dynamic wartime environment that A. Philip Randolph and Chandler Owen co-founded the *Messenger,* a militant journal that styled itself as "the only magazine of scientific radicalism in the world published by Negroes." It was in the pages of the *Messenger* that Randolph worked to refine his ideas about social justice and industrial organization. In these years he began to articulate a view of social justice rooted in the language of universal human rights that forcefully asserted the right of all individuals to benefit equally from society's advances. In the war's aftermath, this conception of social justice and his deep commitment to industrial organization became the central rallying points around which he tried to mobilize black workers.

The *Messenger* was especially important to the evolution of Randolph's thought on social justice. The process of editing the *Messenger* and the opportunity to write on a wide variety of national and international issues helped him distill his criticisms of industrial capitalism into a comprehensive worldview that underscored in stark terms the fundamental connections between social justice, industrial organization, and racial discrimination. Moreover, the *Messenger* attracted a broad array of black and white socialist intellectuals and radicals as regular contributors; Randolph's association with this radical cohort deepened his understanding of and commitment to industrial reform. As he struggled to organize Pullman porters and maids in the mid-1920s and 1930s, it was in editing the *Messenger* in the early 1920s that his understanding of the entwined nature of social justice, industrial organization, and racial discrimination took on more distinct shape.

Although the *Messenger* became one of the most influential radical journals of this period, its origins were rather inauspicious.[1] In the early months of 1917, officials from the Headwaiters and Sidewaiters Society of Greater New York approached Randolph and Owen with a proposal to edit the union's journal, the *Hotel Messenger*. In exchange for free office space to house their Independent Political Council, the waiters expected Randolph and Owen to report on the kind of routine union activities and issues that generally helped to build a labor organization. For Randolph and Owen, whose manuscripts *The Terms of Peace and the Darker Races* and *The Truth about Lynching* had only recently been published, editing the *Hotel Messenger* was an excellent opportunity to develop a regular forum for broadcasting their views about unionization and the pitfalls of capitalism. In a short period of months, however, this mutually beneficial arrangement fell apart over Randolph and Owen's unrelenting editorial criticisms of corruption within the union.

After settling into their new facilities and meeting some of the rank-and-file members, Randolph and Owen began to hear more and more accounts of headwaiters using their position to extort and exploit the side waiters and pantry men who worked under them. As the new editors quickly learned, in addition to low wages and poor working conditions, common waiters were frequently coerced into gambling in dice games run by their bosses. Moreover, several of the side waiters and pantry men explained how they were forced to purchase work uniforms through headwaiters who then took kickbacks from suppliers. Rather than the idyllic vision of working-class solidarity that they imagined, Randolph and Owen came to understand that, for the victims, these kinds of unsavory union practices were as exploitative as any of the tactics generally used by employers. In their early editorials, they scathingly condemned the headwaiters and bluntly challenged the ethical character of the union's leadership. In response, union officials fired them after only eight months on the job.

Despite this unceremonious break with the Headwaiters and Sidewaiters' Union, their exposure of union corruption clearly illustrated for Randolph and Owen the powerful potential of independent journalism. After collecting their equipment and setting up shop in a new headquarters at

513 Lennox Avenue in Harlem, they published the first issue of their recon-
stituted magazine under the title of the *Messenger* in November 1917. They
envisioned publishing a thoughtful journal "devoted to the problem of the
exploitation of the black worker in particular and the exploitation of workers in general." Randolph later explained that the *Messenger* was "basically
socialist-oriented" and discussed the doctrine of socialism as a key factor
in the liberation of workers and the creation of a democratic society.[2] In its
early days, the *Messenger* struggled; it appeared only sporadically until July
1919, when it first began regular monthly publication. The explanation for
its uncertain appearance in this early period is simple. "We had no money,"
Randolph recalled, "and there was no way to get any money" during these
years. Notwithstanding their enthusiasm, Randolph and Owen found little
initial support for their journalistic venture because few organizations "would
give the Socialists any thought whatsoever." In their first year and a half of
operation, Randolph explained, "all we had were ideals."[3]

Notwithstanding these early struggles, the magazine achieved a measure
of prominence among the growing number of radical journalists centered in
New York during and immediately following the war. Closely associated with
the evolving radicalism underlying the Harlem Renaissance and emergence
of the New Negro in the 1920s, the *Messenger* became a prominent outlet
for African American militancy in the postwar period.[4] From its founding
until 1923, when it began to shift away from its original audience of black
and white intellectuals and radical workers and toward the growing black
professional class that made up the black bourgeoisie,[5] few domestic or international issues of significance arose that escaped Randolph and Owen's
editorial notice. While it is certainly important to understand how the *Messenger* came into being as well as the factors that contributed to its decline
in the mid-1920s, it is the breadth and scope of these editorials that give the
magazine its greatest significance.

With America's participation in World War I as a backdrop, *Messenger* editorials consistently pointed to discrepancies between America's democratic
ideals and its practice of racial discrimination against African Americans.
The commentary "Making the World Safe for Democracy," which appeared
in the journal's first issue, set a tone that persisted throughout much of the
Messenger's first years. Contrasting their discontent with that of individuals
like Booker T. Washington, from whom they believed "no radical utterance
ever emanated," Randolph and Owen explained that "their feelings will not
down by prayers of patriotism." They made it clear that they felt very little
urgency to heed appeals for supporting freedom and democracy in Europe

when African American demands to "make the world safe for democracy in that part of the world known as the United States" were so "insistent."[6] Throughout this period, the *Messenger* editors seized every opportunity to expose in the starkest possible terms the contrast between American wartime ultimatums to Germany and its treatment of African Americans. In response to an invitation to present their grievances to the People' Council of America for Peace and Democracy, a national coalition of socialists, social workers, and social gospel clergy organized in 1917, Randolph and Owen turned their focus to black disfranchisement in the South. Because "government by the consent of the governed" should be accorded to all, they explained, the People's Council should join the *Messenger*'s effort to "call attention to the fact that the demand which the President makes of Germany with respect to her people's having a voice in their government is denied to over two million Negroes." Though Randolph and Owen were unable to attend the peace conference, they insisted that there was no mission more important for the People's Council than to help "induce our government to square its practice with its profession."[7]

The underlying hypocrisy of American race policy was common to much of the *Messenger*'s editorial perspective on the war and African Americans' role in it. For example, in a January 1918 column on the execution of African American soldiers who rioted against racial discrimination in Houston, Randolph and his *Messenger* circle acerbically pointed out that the black soldier was "invariably" called upon "to defend rights for others" that he did not himself enjoy.[8] Certainly, American wartime rhetoric extolling the principles of freedom and democracy provided rich material for the *Messenger* to use in making such points. A September 1920 article titled "Americanism" argued that from "the very beginning of our national existence," the Declaration of Independence created a fundamental moral dilemma by attaching "all its lofty rhetoric" to the signatures of slaveholders and "thereby placing the stamp of hypocrisy on the brow of the new born nation."[9] In the particular context of World War I, Randolph and Owen noted that the clear disconnection between American ideals and American racial practices elevated this basic dilemma to new levels. In the pointedly titled commentary "The Hun in America," appearing in the July 1919 issue, they explained that "however much advocates of the cause of the Allies whose slogans were to make the world safe for democracy . . . might plead to the contrawise . . . America, the chief ally in the fight for democracy, stands before the world with her garments dripping with blood and covered with shame as the land of the most criminal HUNS of Christendom."[10]

This view of America's participation in the war dovetailed with the understanding of social justice at the core of Randolph's earlier criticisms of
industrial capitalism. Prior to the war, Randolph and others began to devise
a concept of social justice that maintained that all races and classes of people
were equal inheritors of the social, political, and economic institutions created by civilization's progress because all had contributed their share to man's
development.[11] They sought a participatory democracy open to all that ap-
portioned citizenship rights not by race or class but by the degree to which
individuals were willing to perform the civic duties of a faithful citizen.
Hence, the central hypocrisy of America's participation in World War I was
its demand of loyalty from African Americans, especially black soldiers, while
simultaneously denying them the full rights and privileges of citizenship.
This particularly potent argument framed much of the *Messenger*'s editorial
perspective in these years.

The *Messenger*'s opposition to the war was also connected in significant
ways to a broad pacifist coalition that emerged among some in the Socialist Party.[12] In its inaugural issue, the *Messenger* editors explained that
their "hearts followed the brave band of delegates who unswervingly and
unfalteringly" stood for peace without annexation, indemnities, or regard
to race or color.[13] Throughout this period, Randolph and Owen cemented
relationships with prominent New York Socialist Party intellectuals, including Scott Nearing and Norman Thomas, who published antiwar treatises in
the *Messenger* and regularly participated in the forums held by Randolph's
Friends of Negro Freedom.[14]

Between 1917 and 1923, Randolph and Owen formed as many as a half-
dozen discussion groups and political forums that expounded on ideas expressed in the *Messenger*. This was certainly the case when it came to their
opposition to the war. In addition to the numerous street corner speeches
that Randolph delivered on imperialism and war, he and Owen refined their
antiwar critique in countless discussions and debates organized by Randolph's
League of Darker Races.[15] This connection between the ideas expressed in
the *Messenger* and the discussion groups that Randolph and Owen put together also played out in other instances. The Independent Political Council,
the very first political forum that Randolph and Owen organized, hosted
debates, discussions, and forums on topics ranging from religion to armed
self-defense that helped to shape Randolph's views in myriad areas.[16]

Throughout the war and the years immediately following it, the *Messenger*
continually called on the nation to square its practices with its principles. In
an article titled "An Analysis of Negro Patriotism," William Colson, one of

the magazine's contributing editors and a former soldier in the U.S. Army's all-black 367th Infantry, pointed out that the "treachery of the white American was infinitely more damaging" to black soldiers than fighting abroad. He explained that as black soldiers took up democracy's cause under the "guise" that they were a "common inheritor" of American rights and duties and responsible for "unqualifiedly" joining in "every burst of patriotism," they were "refused a square deal in the Army and Navy" even as discrimination in the South became more "grueling." He explained that for many African Americans, especially black soldiers, there seemed to be "more racial limitation and restriction than ever before."[17] The *Messenger* frequently underscored such points with the oft-repeated contention that white soldiers, "with whom the black men were fighting and for whose liberty they were dying," treated black soldiers worse than the enemy, "whose duty was to kill the Negro soldiers and whom the Negro soldiers were killing."[18]

Throughout these years, the *Messenger* persistently used the nation's call to war as a powerful rhetorical tool in African Americans' cause for equal justice. For example, in a July 1918 editorial titled "American Lawlessness," the two editors explained that their dogged attention to wartime instances of racial injustice was not only intended "to let the government and the public know that it is not giving the Negro a square deal," but also to put the nation on notice that "we do not propose to wink our eyes at these injustices and pretend we are satisfied." Unlike W.E.B. Du Bois who called upon African Americans to "forget our special grievances and close our ranks shoulder to shoulder with our own white fellow citizens and the allied nations that are fighting for democracy," the *Messenger* editor insisted that African American loyalty and service should be conditional.[19] In their view, if America could draft Negroes to fight and expect them to give their lives in defense of their country, then America needed to understand that Negroes did not expect the "lawlessness" of racial discrimination, Jim Crow, and lynching to be the sole reward for "her loyal colored citizens."[20] Otherwise, the "sham democracy about which Americans prate" would be exposed as "a sham, a mockery, a rape on decency and a travesty on common sense" before the world.[21]

In making this basic point about the fundamental disconnection between American ideals and American racial practices, the *Messenger* wove together a broad tapestry of interrelated but distinct themes. First, though implicit in much of their commentary on American hypocrisy, Randolph and his colleagues consistently used the *Messenger*'s editorial page to outline the root causes of African Americans' discontent in clear terms. Much like Randolph's view of social justice that assigned civic rights on the basis of civic contribution, the *Messenger* explained that lynching, Jim Crow, and disfranchisement were especially poor compensation for the loyal service of black soldiers. Likewise, this framework of equal rights for equal sacrifice also shaped the *Messenger*'s exposition of African Americans' postwar expectations. In many instances it suggested, and often stated outright, that black soldiers should not and would not fight and die abroad to protect freedoms they did not possess at home. It was in drawing these distinct but related threads together in its wartime editorials that the *Messenger* most accurately reflected and, to some degree, influenced African Americans' evolving racial militancy.

The *Messenger* editors went on to explain that it was this basic injustice and the sheer brutality of American racial discrimination that stood at the center of African Americans' wartime discontent. In response to concerns about African Americans' loyalty, the *Messenger* published in July 1918 a commentary titled "Pro-Germanism among Negroes." They explained that the general "discontent among Negroes" was rooted in "deep and dark" causes "obvious to all those who care to use their mental eyes." More specifically, they pointed out, "peonage, disfranchisement, Jim Crowism, segregation, rank civil discrimination, injustice of legislatures, courts, and administrators" were the most effective "propaganda of discontent among Negroes."[22] Similarly, editorializing on the spate of racial disturbances that marked the summer of 1919 in a piece titled "An Open Letter to the Union League Club of New York," Randolph bitterly expressed his view that the "chief causes of unrest" among African Americans were the "unjust conditions in this alleged land of the free and home of the brave." He went on to note that America's racial policies systematically eroded the moral integrity of the nation's political, economic, and social foundations. He pointed to the widespread disfranchisement of African Americans "as a complete refutation of our professions of political democracy," the persistence of peonage in the South as a "complete refutation of any claims of industrial democracy," and the Jim Crow railroad car as an institution that "smacks of an unspeakable caste system."[23]

These conditions, especially when compared to America's lofty war aims, helped to fan the flames of Randolph's ire. He and his colleagues never missed an opportunity to editorialize that it was "elementary that the spirit of equality runs neither through the letter nor the administration of American law." Instead, they contended, the "entire warp and woof and fabric of American law" was haunted by a "spirit of inequality, injustice, and prejudiced administration." Throughout this period, the *Messenger* took the nation's political leaders to task for condoning racial discrimination. Rather than live up to their grand pronouncements of freedom and democracy, Randolph and his staff made clear in a commentary titled "Prof. Harry H. Jones—The Crisis in Negro Leadership" that during these most trying of times "the nation showed no ability to respond to any ideals except the ideals of anarchy, lawlessness, mob violence, lynching, autocracy, and falsehood."[24]

In response to claims that their opposition to the war and America's role in it amounted to treason, the *Messenger* explained that "the vice of being traitorous depends entirely upon what one is traitorous to. Treason of the slave to his master is a virtue. Loyalty of a slave to his master is vice. Liberty and justice have advanced in the world in proportion as people have been traitorous to their tyrants and oppressors." African Americans would never gain their just rights, the *Messenger* editors insisted, until they became "thoroughly permeated, saturated, and shot through with treason to the institutions of Jim-Crowism, lynching, race discrimination, segregation, disfranchisement, and to every instrument which maintains, perpetuates, and fosters these pernicious institutions."[25]

The belligerent tone that suffused its discussion of African Americans' discontent also shaped the *Messenger*'s outline of their postwar expectations. The *Messenger* editors explained that African Americans, especially returning black soldiers, wanted "justice and fair play—a chance to work for a decent wage, freedom from discrimination on railroads, street cars, theaters, and hotels, protection . . . from lynching and [protection for] his property from mob violence, the right to vote and education for his children."[26] In an editorial titled "The Negro in Public Utilities," the *Messenger* explained that Negros were like other groups who were "insisting that equality of opportunity" be the "measure and test of democracy"; that the same spirit "to demand equality of opportunity has seized the Negro."[27] In staking this claim to the full rights of citizenship, African Americans' war experience served as a poignant rhetorical backdrop. Hence, in their response to the comments of South Carolina congressman James F. Byrnes that African Americans should be satisfied with their place in American society, the *Messenger* editors explained that

> no one should be loyal to any flag unless the flag is loyal to him. Should we be loyal to lynch-law? Should we be loyal to disfranchisement? Should we be loyal to your Jim-Crow car? Should we be loyal to your flag that never stands between our charred and blackened bodies roasted by your lawless mobs? What we want to do is to make the American flag so just and fair to every citizen in the land without regard to race, nationality, or color that loyalty will flow freely and not have to be exacted by the whip of the lash.[28]

In couching African Americans' postwar expectations in such terms, the *Messenger* clearly sought to turn the nation's professed ideals against its racial practices while also encouraging its readership to accept nothing less than the full measure of equal justice. In a September 1919 editorial responding to calls for the creation of a new holiday celebrating the ratification of the U.S. Constitution, the *Messenger* explained that it was "not very interested in the Constitution as such." It would, however, be willing to join in the celebration if it could "pick out a few specific clauses" for special observation. The *Messenger*'s lukewarm response to this proposed commemoration of the Constitution was rooted in the view that the "only" purpose such a celebration could serve was "first, to continue the enforcement of that part of the Constitution which has been enforced all along, and to begin the enforcement of that part of the Constitution which has not been enforced," especially the Fourteenth and Fifteenth Amendments.[29] These kinds of editorial assaults on the nation's unwillingness to meet the obligations of its basic principles appeared consistently throughout this period and provided a powerful context for the *Messenger*'s insistence on black "leadership of uncompromising manhood." In an August 1919 article titled "Our Reason for Being," which discussed the origins of the National Association for the Promotion of Labor Unionism among Negroes under the leadership of Randolph, Frank Crosswaith, and others, the *Messenger* explained that New Negroes were "not asking for a half loaf but for the whole loaf" in regard to the rights and interests of black workers specifically and African Americans generally.[30]

The strident undertones that shaped most of the *Messenger* wartime editorials paralleled sentiments expressed in other places throughout Harlem. In addition to other radical journals like the *Crusader* founded by Cyril Briggs in 1918 and Hubert Harrison's *Negro Voice,* groups such as Frank Crosswaith's Harlem Labor Committee, a precursor to the National Association for the Promotion of Labor Unionism among Negroes, echoed the *Messenger*'s militant timbre in calling for race-conscious and steadfast black leadership.[31] In a pamphlet extolling the virtues of labor unionism and targeting black workers in the garment industry, Crosswaith explained that the New Negro was a union worker. He argued that "for generations, the Negro has been the victim of all manner of industrial discrimination and social injustice," and insisted that black workers "must be intelligent," "guard against every attempt to use us as children," and end "the days of the Negro who fell for every vulgar barker selling poison to weaken the Negro in his fight for complete equality and justice."[32] The emphasis on equality and justice at the center of Crosswaith's appeal became significant in new and different ways in the years following the war as Randolph and the *Messenger* began to use these twin concepts to redefine the New Negro.

Throughout the early 1920s, the *Messenger* ran more and more columns focused on the rising tide of black militancy rooted directly in the wartime experiences of black soldiers. In this regard, the *Messenger* exclaimed that "the hunger for manhood rights is destined to grow stronger not weaker among Negroes" because "the militant spirit of the New Negro is gradually infecting the wide masses." Randolph and his *Messenger* staff believed intensely that after fighting for freedom in Europe, African Americans would be increasingly driven by a "passionate will to freedom" that would become "more articulate, aggressive and bold from year to year." In their view, "Negroes would be less than human" were they to be otherwise affected and, "by the same token, undeserving of a better lot."[33] This theme, African Americans' deep-seated impatience with persistent racial discrimination, became a mainstay of the *Messenger*'s postwar commentary. For instance, in an April 1923 editorial on Charles W. Anderson, the black Republican appointed as collector of internal revenue of New York in 1921, Randolph and Owen gleefully proclaimed that "the days of the good old Uncle Toms are passing." Rather than continue to accept the occasional "sop" political appointment as "an expiation of the Republicans' treachery to the Dyer [Anti-Lynching] Bill and Negroes' appeals for justice in America," the New Negro understood that "political handouts" will neither stop lynching nor "do for the Negro any of the things they so greatly need."[34]

In many ways, the *Messenger* became the primary mouthpiece for the more assertive racial spirit exhibited by African Americans in the postwar years. Notwithstanding such articles as Du Bois's "Returning Soldiers" or Claude McKay's poem "If We Must Die," it was the *Messenger* that most consistently hailed the changed "demeanor and tactics" of New Negroes intent upon giving "men's account of themselves." In a column that borrowed its title from McKay's poem "If We Must Die," the *Messenger* editors explained that African Americans had come to realize that "force" alone was the most "effective medium to counteract force." Indeed, the *Messenger* continued, they were now prepared to "investigate the curative values inherent in mass action, revolvers, and other lethal devices" in treating the social ills of racial discrimination.[35] To illustrate this point, the *Messenger* eagerly reported on circumstances in which African Americans responded to violent attacks with force. For example, in a December 1921 article titled "Young Negro Dies like Man," Randolph and Owen described how Walter Ware, an African American bootlegger in Virginia, returned fire when the county sheriff and his deputies cornered him in his barn. Despite Ware's criminal activities, Randolph and Owen interpreted his actions as self-defense, explaining that "this new spirit is a Banquo's ghost to the South." This situation demonstrated to them the degree to which "the new crowd of New Negroes is ready and willing to lay down its life in defense of the rights which it regards [as] the just and rightful heritage of all."

In attaching such heroic significance to the Ware case, Randolph and Owen thought to stir the passions of their readers against the racial violence often associated with southern law enforcement. Even as they de-emphasized the criminal activity that brought the sheriff to the Ware homestead, their focus on Ware's willingness to respond with force when pressed into a corner is instructive. As they put it in their recitation of the facts, African Americans had "reached the end of the road" with the racial terror engendered by southern "picnics and roasting parties."[36] Randolph and Owen held up the Ware case, despite its shadow of criminality, as a clear and vivid demonstration of the new militant postwar racial spirit they attributed to the New Negro. In an increasing number of articles in this period, Randolph and Owen cheered the emergence of the New Negro "who will not compromise, surrender, or retreat" from racial oppression and who, "with iron will and an inflexible determination," vowed to secure the full measure of his civil rights.[37] In a December 1919 column titled "Thanksgiving," the *Messenger* reiterated its regard for the "New Crowd Negro" who "has been right on the job" in protecting his home, life, and loved ones and "upholding the dignity of the law" against American lawlessness and anarchy.[38] As the *Messenger* increasingly raised the issue of African American self-defense against racial violence in these years, such expressions helped to identify it as the central mouthpiece of New Crowd Negroes.[39]

Of the many themes raised by Randolph and his staff in the pages of the *Messenger* after World War I, this issue of black self-defense against racial violence was particularly potent. In an August 1919 article titled, "How to Stop Lynching," the *Messenger* appealed to the universal law of self-defense in insisting that African Americans were justified in always regarding their own lives as "more important" than that of the lyncher. "If a choice has to be made" between your life and that of the lyncher, the *Messenger* declared, African Americans should "invariably" choose to preserve their own lives and "destroy that of the lynching mob." While this point of view was not especially new, the *Messenger* changed the nature of such discussions by purposefully connecting this idea to the war experiences of black soldiers. In asserting that the New Negro could "lay down his life honorably and peacefully for himself in the United States" just as those Negroes who "went three thousand miles away to fight for alleged democracy in Europe and for others," the *Messenger* helped to define a new and decidedly race-conscious standard of conduct for African Americans in the postwar years.[40]

This emphatic endorsement of black self-defense fit squarely with Randolph's philosophical development at the time. Going as far back as his early childhood, support for armed responses to white racial violence was a clear feature of his upbringing. Though nonviolence became a central component of his subsequent activism, in the aftermath of the war and in the face of the rising racial tensions that exploded in the Red Summer of 1919, Randolph's take on black self-defense is not surprising. His views also factor into understanding his early support of the 1917 Russian Revolution. Initially he and other Harlem radicals saw in the Bolsheviks' success a model for engineering a racial revolution against international capitalism. For those Harlem radicals like Randolph that were already convinced that imperialism and racism went hand in hand, the Russian Revolution seemed to offer a new solution to the problem of black exploitation and oppression.[41] In this context, then, one can only really see Randolph's later embrace of nonviolence as part of a philosophical evolution on his part.

In various ways throughout the fall of 1919, Randolph and his colleagues insisted that even if the war had not changed white attitudes toward social and political equality for African Americans, "it has nevertheless changed the attitude of the Negro." They repeatedly appealed to the "manly passions" of New Negroes to "act on the manly and lawful principle of self-defense." "Violence must be met with violence," the *Messenger* wrote, "whether that violence is of the individual or the mob."[42] In a November 1921 commentary titled "The Ku Klux Klan—How to Fight It," the *Messenger* editors insisted that African Americans "must be prepared to protect themselves" and "shoot to kill anyone who encroaches upon their lives." In their view, "no tarring and feathering fraternity should be respected except by bullet, brick, bottle, club, or some deadly and maiming weapon." The *Messenger* maintained that only by "hanging together" in teaching New Negro lessons of "good cold steel," especially in the South, could African Americans ensure that they would "no longer hang separately."[43]

In addition to the recurring theme of collective action that was especially central to their articles on the Ku Klux Klan, Randolph and Owen continuously insisted, "if death is to be their portion," New Negroes should be "determined to make their dying a costly investment for all concerned." They repeatedly encouraged their readers to "uncompromisingly" demand "liberty or death." They insisted that "since death is likely to be a two-edged sword," it would be to the "advantage of those in a position to do so" to give African Americans their long-denied civil and social rights. Again, the war experience was a vital component of this new racial spirit, and the *Messenger* specifically underscored the "insistent and vigorous agitation" of younger African Americans, particularly returning black soldiers, in defining the character of the New Crowd Negro. As more and more black soldiers returned home from the war, the *Messenger* became more confident that white America would come to understand that New Negroes were "determined to observe the primal law of self-preservation whenever civil laws break down."[44]

In regard to collective action in black communities, the second component of Randolph's redefinition of New Negroes' racial consciousness, the *Messenger* fervently believed that it could be an effective tool for African Americans not just in terms of self-defense, but in economic and political terms as well. In a March 1920 article titled "Jacksonville Negroes Boycott Big White Insurance Company," the *Messenger* explained how African Americans' "collective money-power, mental, muscle, and moral power" could be employed to "make race prejudice a liability." They commended black Jacksonville, which had collectively canceled insurance policies to protest the alleged participation of company agents in local lynch mob activities, for demonstrating how to "paralyze southern white business" and thereby force a reexamination of Jim Crow. In their view, boycott strategies could give African Americans significant political leverage to demand that federal, state, and local politicians send Jim Crow, disfranchisement, and lynching "aflying" because the "southern white capitalist will allow nothing to stand in the way of his making profits, dollars, and dividends." They concluded that racial prejudice would "be thrown aside" when it "ceases to pay."[45]

Despite the clear emphasis on race that shaped much of the *Messenger's* commentary in these years, Randolph certainly intended to locate his redefinition of the New Negro's underlying philosophy within the framework of his previously expressed views on social justice. In fact, both his description of the New Negro and his definition of New Negroes' most important beliefs fit squarely within the framework of democratic socialism that he and Frank Crosswaith were formulating during this period.[46] In an article titled "A New Crowd—A New Negro," appearing in the May–June 1919 issue of the *Messenger*, Randolph explained that the "New Crowd must be composed of young men who are educated, radical, and fearless." He insisted that essential qualities for joining the New Crowd were "ability, radicalism, and sincerity" and a healthy "expectancy" for the "revolutions ushering in a new world."[47] Though cast in a race-conscious form, these traits paralleled attributes associated with radical labor groups like the IWW in significant ways. In defining the core characteristics of New Crowd Negroes in this way, Randolph tried to bridge the gap between the rising tide of black militancy following the war and the growing labor radicalism of the same period. By connecting these two trends, he hoped to turn New Crowd Negroes into more "effective soldiers in the great army of all races to fight for the achievement of social justice."[48]

In outlining the character of New Crowd Negroes, the *Messenger* devoted special attention to the role of women. Although it did not encourage black women to take to the streets in armed insurrection, the *Messenger* nonetheless insisted that New Negro women had as much responsibility as New Negro men "to fight with increasing vigor, with dauntless courage, unrelenting zeal, and intelligent vision for the attainment of the stature of a full man, a free race, and a new world." Though rooted in the gender politics of home and hearth, the arenas that traditionally defined women's roles, the *Messenger* placed significant value on black women's ability to help "create and keep live" the deep and "consuming passion to break with the slave traditions of the past" in black men. To women the *Messenger* assigned the duty of spurning the "fatal, insidious inferiority complex of the present" that worked to arrest the progress of the New Negro manhood movement. "In politics, business and labor, in the professions, church and education, in science, art, and literature," explained the *Messenger,* "the New Negro Woman, with her head erect and spirit undaunted" must be prepared to march forward "ever conscious of her historic and noble mission of doing her bit toward the liberation of her people in particular and the human race in general."[49]

The ways in which the *Messenger* redefined key aspects of New Negro ideology also suggested direct links to Randolph's earlier vision of social justice. In a key article titled, "The New Negro—What Is He?" appearing in August 1920, the *Messenger* presented a "definite and clear portrayal of the New Negro" that explained his economic, political, and social aims. Arguing that economic justice was the primary basis of social and political equality, the *Messenger* editors maintained that the New Negro "demands the full product of his toil." As a worker, his immediate aims were shorter hours, higher wages, and better working conditions; as a consumer, he insisted on purchasing commodities at the lowest possible price. In politics, the *Messenger* continued, the New Negro "demands political equality" and "stands for universal suffrage." Unlike black Republicans, whom the *Messenger* viewed as "lulled into a false sense of security with political spoils and patronage," New Negroes would not "continue to accept political promissory notes" from political parties that consistently refused to meet their "political obligations" to African Americans. Lastly, the *Messenger* explained that the social aim of the New Negro was "absolute and unequivocal social equality." New Negroes understood quite clearly, Randolph and the *Messenger* pointed out, that a "society which is based upon justice" can only be "composed of social equals."[50]

In many ways, this portrayal of New Crowd Negroes differed significantly from the growing impulse toward racial self-sufficiency that increasingly characterized the sentiments of urban African Americans, more and more of whom were being herded into the expanding ghetto during this period. While they did subscribe to a heightened sense of racial militancy, particularly around issues like self-defense, New Negroes generally accepted the de facto existence of black ghettoes and stopped opposing separate black institutions simply because they were separate.[51] More and more, they refused to view the struggle for equality solely in terms of racial integration while at the same time insisting upon their right to participate fully in the institutional life of the modern city.[52] In connecting their economic and social agenda rooted in a class critique of industrial capitalism to New Negro ideology, Randolph and the *Messenger* hoped to co-opt the growing racial sentiment of the emerging ghetto and direct it toward more class-based outlets.

Thus, while maintaining that New Negroes should have "no armistice" with lynching, Jim Crow, or disfranchisement nor settle for anything less than "complete social, economic, and political justice," the *Messenger* simultaneously pushed New Negroes to consider more class-conscious perspectives in their quest for equal citizenship. As Randolph explained in "A New Crowd—A New Negro," New Crowd Negroes should explore alliances with white radicals in the IWW and the Socialist Party to "build a new society . . . of equals without class, race, caste, or religious distinctions."[53] The central idea of this proposal, that social justice for African Americans was inextricably linked to the struggle of the working class to overcome the exploitation of industrial capitalism, served to locate a distinctly race-conscious aim within a broader class agenda. As the *Messenger* continued to cheer New Negro militancy in these years, Randolph and his staff intensified their efforts to connect racial justice to class consciousness.

Although this push to connect racial justice to a broader class movement seemingly contradicted Randolph's subsequent effort to organize the Brotherhood of Sleeping Car Porters, this tension underscored the degree to which he was divided between the special needs of black workers to protect themselves—sometimes even from white workers—and class-based impulses toward industrial unionism. Yet, the Brotherhood of Sleeping Car Porters should, in part, be understood as an attempt to bring the socialist message of economic justice to a segment of the working class generally left out of this discussion. Randolph certainly thought of the Brotherhood as an important stepping-stone for drawing African Americans more deeply into the labor movement. Moreover, he continually pushed labor groups like the AFL to live up to their class obligations to black workers. Conversely, Randolph also believed that African Americans had an obligation to take steps to solve their own problems before seeking help from others. As he explained in a 1956 letter to Virginia D. Randolph in response to her request for advice on organizing black voters in Norfolk, Virginia, African Americans had to be willing to pay the price of solving their own problems because the "job is not going to be done by labor or anyone else, but by Negroes themselves."[54] Though written in a much later period of his life, this perception of the need for African Americans to act in their own interests clearly shaped Randolph's participation in organizing the porters' union. As the Brotherhood struggled for survival in the midst of the deepening hardships of the coming Great Depression, this tension between organizing an all-black union and inter-racial industrial unionism became more acute.

In situating New Negro militancy in a broader class consciousness, Randolph set out to promote his firmly held belief that the "race question" had an "economic foundation."[55] Even while pushing greater racial awareness among African Americans, the Messenger steadfastly maintained that racial discrimination was primarily a device used by "agencies of reaction to stop the message of working class justice" from reaching black workers.[56] As a result, Randolph and his Messenger staff focused their editorials promoting class consciousness on the ways that class solidarity vitally served the mutual interests of black and white workers. To this end, the Messenger insisted in the February 1920 article "Labor and Lynching" that African Americans' best weapon against racial discrimination was the "solidarity of the working class." It claimed that only "class conscious, militant labor" could permanently change the South.[57] Conversely, the Messenger repeatedly argued, often at great length, that labor could not win its economic demands as long as black workers were left out of unions to be employed as strikebreakers. In Randolph's view, these twin ideas comprised a solid basis for concluding that African Americans' ultimate "emancipation from lynching, Jim Crow, and disfranchisement can only come when the profit system is destroyed."[58]

6

Black and White Unite

Randolph and the Divide between Class Theory and the Race Problem

As with its discussions of New Negro race consciousness, the *Messenger*'s emphasis on the economic roots of racism and the importance of organized labor in the fight against discrimination connected its editorial perspective on class to Randolph's previously expressed views on social justice. In addition to equal access to the social and political fruits of civilization's progress, Randolph also insisted that social justice required the overthrow of any "profit economy" achieved "at the cost of a lower level of income and social well-being for the majority of the population." In his view, any economic system that allowed one group to appropriate all or part of what another produced without "equivalent" compensation amounted to "economic injustice."[1] Randolph used his editorial prerogative to promote an elaborate class-conscious philosophy centered on labor solidarity, the mutual economic interests of black and white workers, and industrial unionism that he hoped could effectively translate African Americans' growing postwar discontent with the racial status quo into momentum for a broader revision of industrial capitalism.

In addressing the first element of this class agenda, labor solidarity, Randolph and the *Messenger* consistently stressed the opinion that individual workers could not effectively challenge organized capital. Just as "one hundred reeds joined together are harder to break than when separate," the *Messenger* argued, "so it was with labor." Concessions from big business had only come, it continued, as a result of workers' "increasing intelligence and solidarity."[2] Through homily and metaphor, the *Messenger* attempted to illustrate for its readers how labor divisions and the lack of effective organization forced workers to accept a "fair day's wage for a fair day's work" instead of according them the "full product" of their toil. The April–May 1920 column titled "When Labor Is Awakened" explained that "capital knows that while labor sleeps," it can be exploited, imprisoned, and pitted against itself. But, when awakened, "trade, religious, nationality, and race lines will cease to divide" organized labor and workers will demand the entire yield of what they produce.[3] Indeed, Randolph and his staff viewed themselves as labor's alarm clock. They insisted that because all workers were equally entitled to all that they produced, black and white workers should unite against their "common enemy," exploitative capitalism. Black and white workers should "form a labor movement of workmen—not white men—but all men who work without regard to race, nationality, or color."[4]

In outlining this notion of class solidarity, the *Messenger* editors based their arguments on straightforward calculations of working-class interests. They repeatedly pointed out that black and white workers shared a common interest in securing higher wages, shorter hours, and better working conditions. They maintained that black and white workers "should combine for no other reason" than to "increase their bargaining power" in pushing forward their economic demands. Because these demands directly opposed the interests of an "employing class" that recognized "no race lines," labor could not afford divisive internal tensions between black and white workers. Randolph and his colleagues believed strongly that only class-conscious collective action could effectively forestall the voracious drive of employers to "exploit any race or class in order to make profits." Another key point made by the *Messenger* in this regard was that non-union workers, whether black or white, were potential scabs who undercut labor's class interests. Randolph and his staff insisted that because "organized labor cannot afford to ignore any labor factor of production" that "organized capital does not ignore," every member of the "industrial machinery must be organized if labor would win its demands."[5]

Though peppered throughout the *Messenger* in this period, these ideas were most clearly delineated in two articles that appeared in the midsummer of 1919. In the first column, titled "Reasons Why White and Black Workers Should Combine in Labor Unions," which appeared in the July issue, the *Messenger* editors stressed these points in outlining their rationale for interracial class cooperation. They explained that because industrial capitalism forces workers to "always seek to improve their conditions" at any cost, it was unrealistic for organized labor to hope or expect unemployed and underpaid black workers "to refuse to scab upon white workers when an opportunity presents itself," especially when white labor unions actively discriminated against them.

Instead, the *Messenger* argued, organized labor needed to ensure that all workers, black and white, were aware of their mutual class interests and to make sure that each worker understood that any future gains by labor could only be "secured through collective action." Indeed, "no union man's standard of living" was safe so long as non-union workers, particularly black workers, were left to scab against striking workers. These two points, the mutual class interests of black and white workers and the importance of collective action, were central to the *Messenger*'s promotion of working-class solidarity.[6]

The emphasis on class solidarity came through even more clearly in the second article, "Our Reason for Being," which appeared in August 1919. In discussing the origins of the National Association for the Promotion of Labor Unionism among Negroes, an organization Randolph and Crosswaith helped to form to counter the divisive impact of racial prejudice on class unity, the *Messenger* confidently asserted that "the combination of black and white workers" would conclusively illustrate that labor was conscious of its mutual interests and collective power. The *Messenger* editors insisted that by turning away from racial prejudice, organized labor could successfully "convert a class of workers which has been used by the capitalist class to defeat organized labor into an ardent, class conscious, intelligent, militant group." In so doing, organized labor would decisively demonstrate to black workers "that unions are not based upon race lines, but upon class lines" and present "a powerful lesson to the capitalist of the solidarity of labor."[7]

The organization's insignia was an important element in emphasizing these points. Its emblem presenting two hands—one black and one white—clasped in fraternal union helped the National Association for the Promotion of Labor Unionism among Negroes create a memorable visual depiction of the class spirit captured in the slogan "black and white workers unite."[8] As Randolph and the *Messenger* continued to push ideas about interracial class cooperation even as tensions between black and white workers increased in the 1920s and beyond, such images became even more important to their message.

The *Messenger* also tried to bolster its readers' sense of class solidarity in these years by drawing very clear distinctions between workers and employers. In editorial after editorial, Randolph and his staff forcefully asserted that the capitalist interests that "dominate and control the government" did not care about workers, black or white. In the March 1919 column "The Deportation of Agitators," the *Messenger* insisted that employers were just as eager to "coin the blood" of the whites as blacks in their merciless pursuit of profits. "Reactionary plutocrats" invariably set out to "ruthlessly and relentlessly" crush either race when one of them "rises to protest against exploitation or adopt measures for relief or improvement."[9] In another instance, the *Messenger* explained, "no sane working man can afford to support the party of his bosses." Though it considered both the Republican and Democratic parties to be opposite "wings of the same foul bird," the *Messenger* insisted that the "average man—white or black—has about the same thing in common with the Republican Party that a dog has in common with a flea." Just as it was in the interest of the dog to rid himself of the flea, it was in the interests of workers to rid themselves of a Republican Party intent on sucking "blood out of the people [and] exploiting the masses for . . . unscrupulous, wicked, and mercenary special interests and labor haters."[10]

This description of the Republican and Democratic parties as common enemies of black and white workers again highlighted a key rationale for the class unity articulated by Randolph and his staff. They consistently argued that all workers, regardless of race, creed, or nationality, should join together "as a matter of course" because of the formidable array of capitalist forces aligned against them. In the September 1920 article, "Should Black Workers Join White Unions?" the *Messenger* explained that while it was "utterly impossible" for white workers to win their demands so long as African Americans were employed as scabs, it was equally clear that "there is every reason why the Negro as a race should support the workers as a class." Both common sense and "enlightened self-interest" dictated that "the organized labor movement of America accord the Negro worker justice." The *Messenger* concluded that "black workers should join white unions and white unions should organize black workers" because to remain divided by the "virus of race prejudice" enabled the "master class to rob both more easily."[11]

In addition to such racialized calculations of class interests in promoting labor solidarity against capital, the *Messenger* also routinely emphasized the more doctrinaire view that a "partnership between labor and capital was about as feasible as a partnership between a cat and a mouse." Because capital sought to maximize its profits by manufacturing goods and services at the lowest possible cost and labor sought the highest wages, improved working conditions, and the shortest hours possible, there was no possibility of reconciling these two "diametrically opposed" goals. Randolph and his colleagues strenuously argued that so long as the "right of one man to make profits out of another man's labors" guided the nation's economic course, black and white workers needed to organize to challenge capital's control of industry. In their view, the "present masters of the industrial foundations of wealth production" held no legitimate claim on the product of labor's sweat, blood, and toil. Because labor wanted nothing that capital was willing to concede and capital adamantly refused to meet any of labor's demands, Randolph and his colleagues maintained that class solidarity in the form of militant, organized labor was the only genuine recourse for workers in pursuing their economic interests.[12]

The bright spotlight that Randolph and the *Messenger* focused on the issue of labor solidarity in large measure reflected the degree to which race prejudice divided black and white workers. Throughout this period, the *Messenger* diligently sought to counteract working-class racial tension by insisting that such division was a significant "menace" to workers' interests. In an article titled "The Task of Local 8—The Marine Transport Workers of Philadelphia," the *Messenger* commended the quick and efficient response of white dockworkers in Philadelphia who began conducting educational forums to quell increasing racial prejudice between black and white workers. They explained that, while the "masters" of the country's economic life allowed no such distinctions to undermine their drive for greater profits, they deliberately fanned the "sinister flames" of race prejudice among workers to "rob them all." Until workers put aside racial differences and established real working-class unity, they would never succeed in any serious struggle for economic emancipation.[13]

This insistence on the fundamental importance of interracial class cooperation did not undermine Randolph's subsequent effort to organize the Brotherhood of Sleeping Car Porters. First of all, the Pullman Company's custom of only hiring African Americans as porters and maids dictated that any union looking to organize these workers would necessarily be an all-black one. When the company briefly turned to hiring Filipinos as replacements for black workers to discouraged union participation, Randolph began exploring plans for incorporating the newcomers into the Brotherhood and became even more determined to press forward with the cause of independent organization.[14] Also, the racially discriminatory practices of the large railroad brotherhoods affiliated with the American Federation of Labor (AFL) left the porters few other options than organizing their own union.[15] Last, and most important, Randolph never considered the organization of all-black unions as an end unto itself. Rather, he initially viewed the Brotherhood as one key step in the process of drawing black workers more deeply into the American labor movement.

This intent comes through quite clearly in Randolph's early orientation toward "black unionism." Prior to his deep involvement with the porters' union, he fervently believed that the essence of a union's effectiveness in protecting workers' interests rested in the power it drew from the "unity of all workers in a given industry or craft." As such, black unionism, which he defined as implying that the "effective role of trade unions for Negroes is only possible . . . through black unions," was the very "negation" of the basic strength of trade unionism. He explained that black unionism served only to "fracture" workers in a given industry into various ethnic groups, resulting in "trade union weakness instead of trade union power." Such racial division only resulted in the "victimization" of all workers involved in the particular industry or trade. Moreover, the "immense" resources created by the emergence of horizontally and vertically integrated corporations meant that trade unions had to adopt more comprehensive organizational strategies to challenge the growing economic power of capital. Without strong class ties to other workers in their industries, Randolph maintained, "Negro unions would stand helpless before such economic juggernauts."[16] With this point of view in mind, it becomes increasingly clear that Randolph intended the Brotherhood to serve as a point of initiation for black workers into the broader labor movement.

The emphasis on labor unity at the center of this critique of black unionism also shaped the *Messenger*'s insistence that race prejudice was a capitalist device for dividing the working class. Throughout this period, Randolph's magazine tried to frame working-class racial tension in ways that resonated with black and white workers and caused them to reexamine the sources of their mutual antipathy. This reasoning clearly shaped the August 1920 column titled "The Fight of the Negro Worker," wherein the *Messenger* contended that "white and black workers do not fight each other because they hate each other, but hate each other because they fight each other." It continued, "capitalists will spare no pains" in seeing that this fight went on because it made it "unnecessary" for them to worry about significant working-class unity. Regardless of how accurate this interpretation of the race question was, Randolph and his editorial staff consistently promoted it and hoped that it would encourage black and white workers to view their hostility in new ways; the *Messenger*, in short, sought to produce greater class solidarity. By succumbing to racial prejudice, the *Messenger* noted, black and white workers helped to advance the divide and conquer strategy of capitalists that recognized no racial, religious, or national differences. Only by acknowledging their mutual class interests could black and white workers hope to protect themselves against a "master class" that viewed the world as their country and robbing labor as their religion.[17]

Two articles in particular, "Lynching: Capitalism Its Cause, Socialism Its Cure" and "Negro Workers: The A.F. of L. or I.W.W.," outlined in detail the *Messenger*'s distinctive explanation of the root cause of working-class racial animosity. Writing on the causes of lynching in the South in March 1919, Randolph asserted that racial discrimination was the "chief weapon" employed by capitalists "to exploit both races." By fostering race prejudice between black and white farmers, both of whom are "fleeced" by southern financial systems, he argued that capitalists hoped to ensure that blacks and whites would not cooperate to overthrow a crop lien system that exploited them both. He explained lynching as a practice encouraged by southern capital "to foster and engender race prejudice to prevent the lynchers and the lynched, white and black workers, from organizing on the industrial field and voting on the political field to protect their labor power."[18] This point echoed loudly through the commentary of the second article, "Negro Workers: The A.F. of L. or I.W.W." Because race prejudice still "haunts the trail of labor," the *Messenger* lamented, white and black workers, especially in the South, still fought each other "while rich white plutocrats pick the pockets of both."

For the *Messenger* editors, the pressing question facing labor was not whether one's co-workers were black or white, but rather how to improve working conditions, wages, and hours and "gain something more of freedom" from the owners of industry. The *Messenger* argued that it was this understanding on the part of capital that led the employing class to seek "to engender race hatred" between black and white workers and, thus, "keep both divided and enslaved." In fact, the *Messenger* insisted that any difference between black and white workers was simply a distinction of degree rather than kind. They maintained that white workers were "little, if any, better off" than black workers in that they were regarded by employers as no more than a "means of making profits." Like the black worker, whose change from chattel slavery to wage slavery "benefited no one but the masters of industry," who could now put him to work "at the hardest and most hazardous labor" without any concern for his "health or welfare," the white worker was "but a machine for producing profits" to be replaced by "another wage slave on the same terms" when he became too old or broken in health or strength. For the *Messenger,* this indiscriminate application of profit calculations to black and white workers demanded a unified response because it demonstrated that the working class could not "depend upon anyone but itself to free it from wage slavery."[19]

While this distinctive explanation of the root cause of working-class racial antipathy overlooked significant aspects of the race problem, it was a fairly creative response to the rising racial tension of the period. Throughout these years, but particularly in the summer of 1919, race riots rocked major urban industrial centers across the country. Often these disputes grew out of simmering tensions between black and white workers as more and more returning soldiers entered the job market. In May 1919, for example, the city of Chicago erupted in violence when black workers were brought in by a local employers' association to break a citywide teamsters strike.[20] The *Messenger's* general response to such events was that every race riot served the interests of capital by driving the "wedge of race prejudice just so much deeper, making it more and more impossible for labor to achieve solidarity." By casting such uprisings as the deliberately engineered result of strategies to divide the working class by industrial employers, Randolph and his editorial staff hoped to convince black and white workers that they had "nothing to gain" from race wars and should, therefore, "drop their daggers and join hands against their common enemy."[21]

This effort to harness the raw emotions that drove these urban race riots and to turn them against industrial capitalism led Randolph and his staff to consistently emphasize the common class interests and status of black and white workers while downplaying, for the most part, deep and long-standing racial divisions within the labor movement. While the *Messenger* did not hesitate to level harsh criticism at the racial policies of the AFL and its craft-oriented focus, it routinely asserted that "even the southern working man will change" his racial views when shown that the "Bourbon master class of the South keeps him in ignorance and poverty by playing race against race." By redefining the players and stakes involved in the South's racial hierarchy, Randolph and his staff hoped to convince black and white workers that it was the white employing class of the South that was labor's "worst enemy." They insisted that both black and white workers would benefit from the destruction of racial barriers that were so effective in dividing organized labor.[22] This effort to link race prejudice to a deliberate strategy pitting black and white workers against each other became a central element in the *Messenger's* struggle to transform working-class racial animosity into genuine working-class consciousness.

Throughout these years, Randolph and his *Messenger* colleagues also used editorial cartoons to illustrate their view of the true nature and cause of working-class racial antagonism. In one instance, the *Messenger* drew parallels between black and white workers and squabbling dogs. In depicting workers as dogs wrangling over a bone while the capitalist dog made away with the ham of "profits," Randolph and the *Messenger* intended to emphasize visually how interracial class tension and petty conflicts worked to distract black and white workers from more important and mutually beneficial goals. "So long as the white dog and the black dog—laborers—fight over the bone," the *Messenger* repeatedly asserted, the "third capitalist dog will surely run away with it."[23]

This point certainly inspired another editorial drawing appearing in the August 1919 issue of the *Messenger* under the heading "When They Get Together They'll Dump Us Off." With this illustration of how employers kept black and white workers separated, the *Messenger* tried to impress upon workers why they could not afford to be "deceived" by race prejudice. In this instance and numerous others throughout the 1920s and beyond, Randolph and his staff insisted that black and white workers had to put aside interracial conflict and recognize their fundamental common class interests. As the *Messenger* repeatedly tried to illustrate, employers were determined to "beat down, mob, and starve" white workers "just as readily as" they did African Americans.[24]

This understanding of the symbiotic nature of black and white working-class interests also framed the *Messenger*'s view of industrial organization. Randolph and his editorial staff maintained that because employers indiscriminately sought to exploit labor to boost their profit margins, black and white workers could get only so far in their demands for better wages and work conditions as their "intelligence and power" would carry them. The *Messenger* insisted that no single individual could effectively challenge organized capital and that any concessions workers managed to extract from employers came only as a result of class-conscious labor solidarity. The worker, regardless of race, gender, or religion, could only "get what he has the power to take" through the organized action of an industrial union. History clearly demonstrated, the *Messenger* argued, that "no advantage, no benefit, no improvement ever came to labor except through organized action." Despite the rampant racial discrimination that plagued the American labor movement, Randolph and his associates enthusiastically encouraged black workers to organize themselves "to fight organized capital, on the one hand, and to force white labor to practice the principles of brotherhood, on the other." In their view, industrial action was the "most effective weapon" that the Negro possessed in protecting "himself as a worker and a race."[25] In the years to come, this dual characterization—one emphasizing race and class instead of Du Bois's race and nation construct—would come to aptly describe Randolph's organization of the Brotherhood of Sleeping Car Porters.

This promotion of industrial unions as a method of race and class advancement connected the *Messenger* to ideas Randolph formulated in previous years. Prior to founding the *Messenger*, Randolph had begun to think about the conflict between labor and capital in terms of purchasing power. In his view, the "fact that the wage scale was never high enough" to enable workers to consume the things they manufactured was the "beginning of trouble for American industry." Labor could never effectively "push wages up to the necessary point to purchase the goods created" because capital always managed "to take back most of labor's gains through the manipulation of prices."[26] Nonetheless, Randolph insisted that workers' only real opportunity to improve their living standards and get a larger share of the wealth that they produced was through class-conscious industrial organization. As he and others pointed out in various editorials, they viewed "mass action" as "labor's only effective weapon" against organized capital.[27] Just as its commentaries on racial discrimination, New Negro race consciousness, and class consciousness clearly drew on Randolph's earlier notions about social justice, the *Messenger*'s discussions of the importance of organized labor directly connected with his early ideas about industrial organization.

In emphasizing the importance of mass action to labor's ultimate victory over capital, Randolph foreshadowed a central feature of the black protest strategy that he would develop in the years to come.[28] Beginning with the porters' union and continuing through his threatened 1941 march on Washington and subsequent Committee Against Jim Crow in Military Service and Training, Randolph articulated a program of mass action and civil disobedience that in many ways built on ideas first put forward in his 1920s *Messenger* editorials on industrial unionism. Just as he would insist that mass action in the context of interest group politics gave African Americans the best chance to push for social change, Randolph argued that mass action in the form of industrial unionism was the only real mechanism for workers to exert pressure on industrial capitalism to take note of their concerns. In recognizing the potential of mass action in the form of industrial unionism to generate significant leverage for social change, Randolph took important steps toward developing aspects of the protest strategy that would shape the 1950s and 1960s civil rights movement.

Another key reason put forward by the *Messenger* for labor to form interracial unions was that such organizations gave workers the ability to affect industrial production. "The strike," insisted the *Messenger*, "is the chief weapon in the hands of labor in the class war" because it "enables labor to enforce a loss upon capital by arresting production." Because the sole purpose of big business was to generate profits, the *Messenger* maintained, organized workers' ability to manipulate industrial output at its source of production was a powerful means of attacking the pocketbooks of the exploiting class. It explained that, when organized properly, unions were not only effective in securing economic objectives like better wages but could be equally effective for political action.[29] This ability, however, depended directly upon labor's success in drawing each and every worker into effective unions. The *Messenger* insisted that "it is too true that so long as one worker is out of the ranks of organized labor, the interests of the workers inside are not secure."[30] Randolph and his staff believed that the unity of purpose fostered by class consciousness meant very little without the unity of action that came with industrial organization.

Furthermore, Randolph and his associates viewed unionization as a "logical and revolutionary" response to capitalism's gigantic combinations of trust, cartels, and financial syndicates. They argued that the size, resources, and influence that such organizations placed at the disposal of big business meant that individuals had no hope of challenging such economic and political hegemony without combinations of a similar nature. In the September 1919 article titled "The March of Industrial Unionism," the *Messenger* stressed that the "slowness and inadequacy of political action" in a system so dominated by capital meant that class-conscious labor had to rely more and more on industrial solidarity as its "omnipotent weapon" for the achievement of workers' immediate aims and ultimate liberation. Yet, instead of depending on their industrial power, workers continued to rely upon a political system whose efforts to "legislate justice for the working class" were, at best, "clumsy." More often than not, the *Messenger* continued, these efforts "proved barren of real results." The *Messenger* insisted that workers had to turn to industrial organization and strikes to produce "maximum" pressure on politicians and business leaders to act on workers' demands. Class-conscious, industrial unions were the best "antidote" for the "capitalist poisons" that had corrupted the nation's key social, political, and economic institutions.[31]

Randolph and the *Messenger* also maintained that industrially organized unions were especially important for African Americans whose largely unskilled status generally left them with "no strategic position in the industrial scheme" and outside the craft-oriented structure of the AFL. Like the United Hebrew Trades that served to protect Jewish workers,[32] Randolph believed that it was even more important for black workers to cultivate "a sort of Negro Federation of Labor" to protect themselves from employers as well as to fight racial discrimination in white labor unions. In various ways throughout this period he argued that such organizations were the "only salvation" for black workers, the most exploited of all classes of people.[33] The *Messenger* also explained that effective unionization served to create a certain degree of leverage for workers by establishing monopoly control over the available labor supply. So long as management can secure replacements, the *Messenger* explained, it was hopeless for workers to press their case for better wages. But with an effective union able to force every potential scab into its ranks, labor could bargain with management from a position of strength.[34]

As part of this discussion of the importance of industrial organization in improving workers' wages and work conditions, the *Messenger* made it clear that it favored the industrial unionism practiced by the Industrial Workers of the World (IWW) over the craft structure of the AFL. In its view, the "chief weakness" of the craft system, where workers are organized by craft or tasks rather than by industry, "lies in the fact that the skilled are cut off and isolated from their unskilled brothers."[35] The *Messenger* pointed out that such division served only to undercut the potency of strikes, especially those staged by un-skilled labor, by permitting different groups of workers in the same industry to continue working while others walked off the job. The *Messenger* explained, for example, that if pressmen walk off their jobs, but linographers remain hard at work, employers needed only to replace the pressmen to keep the printing operation running smoothly and, thus, break the strike.[36] However, if workers in the printing industry were organized industrially, combining everyone regardless of craft into one big union, employers would either have to replace every employee, including highly skilled ones, or meet the unions' demands. Randolph and his colleagues maintained that by recognizing com-mon class interests and organizing industrially rather than by craft, workers could dramatically enhance their leverage against management and ensure that employers responded to their demands for better wages and work condi-tions.

Moreover, the *Messenger* argued that craft-oriented unionization made workers more susceptible to "a sort of grade-working class prejudice between skilled and unskilled groups" that employers artfully cultivated "to attack and conquer" workers one group at a time. As an example, the editorship pointed to employers' efforts to reduce workers' wages in the prewar years. The *Messenger* explained that management first targeted unskilled labor not only because they were the weakest group but, more importantly, because "a victory over the lowest paid workers gives them some color of justification" for subsequently "reducing the [wages of] more highly paid skilled work-ers."[37] However, if workers were organized by industry, employers could not successfully implement such divisive tactics because even the least skilled workers in the union would be in a position to shut down all production. By drawing together every worker in a particular industry into one organization, the *Messenger* argued, industrial trade unionism put to rest the "jurisdictional jealousies" that supported "deluded" ideas of a craft aristocracy and made it possible for labor "to avail itself of its entire strength."[38]

While the *Messenger* maintained that industrial unionism would benefit all workers, it also understood that African Americans especially would gain from this form of organization. As a large portion of the nation's unskilled labor force, black workers generally found themselves left out of the most powerful unions, particularly the railroad brotherhoods affiliated with the AFL.[39] In fact, several of these AFL unions maintained explicit racial bars against black workers in their constitutions. Because it openly condoned these "unsound principles," the *Messenger* renamed the American Federation of Labor the "American Separation of Labor" and charged it was one of the "most wicked machines for the propagation of race prejudice in the country."[40] Randolph and his staff pointed out that industrial unionism, in contrast, "would necessarily include in its organization any Negroes in an industry."[41] The *Messenger* insisted that this "one big union" principle was the only basis for developing a "real constructive labor movement" that would be "feared and respected" instead of being "an object of ridicule" all over the world.[42]

As this "one big union" philosophy of industrial organization suggests, Randolph and the *Messenger* began to promote labor solutions that placed them near the more syndicalist elements of the Socialist Party. Most closely associated with William Haywood and the Industrial Workers of the World, syndicalism focused almost exclusively on labor's immediate demands, endorsed industrial sabotage as an acceptable form of class protest, and called for a general strike to reorganize society around the key means of industrial production.[43] Yet, for Randolph, the issue of race acted to temper his labor radicalism somewhat. He clearly understood that the injudicious advocacy of violence in any form was exceedingly dangerous for black workers, individually and collectively, because such arguments could easily translate into justifications for acts of racial violence. Nonetheless, Randolph and his staff continued to develop and promote criticisms of industrial capitalism and class-based solutions that closely paralleled the views of the Socialist Party's most radical factions.

In this regard, the *Messenger* contended that industrial capitalism was responsible for promoting "certain socio-economic conditions" that inevitably led to peonage, the crop-lien system, tenant farming, and peasantry, all of which exploited African Americans more than any other group and was an "immediate" cause of lynching. Arguing that "material gains" are the key "motor-forces of individual and social action," the *Messenger* explained that capitalism's "exploitation of human labor power and the natural resources of the country for private profit" promoted the kind of "crass, materialistic economic" factors that placed various working-class ethnic and racial groups at odds with each other.[44] Not only were workers left to divide a continually shrinking portion of the wealth that they produced, Randolph and his staff argued, but the wide-scale poverty that resulted from the private ownership of the means of production and exchange was the primary source of crime, prostitution, and, especially, racial prejudice. They pointed out that "socialism would abolish poverty and its consequences" by replacing the profit system. Socialism would undercut the value of racial discrimination and, therefore, would "remove Negro workers from the base of the working world."[45]

The commitment to socialism that the *Messenger* exhibited in selling industrial unionism and interracial class consciousness to African Americans also shaped the increasingly contentious divide that began to develop between Randolph and the small but vocal band of black communists that emerged in Harlem in the early 1920s. Randolph's initial enthusiasm for the Bolshevik Revolution had faded significantly in the aftermath of the Socialist Party's split in 1919, and the American Communist Party began implementing its own program of interracial organization. Increasingly concerned about the Comintern's impingements on black self-expression and independence, Randolph boycotted the founding convention of the American Negro Labor Congress in 1925 and maintained a wary distance until the 1930s, when he embraced a kind of militant anticommunism that set the tone for the rest of his career.[46]

Randolph's growing ambivalence toward communism in the 1920s cannot be separated from the distinct anti–West Indian sentiment that shaped his part in his heated drama with Garvey. At the same time that his suspicions of communism began to take root, his questioning of Garvey's ethics, intelligence, and race loyalty increasingly veered toward the personal.[47] For the core group of black radicals in Harlem that embraced communism, all of whom were West Indian immigrants, Randolph's denunciation of Garvey and contention that Garvey's ideas for establishing a Negro nation "could emanate only from the diseased brain of this Supreme Negro Jackass from Jamaica" seemed completely over the top.[48] Even as West Indian radicals like Cyril Briggs, Richard B. Moore, and others raised their own concerns about Garvey's program, Randolph's growing propensity to turn his criticism in an anti-Jamaican direction offended even his closest West-Indian associates. As the hostility between Randolph and the Communist Party deepened, the deep-felt bitterness that his anti–West Indian tone engendered among these early black converts to communism should not be ignored.

Ironically, though, in organizing the Brotherhood of Sleeping Car Porters in the mid-1920s Randolph became much more sympathetic to some of the racial sensitivities that led Briggs, Moore, and W. A. Domingo to embrace communism. As the porters struggled for union recognition, the class sensibilities that characterized Randolph's early association with the Socialist Party ran headlong into the entrenched racial discrimination that constrained African Americans' lives. Indeed, the challenge of organizing Pullman porters and maids would test Randolph's core class convictions in fundamental ways. Ultimately he would begin to articulate a kind of dual race and class consciousness as the best prescription for the problems plaguing black workers.

PART 4

Blending Race and Class

7

Ridin' the Rails

*Randolph and the Brotherhood
of Sleeping Car Porters' Struggle
for Union Recognition*

When a group of Pullman porters approached A. Philip Randolph about helping them form a union in August 1925, he quickly envisioned the radical potential of such an enterprise. Randolph believed that not only could the nascent Brotherhood of Sleeping Car Porters mark "an epochal stage in the life of the Pullman porter," but that it could also serve as "a significant land-mark in the history and struggle of the Negro workers in America."[1] Equally important, however, was the practical opportunity it created for him to put into action his ideas about the relationship between socialism and the race problem. Previously, he had come to view social justice as a function of workers' ability to extract economic concessions from industrial capitalism through labor unions.[2] He initially believed that the Brotherhood would be an ideal way of illustrating the common class interests that black and white workers shared; he saw the porters' union as central to drawing African Americans more deeply into the general labor movement. Instead, he discovered that in corporate boardrooms and on the shop floor, race still trumped class in that racial discrimination severely limited the effectiveness of strict class theory in addressing the needs of black workers.[3] As the impact of the Great Depression spread in the late 1920s and 1930s, this realization forced Randolph to revise his views on industrial unionism and insist that black workers simultaneously pursue their general class interests while also attending to their particular racial needs.

Though the idea of forming a porters' union may have seemed like a radical notion at the time, Randolph's Brotherhood of Sleeping Car Porters (BSCP) was in fact only one of many attempts by black railway workers to organize bona fide trade unions.[4] As Randolph explained, as far back as 1910 there were perhaps as many as "a half dozen or more Pullman porters' movements . . . started from time to time."[5] Two unions in particular succeeded in recruiting significant memberships. The Brotherhood of Sleeping Car Porters' Protective Union and the Railway Men's International Benevolent Industrial Association both were organized in the years surrounding World War I when the federal government nationalized railroads under the National Railroad Administration and began to endorse union activities among railroad workers.[6] Unfortunately for Pullman porters, neither organization made much progress in protecting their interests. As with previous attempts to organize black Pullman employees, both the Porters' Protective Union and the International Benevolent Industrial Association failed. In both cases, Randolph explained, either porters were "maneuvered into accepting Company benevolence," or the company's well-maintained spy system exposed and victimized the organizations' leadership with "intimidation through the loss of jobs."[7]

In place of these kinds of independent labor organizations, the Pullman Company offered its porters membership in the company-run Employee Representation Plan (ERP). A typical company-sponsored employee association, Pullman's plan fit squarely with the business spirit of the American Plan of labor relations that sought to defuse labor radicalism through welfare capitalism and the anti-labor tone of the Transportation Act of 1920, which restored the railroad industry to private ownership.[8] Under the ERP, the Pullman Company offered its porters and maids a small wage increase and sought to co-opt features of the Porters' Protective Union by also providing its black employees modest sickness and death benefits. Though the Porters' Protective Union continued to exist into the mid-1920s, the Employee Representation Plan effectively quelled discontent among most porters. As Randolph put it, "this welfareism of the Pullman Company appeared not only plausible to the Pullman porters and their families, but desirable," and for some it served as "evidence of the high generosity and big-hearted spirit of the Company to the porters."[9]

Yet, Randolph also understood the real intent behind the ERP. He noted that by offering its black service workers free membership in this company plan, Pullman officials hoped to blind porters and maids to their fundamental interests in building independent labor organizations that could "rescue them from the bog and swamps of industrial charity and ruthless exploitation."[10] This view of the plan's underlying intent became more evident to an increasing number of porters as well after 1924 when company officials organized a wage conference to respond to porters' petitions for pay raises. Insisting that all workplace complaints be presented through the ERP's grievance structure, Pullman set out to ensure that it maintained complete control over labor negotiations with its porters and maids during this conference. Since the Employee Representation Plan was a company-sponsored employee organization with company-endorsed representatives bargaining on behalf of porters, this wage conference ostensibly placed company men on both sides of the negotiating table. Moreover, because the porters representing the plan were subject to dismissal by management with whom they were bargaining, some porters came to agree with Randolph's assessment that the ERP and the deals reached through it "amounted to sheer mockery." Despite the small wage increase that resulted from the 1924 wage conference, more and more porters came to believe that the impotence of the plan in securing higher wages and other benefits in effect robbed them of even more meaningful upgrades in their livelihood.[11]

Certainly none of the core issues that Randolph and the Brotherhood would later raise were ever considered under the ERP. For instance, not only were porters poorly compensated for the services they provided, but they were also required to work long hours. In addition to the duties they performed during the day attending to passengers' needs, on long trips porters were expected to be equally available to passengers at night. In many instances, this meant that they got little or no sleep. For the four hundred hours of road service it required porters to put in each month, Pullman paid an average wage of only $78.11. A significant portion of porters' time went to preparing Pullman cars before passengers arrived for boarding and cleaning up the cabins after each trip. Yet, they were not paid for this time. Likewise, they were not paid for layovers on long trips or for return trips to their home stations when no passengers were riding in their cars, a procedure called "deadheading." Porters were also expected to provide their own meals and sleeping quarters on overnight runs. While services like shoe shining were part of a porter's job, each man was responsible for supplying his own polish, brushes, and cloths.

Working conditions and compensation were even worse for the two hundred or so maids that Pullman employed during this period. According to a pamphlet titled "The Pullman Porter," issued by the Brotherhood in conjunction with its 1926 appeal to the U.S. Mediation Board, Pullman maids received a minimum wage of only $70 a month. While the average porter earned on average about $58 a month in tips to supplement his paycheck, opportunities to earn tips for Pullman maids were "necessarily limited." Even though they like porters were frequently required to make overnight runs,

Pullman made no sleeping provisions for its maids, and maids were given even "shorter rest periods than porters on the same run." Thus, irrespective of the small pay increases that porters and maids received under Pullman's ERP, by purposefully leaving all of these other workplace issues unaddressed, the plan clearly left porters and maids vulnerable to company exploitation. As the Brotherhood pamphlet explained, the utter lack of regard that Pullman's Employee Representation Plan exhibited toward these issues was "a constant source of dissatisfaction to the porters."[12]

Randolph understood early on the fundamental shortcomings of the Pullman employee plan. In his presidential report to the Third National Convention of the Brotherhood of Sleeping Car Porters, he described the Employee Representation Plan as an "iniquitous system of economic servitude" whose "alluring facade" of industrial welfare effectively "chloroformed many well-meaning but misguided men and women in the Pullman service."[13] In Randolph's account of the Brotherhood's origins, he pointed to the duplicitous nature of the Pullman plan as the central catalyst for galvanizing support among some porters for an independent labor organization.[14] The "flagrant injustices" of the ERP "exposed" its futility as an instrument for securing economic justice and helped to crystallize porters' determination to form a "bona fide" labor union to bargain collectively on their behalf.[15] This disillusionment was particularly strong among porters headquartered in New York City, where the influence of journals like the *Messenger* and the radical atmosphere of the Harlem street corner continued to shape the community. Following the 1924 wage conference, a group of New York porters that included Ashley Totten and Roy Lancaster, two future national officers of the Brotherhood of Sleeping Car Porters, began to meet to discuss issues of economic security and workplace dignity for black Pullman employees. They concluded that the porters' interests could only be effectively protected by an independent labor union and turned to the question of how to go about building such an organization.[16]

One of the central ideas to emerge from these initial discussions was that any new effort to organize porters had to be spearheaded by someone beyond the direct influence of the Pullman Company.[17] The company had successfully undermined previous attempts to form independent porters' unions, and Totten, Lancaster, and the other members of this founding group wanted to insulate their new organization from such tactics. By bringing in someone to lead the organization who was not on the Pullman payroll, they hoped to neutralize this potential problem. Since such a person would not be dependent upon Pullman for his livelihood, they reasoned, he would truly be free

to operate independently and on their behalf.[18] The responsibility for identifying and recruiting a competent, independent union organizer fell to Totten,
the most radical of the founding members. However, the degree to which
Totten initially considered Randolph for the job is not exactly clear. Totten
and his fellow porters were certainly familiar with Randolph's writings and
frequent lectures and forums in Harlem. But as Randolph later explained,
after his first meeting with Totten and the other New York porters in August
1925, they then questioned Fred R. Moore, publisher of the *New York Age* and
a key spokesman for the old Booker T. Washington Tuskegee Machine, as
to whether he thought Randolph would be a good person to organize their
union. Though Moore endorsed Randolph for the position, this support was
not a sure thing. As Randolph recalled, he and Moore were at "loggerheads"
at the time because Moore considered him "an extreme radical."[19]

With this qualified endorsement from Moore, Totten and the porters ar-
ranged a second meeting with Randolph where they offered him the job of
general organizer for the new union. Randolph accepted the position and
explained that before he began any actual organizing he would need to conduct a broad-based propaganda campaign in the *Messenger* against Pullman
and the Employee Representation Plan to underscore for porters the merits
of an independent union. While some have speculated that this early strategy
indicated that Randolph initially saw the porters' movement as a means of
rejuvenating the *Messenger's* flagging circulation, it seems clear that Randolph
thought that no effective organizing among porters could take place "until
the Plan of Employee Representation or company union was completely
scrapped and thrown into the ashcan of annihilation."[20] He explained that
as a "virgin group so far as their knowledge and belief in the great value of
labor organizations to workers . . . was concerned," the Brotherhood first had
to overcome the "mass of propaganda" against unionization from the black
press and pulpit and the insidious tactics of the Pullman plan in convincing
porters that it could be more effective in securing higher wages and better
working conditions for them.[21]

With this understanding in place, Randolph set about interviewing Totten and other porters to get a sense of the scope and scale of the workplace
problems that they faced. As he noted later, the nature of the porters' job
as it was explained to him in these interviews made clear that being a Pullman porter was a "tough road to travel." In addition to the media campaign
against Pullman and its employee plan, Randolph also conducted a series
of union meetings intended to educate porters in New York, Chicago, St.
Louis, and other key Pullman hubs about the merits of the Brotherhood.

At the first meeting of porters in New York, Randolph set out to present "the whole course of the struggle of the worker to emancipate himself from exploitation" with specific emphasis on African Americans' special need for the power achieved through industrial unity. As he recalled, the first meeting was particularly delicate because of the certain presence of company spies in the audience whose task was to mark any porter who showed an interest in joining the Brotherhood. Despite the very real threat of being fired, porters packed Harlem's Elks Hall to hear what Randolph and the Brotherhood had to say. [22]

In some ways Randolph's selection to head up the organizing campaign among Pullman porters was an odd choice. Though he had some limited experience working on the railroads, he was not a porter and had no real understanding of their specific grievances. In fact, the strongest recommendation for approaching Randolph might have been his renown as an economic radical whose editorial polemics and street corner harangues against capitalist exploitation and economic injustice were widely known. There were also veteran porters like Robert L. Mays, founder of the Railway Men's International Benevolent Industrial Association, with practical experience in organizing black workers that were perhaps better suited and situated to lead the new union.[23] It is not surprising, then, that Randolph may not have been the first choice for the job. In fact, evidence suggests that Randolph became the leading candidate only after delivering a speech to the Pullman Porters' Athletic Club, a social group associated with Totten and the other founding Brotherhood members, in which Randolph first raised the possibility of building an international porters' union on the scale of other international railroad brotherhoods.[24]

The most comprehensive accounts of Randolph's organizing campaign among Pullman porters typically paint a picture of an idealistic crusader determined to make the nation live up to its fundamental principles of justice and freedom. These accounts emphasize Randolph's efforts to use every provision of the 1926 Railway Labor Act and the new mediating agencies it created to resolve labor disputes to force Pullman to negotiate with the Brotherhood; Randolph even presented the Brotherhood's case to the Interstate Commerce Commission (ICC) in an attempt to increase wages. Despite the repeated setbacks the Brotherhood encountered in petitioning these agencies for relief, these accounts highlight Randolph's continued efforts to enlist federal intervention on the porters' behalf as a central feature of his campaign to establish the Brotherhood's credentials. For some observers, these repeated appeals for federal mediation and intervention in the face of repeated setbacks is strong evidence of his faith in the law and idealistic belief in justice and fair play.[25]

But, while such accounts of the Brotherhood's struggle for recognition present a thorough outline of the union's founding, the emphasis on Randolph's faith in notions of justice and fair play is misplaced. Such idealism does not at all fit with the harsh criticism that he leveled at the nation, the American labor movement, and white Americans for their treatment of African Americans. Beginning with the *Messenger*, Randolph's many speeches, essays, and articles uniformly argued that despite the nation's "dazzling" technological achievements, the "deprivation of civil rights for the Negro" frustrated the development of the "democratic process" in the nation's social, political, and civil institutions. From 1917, when the *Messenger* first appeared, through the late 1960s, Randolph consistently argued that "for too long" white Americans had placed "the burden of democracy's advance" on the shoulders of African Americans and refused to recognize that "the fight [for equality] belongs to all Americans who cherish representative government and whose ancestors fought for freedom under the banner of equality and equal representation."[26] While numerous studies thoroughly examine the origins and evolution of the Brotherhood of Sleeping Car Porters, Randolph's repeated attempts to mobilize federal agencies in support of the porter's cause most certainly did not reflect any great faith in American-style justice.

Instead, it was Randolph's growing conviction that most whites were only prepared to treat African Americans fairly when required to do so by some compelling force that shaped his efforts to mobilize the mediation provisions of the 1926 Railway Labor Act. With the Employee Representation Plan firmly in place and Pullman content to ignore completely the demands presented by the Brotherhood, there was no real way for Randolph to break through with his organizing efforts without some significant external leverage to compel company representatives to acknowledge the Brotherhood's legitimacy. Rather than reflecting any abiding faith in American justice, Randolph's repeated appeals for federal mediation were part of a calculated effort to force Pullman into recognizing and negotiating with the Brotherhood. His understanding of the need for external pressure to compel company representatives to acknowledge the Brotherhood also shaped his efforts to affiliate with the American Federation of Labor. Despite its clear record of racial discrimination, Randolph hoped that AFL membership would make Pullman look even more unreasonable by legitimizing the Brotherhood and the porters' case and, thereby, would persuade company officials to capitulate. Rather than exhibiting an abiding faith in justice and fairness, Randolph's efforts to enlist federal mediation in the porters' case as well as his push to join the AFL reflected a practical and deliberate plan to generate the leverage necessary to secure fair treatment for black workers.[27]

Unfortunately for the porters, Randolph and the Brotherhood discovered that federal authorities were no more sympathetic to their claims than were Pullman managers. Certainly the sheer apathy that Randolph encountered in lobbying the federal agencies created under the Railway Labor Act was a significant factor in his eventual reevaluation of the effectiveness of class theory for African Americans. Prior to his involvement with Pullman porters and maids, Randolph had a dim view of black unionism. He steadfastly opposed any suggestion that trade unionism was only effective for African Americans when they were organized in all-black unions. He insisted that such ideas fundamentally undercut the basic strength of industrial unions. "Black unionism," Randolph maintained, served only to "fracture" class unity and undermine union power.[28] But the Pullman Company's adamant refusal to recognize the Brotherhood along with the reluctance of federal agencies to intervene on the porters' behalf, despite their having fulfilled the necessary requirements under the law for union recognition, unequivocally demonstrated for Randolph that there was a special need for concerted action by black workers. As the Great Depression stretched into the 1930s, Randolph came to recognize more and more that racial discrimination posed unique challenges for black workers that could not be effectively addressed in a strictly class-conscious way.

This point that Randolph made about black unionism is also significant because it stands in stark contrast to the position that he would later take as a result of the Brotherhood's struggle for recognition as the official bargaining agent for Pullman porters and maids. In subsequent letters and speeches throughout the period, Randolph began to assert that in the "struggle of the Negro for freedom and justice and equality in the United States," African Americans "must fight every inch of the way" for their rights. More and more after the failure of the Brotherhood to secure federal mediation under the Railway Labor Act, he began to insist that the continuation of racial discrimination "ought to arouse the Negro to the realization of the fact that they must organize and fight" if they were to secure the full measure of their civil rights because "they are not going to get them any other way."[29] While it is not surprising to see Randolph raise the issues of equal justice and organization, the distinguishing feature of this new point of view was the growing emphasis on racial identity over class identity. Even though shades of this same racial language appeared from time to time in his earlier writings, particularly in the *Messenger*, and in various speeches that he delivered in Harlem and other key porter cities, it was only after the prolonged battle with the Pullman Company that Randolph began to see race as a special and distinct element of the broader effort to secure social justice for black workers through labor organization.

This fundamental shift in Randolph's understanding of the intersection of race and class in the porters' case against Pullman also affected the public's view of the Brotherhood. As Randolph and the porters argued their case before federal mediators, Brotherhood supporters began to echo Randolph's assertion that the porters' cause involved both the "future of Negro workers in American industry" and the potential for "better race relations." In a pamphlet titled "High Points of Deep Interest in the Pullman Porters' Struggle: The Story of a Race's Exploitation," the Boston Citizens' Committee—an interracial group of concerned New Englanders—equated their support for the Brotherhood with the "illustrious sons" of New England who played such a "prominent role in the struggle to achieve the emancipation of the Negro from chattel slavery." In freedom, wrote the Boston Citizens' Committee, the Negro still faced problems of segregation, lynching, disfranchisement, and civil injustice that "haunt his life," but the formation of the Brotherhood indicated that he was beginning to "stir" himself against forces that have "systemically kept him from earning a livelihood." In lending support to the porters' cause, the Boston Citizens' Committee explained that they acted to continue the "glorious and illustrious tradition" of New England abolitionism that fought to "rid the Republic of that blot upon its banner."[30]

This new emphasis on racial identity over class identity came through even more clearly when Randolph turned his attention beyond the shop floor. In these years and beyond, Randolph explained that he was "absolutely" convinced that even the most "honest white American who believes in Negroes rising" expected "Negroes to spearhead their own cause." More importantly, perhaps, Randolph went on to insist that "the only movement I would be interested in developing would be an all-Negro movement fighting for all our civil rights for first-class citizenship but with absolute dependence upon Negroes to furnish the money, the brains, and direction."[31] Race became the central organizing theme for Randolph even as he maneuvered black workers toward the broader class movement of organized labor. "As I see it," Randolph explained, even if black and white workers shared similar class interests and organized labor sympathized with efforts to challenge the status quo of industrial capitalism, the specific challenge of overcoming Jim Crow "is the Negro's problem and he has got to pay for it." Even while pushing anti-poll tax resolutions on the AFL convention floor through the 1940s and 1950s,[32] Randolph continued to maintain that the job of organizing black voters in the South was "not going to be done by labor or anybody else." It had to be done "by Negroes themselves."[33] It is this sea change in his thinking about racial organization and independent racial action that gives his involvement with the Brotherhood of Sleeping Car Porters and other black labor organizations in Harlem in the interwar years new significance.

While the organizational history of the Brotherhood is undoubtedly significant, it is equally important to understand how the evolution of the porters' union, especially the unique racial challenges faced by black workers, fundamentally reshaped Randolph's thinking about industrial organization. Certainly the connections between the various twists and turns of the Brotherhood's struggle for recognition and Randolph's shifting thoughts about race and class is central to reconciling his early insistence that black unionism was the "highest form of irrational economic philosophy" with his later views on the necessity of independent black action against racial discrimination. Similarly, Randolph's involvement with the Negro Labor Committee and other black labor organizations in Harlem in these years also requires substantial explanation to understand how it fit with his critique of black unionism as a "tragic misconception of the origins and purpose of trade unions."[34] Without a comprehensive framework for pulling these disparate views on industrial organization and independent black action into alignment, the full significance of Randolph's accomplishment in building the Brotherhood of Sleeping Car Porters is easily underestimated.

Moreover, it is equally important to reexamine the history of the Brotherhood of Sleeping Car Porters in terms of Randolph's evolving understanding of race and class to make sense of how the issue of race ushered in a new phase in the post–World War I labor movement. Though the Pullman Strike of 1894 was ultimately broken by a combination of court injunctions, federal troops, and corporate intransigence, the principle of industrial unionism survived to challenge the craft orientation of the AFL under Samuel Gompers in the postwar years. However, it was only after Randolph and the Brotherhood began to highlight the discriminatory treatment that black workers faced from both corporate managers and the AFL's railroad brotherhoods that organized labor began to take real note of racial issues. As such, the Brotherhood's struggle with Pullman is not only central to understanding African Americans' push for equal justice but is also at the center of one of the postwar labor movement's primary tensions, the integration of racial minorities into labor unions.

This struggle to reconcile race and class in the American labor movement extended back to the nineteenth century when skill level and ethnic, familial, and religious ties more so than trade unions helped to dictate the structures of the workplace. As white workers internalized the "wages of whiteness as an entitlement," job competition between blacks and whites took on new significance.[35] Racial proscriptions in organized labor took shape in this context, and even when unions did not include racial bars in their constitutions, they often functioned along ethnic or religious lines to preserve racial prerogatives. The AFL became deeply invested in this kind of racial segmentation even as it paid lip service to racial equality. It was this deep-seated heritage of racial antipathy that Randolph and the Brotherhood had to overcome in their quest for full-fledged union recognition.

In December 1926, the Brotherhood presented an appeal to the U.S. Mediation Board set up under the Railway Labor Act of 1926 that focused primarily on the porters' wage and workplace grievances. But the appeal also carried a subtle but significant racial message that would become more pronounced as its struggle for recognition stretched into the 1930s. In strategic places throughout its "Skeleton Brief of the Case in Support of the Demands of the Brotherhood of Sleeping Car Porters," Randolph and the porters pointed out that the Brotherhood's demands for better wages and work conditions were no different than those presented by white Pullman conductors to the Industrial Relations Commission in 1915. The porters' brief insisted that "in considering the demands still put forward by the Brotherhood of Sleeping Car Porters," federal mediators should not look upon them as "novel and unreasonable requests" but rather as a genuine attempt to remedy a long-standing accumulation of grievances. "That any organization must fight for the achievement of ends so modest as these now asked [for] by the Pullman porters and maids," insisted the Brotherhood, "is in itself a grave indictment" of the Pullman Company.[36]

In fact, this comparison between Pullman porters and conductors underlined most, if not all, of the grievances enumerated by the Brotherhood in its appeal for federal mediation. For instance, the porters' petition pointed out that "transportation workers in general, Pullman conductors, and workers in general industry have all advanced much more rapidly in their wages than have the Pullman porters." Though not explicit, the clear intent of such comparisons between Pullman's black service personnel and its white employees highlighted the racial discrimination that porters faced in challenging the workplace status quo. Likewise, Randolph and the porters argued that the "American standard of living" should be accessible to all workers, "regardless of race or color," but in the case of porters, the Pullman Company seemed to believe that "the Negro worker can live on less than can the white." The Brotherhood's brief also pointed to distinctions between Pullman's treatment of white conductors and black porters in resolving complaints over work hours and compensation for service time. If the pay scale for white Pullman conductors could be pegged to a 240-hour working month that included service time prior to departure and after arrival, the Brotherhood maintained that the company should put in place similar conditions for porters "without discrimination."[37]

This theme of racial discrimination was also a central element of the argument that Randolph and the Brotherhood made in support of their case for recognition as the official bargaining agent for Pullman porters and maids. "It is important to note," the brief explained, "that the Pullman Company deals with its conductors through their self-formed, self-managed, and self-financed Order of Sleeping Car Conductors, while it deals with its porters and maids through the company-formed, company-managed, and company-financed Plan of Employee Representation." Beyond merely emphasizing such discrimination in dealing with Pullman's black employees, Randolph and the porters insisted that "by comparing the two representative mechanisms and testing their comparative advantages to the employees concerned," it should be clear that it was the Plan of Employee Representation's obvious "shortcomings" that led Pullman porters and maids to demand recognition of an independent organization "similar to that of the conductors." The brief explained that while all Pullman employees had been pushing for increased pay, fewer hours, and better working conditions, only the white conductors working through their independent union had managed to secure most of their demands. Porters were still fighting for the same concessions "in spite of the operation of the Plan of Employee Representation since 1920."[38]

In defining porters' grievances as similar to or exactly like those previously presented by white conductors, the Brotherhood's brief set out to undercut company claims that the porters' case was unreasonable. In the Brotherhood's view, porters and conductors did similar work under similar conditions and deserved similar treatment.

> Indeed, conductors and porters travel on the same trains, over the same routes, and under the same conditions. If a 240-hour basic month is necessary for the conductors and just for them, it is also necessary and just for the porters. If conductors should be paid for preparatory and terminal time . . ., porters and maids should also be paid for these things. If conductors require definite

provision for sleep on the road, porters and maids also require such provisions. If conductors may be represented in negotiations with the company by an independent union . . . , porters and maids should also be thus represented.

Having outlined this comparative framework in detail, Randolph and the porters concluded by insisting that the "continued refusal on the part of the [Pullman] Company to establish and maintain comparable conditions for comparable work stands as a clear-cut case of discrimination."[39]

By hinging their arguments to the Mediation Board on this comparison with white Pullman conductors, Randolph and the Brotherhood best illustrated their contention that the Pullman Company's opposition to the Brotherhood was strictly motivated by race. Since the Railway Labor Act of 1926 specifically sanctioned collective bargaining for railroad workers and the creation of independent labor unions, Randolph and the porters reasoned that they too were entitled to the rights and privileges enumerated in the law.[40] This appeal for federal mediation was intended to force government officials into applying the law as it was written rather than allowing the Pullman Company to continue to manage its workforce under long-standing racial custom. For Randolph and the porters, federal intervention was the only possible way of forcing the Pullman Company to treat its black workers fairly. The "Skeleton Brief of the Case in Support of the Brotherhood of Sleeping Car Porters" was simply the first of many attempts to enlist the support of federal agencies against racial discrimination.[41]

When it became apparent that the Mediation Board would not act on the porters' behalf, Randolph immediately began to consider other ways to activate the emergency provisions of the Railway Labor Act to force some resolution of the Brotherhood's grievances. Without any other means of pressuring Pullman to negotiate, the Brotherhood issued a call for a nationwide strike to give porters "a new sense" of power and industrial importance and to present to the public for the first time "the problems of the porters . . . in dramatic form."[42] Randolph clearly hoped that the public fervor a strike threat might create would put pressure on Pullman to negotiate a settlement. The evidence clearly demonstrates that he never seriously entertained thoughts of following through on the strike. Instead, with an affirmative strike vote from porters, he thought that federal mediators would have to act on the emergency provisions of the Railway Labor Act and insist that the two sides begin negotiations.[43] Again, the point here is that Randolph looked to federal intervention on the porters' behalf as a concrete regulatory mechanism for forcing the Pullman Company to deal with the Brotherhood.

Throughout the 1920s and into the 1930s, Randolph and the Brotherhood continued to argue that Pullman's Employee Representation Plan violated the provisions of the Railway Labor Act. In a 1930 suit filed in a federal district court seeking a temporary restraining order against ERP elections, the Brotherhood asserted that the continued maintenance of a "company union" violated federal statutes governing labor unions that expressly barred "acts of interference, influence, and coercion" by interstate carriers. "By the conducting of elections of employee representatives," the Brotherhood alleged, Pullman's plan "does interfere, influence, and coerce its employees in their statutory right to select their own representatives for the purposes of the Railway Labor Act." Specifically, Brotherhood lawyers David E. Lilienthal and Walter F. Lynch argued that by controlling the election process, requiring porters to vote, and soliciting votes for particular candidates, Pullman "irreparably" threatened porters' legal right to select without "interference or influence" their own representatives—an ability already deemed a "property right" by a federal circuit court of appeals.[44]

In response to the charges outlined in the Brotherhood's filings, Pullman officials essentially argued that Randolph and the porters misunderstood how the ERP worked and that the Brotherhood had no legal standing to challenge its operation. In a memorandum prepared for G. A. Kelly, Pullman's general counsel, in response to the Brotherhood's 1930 injunction application, Pullman director of labor relations, F. L. Simmons claimed that Randolph and the Brotherhood "erroneously interpreted" the ERP and deliberately "issued false statements" to porters and the public.[45] In Pullman's responding brief, Kelly asserted that the porters' case should be summarily dismissed because the Brotherhood had no legal standing to act on behalf of Pullman porters because it was not "a duly organized voluntary association with the capacity to sue."[46] Rather than engage the Brotherhood's core assertion that Pullman discriminated against porters solely on the basis of race, company officials routinely argued that Randolph and the Brotherhood were simply opportunists. They asserted that Randolph and the Brotherhood were trying to "break" into Pullman's labor negotiations "to disrupt the friendly relations" between the company and its porters. All claims against Pullman should be dismissed, Kelly argued, because Randolph and the Brotherhood fundamentally misunderstood how the ERP operated, and neither had any legal standing to act on behalf of Pullman porters.[47] Ultimately, the court sided with Pullman and denied the porters' injunction request.

Following the failed appeals for federal mediation or adjudication, Randolph and the porters took a new tack in attempting to force the Pullman

Company to negotiate on wages. In 1927 the Brotherhood submitted a complaint to the Interstate Commerce Commission (ICC) against the practice of tipping. As Randolph explained in his report to the Brotherhood's Third National Convention, the porters deliberately "sought the intercession" of the ICC in the form of an examination of Pullman's financial structure as an "indirect" means of pressuring the company to raise wages and negotiate on other workplace issues.[48] Though the ICC determined that it had no jurisdiction over the matter because it fell within the scope of the Railway Labor Act, the Brotherhood's petition to the ICC should be viewed as another attempt to mobilize administrative mechanisms to compel the Pullman Company to deal fairly with its black employees. Randolph took the porter's case before the ICC because he felt that for the porters the "value and utility" of the Mediation Board created by the 1926 Railway Labor Act had been "shown to be futile."[49] The ICC petition was simply a new and novel effort to enlist federal intervention in the porters' cause.

This view certainly best explains the circumstances surrounding the final resolution of the Brotherhood's dispute with the Pullman Company. As the country sank deeper into economic depression in the early 1930s, Congress tried to stabilize industrial production by passing new legislation regulating the workplace. In 1933, it passed the National Industrial Recovery Act (NIRA), which guaranteed industrial workers a minimum wage, maximum hours, and union representation of their own choosing, and the Emergency Transportation Act (ETA), which strengthened provisions for independent unionization by prohibiting railroad carriers from using company funds to support company unions.[50] Together these two pieces of legislation seemingly addressed all of the porters' main grievances, but to Randolph's "amazement and surprise" the federal transportation coordinator in charge of administering the new labor laws, Joseph Eastman, explained that neither law applied to Pullman porters. Randolph recalled that when he and Milton P. Webster, the Brotherhood's first vice president, met with federal authorities to seek redress of the porters' case under these new laws, they were told that porters were not covered under the NIRA. Pullman, they were told, was a carrier, not a railroad company. This technicality was equally devastating to the porters' case under the ETA because, as a carrier company rather than a railroad company, Pullman was not covered under this law either. Without congressional amendments specifically including Pullman porters under one or both laws, the Brotherhood had no legal recourse for challenging Pullman's Employee Representation Plan.

Randolph made this very point in a May 15, 1934, letter to Congressman Oscar DePriest, a representative from Illinois and the first African American elected to Congress from the North. Randolph explained that without specific amendments to include railroad service workers, porters would be left out of both the NIRA and the ETA and "hence utterly without means of adjusting their grievances."[51] Recalling these events in a press release titled "The Story of the Brotherhood of Sleeping Car Porters," Randolph emphasized that it was clear to him that "porters would never be able to build an independent and bona fide labor organization unless they were named in the law . . . just as the engineers and train conductors and firemen were named in the law."[52] Though porters were covered under the Railway Labor Act of 1926, which created a federal infrastructure for mediating labor disputes in the railroad industry, Randolph and the Brotherhood quickly recognized that this law had "no teeth in it and is practically valueless" for porters. The Railway Labor Act neither disqualified company unions nor provided mechanisms for forcing Pullman to negotiate with Brotherhood representatives. Conversely, both the NIRA and the ETA provided for collective bargaining and independent organization. As Randolph explained to DePriest, these provisions were the "chief" reasons for pushing Congress to include the porters under these laws.[53]

It was this need to amend New Deal labor legislation to include Pullman porters that pushed Randolph to lobbying Congress. Just as the Brotherhood's past appeals for federal mediation were designed to pressure the Pullman Company into negotiations, the various legislative changes that Randolph and the Brotherhood sought were intended to give porters greater leverage to force Pullman into recognizing their right to independent representation and to negotiate with the Brotherhood. With federal mediators refusing to act and the federal courts dismissing its lawsuit against Pullman, Randolph and the Brotherhood recognized that only congressional amendment of the Railway Labor Act that extended collective bargaining rights that "placed the sleeping car porters and dining car employees upon a basis of equality in the law with all other railway employees" could help their case. In fact, it was only after Congress amended the Railway Labor Act in 1934 that Pullman was finally forced to recognize the Brotherhood of Sleeping Car Porters as the porters' official bargaining agent and begin fairly negotiating labor contracts with its black service employees.[54]

Randolph and the porters learned several key lessons from this prolonged battle with the Pullman Company for recognition of the Brotherhood. First, the company's sheer resolve to deny its black workers the same rights it granted to white workers was a clear indication of how the special obstacle of racial discrimination affected African Americans in the workplace. Second, the general hesitancy of federal authorities to intervene on behalf of the porters exposed the weaknesses of American labor law in meeting the needs of black workers. And lastly, the propensity of Congress to leave black workers out of federal labor legislation underscored the need for concerted political lobbying specifically on behalf of African Americans. Together such factors forced Randolph to rethink his views about independent black organization and action. Independent black unionism now seemed less a "menace" to genuine radicalism than a necessary component of any serious program for economic justice and industrial reform.[55] The Brotherhood's early interaction with the American Federation of Labor pushed this revaluation even further. The porters' struggle for recognition illustrated the particular importance of compelling external force to press companies like Pullman to accord black workers the same treatment extended to white workers, and Randolph's initial efforts to bring the Brotherhood into the AFL demonstrated that, in many respects, black workers stood alone in their fight for equal justice.

8

Where Class Consciousness Falls Short

Randolph and the Brotherhood's Standing in the House of Labor

After Pullman's stalling tactics effectively undercut the Brotherhood's appeal to the Mediation Board, Randolph and the porters devised a new strategy to compel Pullman to negotiate. In April 1928, the Brotherhood organized a strike vote among porters and maids to trigger emergency provisions of the 1926 Railway Labor Act that sought to force Pullman into arbitration. The Pullman Company retaliated by laying off hundreds of porters and hiring strikebreakers to make sure that its operations would not be disrupted. Convinced that rail service would continue with no serious interruption, federal mediators determined that there was no emergency and, thus, refused to convene an emergency board to hear the porters' grievances. With no arbitration pending and porters possibly facing additional layoffs, the Brotherhood decided to call off its strike. The clear ineffectiveness of established labor law to remedy the porters' long list of complaints led Randolph to pursue new lines of attack on Pullman and its Employee Representation Plan.[1]

Following the aborted porters' strike, Randolph began to push harder for affiliation with the American Federation of Labor (AFL) as a way of bolstering the Brotherhood's labor credibility. Despite the AFL's long-standing racial hostility toward black workers, Randolph was somewhat desperate to regain some of the momentum lost by calling off the strike. He hoped that membership in the AFL would demonstrate that porters "were serious-minded working men" who were "concerned about building a trade union with which to fight for decent wages, better hours of work, and improved working conditions and all other interests, advantages, and benefits other organized railway workers sought."[2] The leadership changeover that brought in William

Green as president of the AFL in 1924 gave Randolph some hope that black workers would be better received than in past years. In correspondence with Green, Randolph acknowledged that he and the Brotherhood recognized that "practically all other railroad unions are in the A.F. of L" and that it served the porters' interests to secure AFL affiliation as well.[3] Although Randolph understood that Green "was not any great advocate" of the porters' cause, the new AFL president did lend the "great prestige of his position" to the Brotherhood after it set a strike date and assured Randolph that "he would give us support" if the porters did indeed decide to strike.[4]

Unfortunately, the results of this strategy to align the Brotherhood with the AFL were not nearly as beneficial as Randolph had hoped. While he was able to call upon Green's "good offices" in weathering the strike crisis and the AFL president did participate in Brotherhood recruiting efforts in major porter cities, there was considerable resistance from many of the AFL's international brotherhoods to admitting the porters.[5] Instead of receiving a full international charter, the sixteen Brotherhood locals were given federal charters that brought them into the AFL without opening up leadership positions to black delegates; federal charters allowed the AFL to bypass the Brotherhood's national officers and oversee each local separately.[6] While this new affiliation certainly gave porters the opportunity to attend AFL conventions, where they could tell their "story of Pullman oppression" on the convention floor and introduce "resolutions condemning the despotic economic policies of the Pullman financial and industrial hierarchy," Randolph recognized that the tactic of chartering Brotherhood locals under a federal system served primarily as "a substitute for real unionism."[7]

Part of the reason for admitting the Brotherhood under this federal charter system was that there were some AFL members who challenged the legitimacy of the porters' application. They believed that the porters should fall under the organizational jurisdiction of the Order of Sleeping Car Conductors. "It was unsound trade union practice," leaders of the conductors union reasoned, "for two organizations on the same cars to negotiate agreements with the same company concerning rates of pay and working conditions." Randolph and the Brotherhood obviously had quite a different point of view. Randolph pointed out that in raising this claim of jurisdiction over porters, Pullman conductors exhibited "astonishing presumption" given that they had "carefully ignored" Pullman porters and their interests for "some seventeen or more years." Moreover, the reasoning underlying the conductors' claim was seriously flawed. Randolph noted that the conductors' allegation that it was unsound for two separate unions working on the same car to organize and negotiate independently was made in the face of the fact that engineers and firemen, working in the same engine cars, did just that. In addition to such "fallacies," Randolph explained, "the Sleeping Car Conductors Union is saturated with race prejudice as shown by a clause in its constitution barring Negroes from membership." He concluded that the conductors' union was entirely unsuitable as a steward of the porters' interests. "If the Executive Council and the A.F. of L. Convention upholds the right of jurisdiction of the Order of Sleeping Car Conductors over sleeping car porters," Randolph asserted, "the Brotherhood will have no other honorable alternative before it but to withdraw from the A.F. of L."[8]

Despite the clear disadvantages of the Brotherhood's position in the AFL, Randolph continued to press the porters' case with AFL leaders and on the convention floor. With the country "locked in a great struggle to beat back the menacing tides of aggression from Japan, Germany, and Italy," Randolph emphasized the profound consequences for the "preservation of our democratic ideals and traditions for organized labor to take the lead in making the democratic process work" effectively for black workers.[9] He and the Brotherhood's first AFL delegates quickly came to see their place in the organization as "the beginning of a vigorous war against racial bias in the trade unions."[10] Without fail, Randolph stood up at national conventions and "denounced the discrimination in the trade unions against Negroes because of race and color." From the 1930s through the 1950s, he strenuously argued that "until the A.F. of L. realistically attacks this question of racial discrimination, it cannot mobilize the complete strength of American labor or develop a healthy and sound and progressive existence."[11] At the 1939 AFL convention in Cincinnati, for example, Randolph and the Brotherhood introduced a resolution that called for the revision of "any constitutional provisions which serves to exclude workers from membership on account of race or color."[12] Though this resolution was ultimately voted down, it was indicative of the Brotherhood's convention maneuverings in these years. In addition to antidiscrimination motions, Randolph introduced convention resolutions calling on the AFL to create a civil rights information center, support fully the Supreme Court's ruling in *Brown v. Board of Education,* and oppose Jim Crow housing and policies that promoted it. As the Brotherhood's 1955 resolution on civil rights made clear, Randolph and the porters consistently pushed the AFL to "go on record as unequivocally condemning terrorism, lynching and mob law" and stand squarely "for the protection of the constitutional rights of Negro citizens."[13] He was so persistent in calling attention to racial discrimination in organized labor that many AFL leaders had difficulty containing their exasperation. In reflecting back on his convention activities, Randolph recalled that George Meany, future president of the AFL-CIO, got so frustrated with him that in the midst of a heated debate of a Brotherhood resolution to dissolve racially segregated locals, Meany snidely asked Randolph when he had been "elected to speak for all Negroes."[14] Despite the deeply rooted opposition that he and the porters faced from the sleeping car conductors and others within the AFL, Randolph's fight for racial justice in organized labor eventually made some progress. At its fifty-third annual convention held in San Francisco in 1934, the AFL adopted two resolutions put forward by the Brotherhood delegation that endorsed federal anti-lynching legislation and condemned wage differentials for black workers. The Brotherhood of Sleeping Car Porters was eventually granted a full international charter, and Randolph was installed as an executive vice-president of the AFL-CIO.[15]

Just as Randolph's persistence in seeking federal mediation of the porters' case was part of a calculated strategy to pressure Pullman into negotiating with the Brotherhood, Randolph sought AFL affiliation primarily as a means of further legitimizing the porters' case. Not only would AFL membership bolster the Brotherhood's labor credentials, but Randolph hoped that it would also give porters a more prominent public profile and make it more difficult for them to be left out of subsequent labor legislation. Despite clear-cut racial discrimination in organized labor, Randolph insisted that AFL affiliation "served to infuse new life" into the Brotherhood by dramatically placing the cause of the Pullman porter before the American public.[16] Randolph hoped to use the platform created by AFL membership and the public exposure it brought the porters to demonstrate that it was Pullman, not the porters, that was acting unreasonably in its treatment of Pullman porters. As Randolph and the Brotherhood had been arguing since the mid-1920s, race was the only difference between the workplace demands made by the porters and those of other railroad brotherhoods, and Randolph believed that AFL affiliation strengthened this assertion.

The initial reception that the porters received, however, once again underscored the unique circumstances that racial discrimination created for black workers. Hostility toward the porters in the AFL highlighted the special need for independent black industrial unionization. Indeed, by the 1930s Randolph had a much clearer sense of the special challenges racial discrimination posed for black workers. Pressing the porters' case before AFL executives in the 1930s and 1940s led Randolph to think seriously of the Brotherhood's struggle as "not only fighting the battles of the sleeping car porters but for black workers throughout the entire nation."[17] This new understanding marked the beginning of a shift in his thinking away from an exclusively class-conscious perspective to one that emphasized the importance of both race and class identity. As the Brotherhood ran into more and more roadblocks in its dispute with Pullman in the late 1920s and 1930s and faced continued hostility from the rank-and-file AFL membership through the 1940s and 1950s, it became clear to Randolph that straightforward class consciousness was insufficient for overcoming racial discrimination.

Although initially drawn to the porters' cause out of a desire to emphasize the "importance and value of trade unionism" to both black and white workers, Randolph realized by the early 1930s that this mission was significantly more complicated than just pointing out that black and white workers shared common class interests.[18] Racial discrimination meant that African Americans faced considerably more resistance than white workers in pushing for better wages and work conditions. And though this was not a new revelation, the porters' fight with Pullman and the deep-rooted opposition of much of the AFL membership did demonstrate for Randolph the very real need for "all sections of the Negro race" to be engaged in supporting "morally and financially the fight of every section of the Negro workers in their struggle to organize for higher wages, better working conditions, and self-reliance."[19] Consequently, in his recommendations to the Third National Convention of the Brotherhood of Sleeping Car Porters, Randolph issued a call for the Brotherhood to sponsor a national Negro conference to stir and reawaken public opinion generally, but especially to impress upon porters and other black workers "the grave necessity of the development of labor organization among Negroes" to fight for economic and social justice.[20]

In some ways, this call to mobilize African Americans behind black workers was not particularly new for Randolph. As early as 1925, he had joined forces with Frank Crosswaith and other black labor organizers to form the Trade Union Committee for Organizing Negro Workers (TUC). With hopes of doing "for Negro workers in New York City what the Women's Trade Union League does for women workers," Randolph and Crosswaith intended "not only to organize Negro workers, but also to secure justice for them inside unions and to educate both Negro and white workers toward a realization of their common economic interests."[21] After the administrative and legal setbacks of the late 1920s and early 1930s, however, Randolph's focus on mobilizing African Americans took on new tones. In a December 1930 letter to Harry W. Laidler of the League for Industrial Democracy outlining the intent of a black labor conference sponsored by the Brotherhood, Randolph explained that "the purpose of this conference is to discuss the problems of the Negro worker in relation to industry, organized labor, and other social and political movements." Whereas the TUC focused on the shared class interests of black and white workers in promoting trade unionism in Harlem, the Brotherhood's 1931 Negro Labor Conference in Chicago sought to be "instrumental" in stimulating labor organization among African Americans and also to address "worker and adult education among Negroes by bringing together . . . experts on problems of labor, social, economic, and political interests to discuss questions that are vital to the life of the Negro worker."[22] This 1931 conference and other black labor meetings sponsored by the Brotherhood in the 1930s deliberately moved beyond straightforward union organizing to address the "professional, business, cultural, educational, civil, and political life of the Negro" in relation to "the well-being of the Negro worker who constitutes practically ninety-eight percent of the race."[23]

Randolph's effort to expand the purpose of black unionism to include other major racial concerns helped to shape the founding of the National Negro Congress (NNC) in 1935. Organized by Ralph Bunch, chairman of Howard University's Department of Political Science, and John P. Davis, the executive secretary of the Joint Committee on National Recovery, which was responsible for representing the interests of black workers before New Deal agencies, the NNC was organized "to add strength and to give support to every progressive and meaningful program in aid of the Negro people in their just demand for equal opportunity and complete social and economic rights."[24] In his remarks to the NNC's first convention, Randolph, who presided over the NNC from 1936 to 1939, insisted that African Americans, the "submerged tenth of the population," needed to become more self-reliant in protesting civil, political, and economic discrimination. As "victims of both class and race prejudice and oppression," he explained, African Americans were "caught between the nether millstones of discrimination." As workers, they "are browbeaten, bullied, intimidated, robbed, exploited, jailed, and shot down," and as African Americans "they are hated, maligned, and spat upon; lynched, mobbed, and murdered." Increasingly, Randolph began to push for greater community involvement in organizing black workers because the twin hostilities of race and class oppression made it clear to him that "in the final analysis, the salvation of the Negro," like that of workers generally, "must come from within."[25]

This explicitly racial theme was even more evident in a 1937 commentary that Randolph wrote for the *National Negro Congress News*, the organization's monthly newsletter. Placing the NNC in the same "spirit of revolt" as Nat Turner, Denmark Vesey, Gabriel Prosser, Harriet Tubman, Sojourner

Truth, and Frederick Douglass, Randolph exhorted African Americans "in the mines and mills, factories and farms, on the railroads and docks, in merchandise marts and homes, in church and school rooms, in fraternal lodges and women's clubs, in trade unions, and college fraternities" to participate in formulating "programs and proclamations of appeal and action for the liberation of the Negro." And though he also invited "all lovers of freedom and democracy among the white people" to join this second congress, Randolph made a special effort to underscore the "menacing magnitude and pressing urgency" involved in addressing the overwhelming impact of racial discrimination on all facets of African American life. "The task of winning true freedom for black Americans is still unfinished," he said. Despite the Fourteenth and Fifteenth Amendments, he explained, neither civil nor political rights for African Americans were "yet secure," the continuation of peonage still "mocks" the Thirteenth Amendment, "and the Ku Klux Klan, the Black Legion, and southern judicial terror render the Bill of Rights to the Negro people of little avail." For Randolph, the presence of color bars in the constitutions and rituals of labor unions and racial discrimination in the assignment of jobs to black workers only made the "man-sized" task of the Second National Negro Congress convened in 1936 all the more urgent.[26]

Throughout the 1930s and into the 1940s, this evolving connection between social justice for African Americans and industrial democracy secured through labor unions continued to shape Randolph's activities in a significant way. In 1935, he and Crosswaith helped to form the Negro Labor Committee (NLC) to promote trade unionism in Harlem. In addition to assisting with local union activities for a variety of groups, the NLC also recognized "the necessity for an educational program" to "popularize trade unionism in Harlem" and worked with the staff of the Works Progress Administration in New York to put together a lecture series on workers' problems.[27] Randolph, who served as a vice chairman of the committee, and other members of the NLC believed such endeavors to be "of inestimable value not only to the Negro but to the general labor movement and the nation" because of their utility in "turning the tide of Negro thought toward industrial organization as the basis of manhood rights and equality." Though all minority groups had to sacrifice and struggle to secure for themselves equality and fair play, Randolph and the committee insisted that African Americans' particular "spiritual and cultural gifts . . . are needed in the American labor movement now more than ever" and that labor would "be richer and more impregnable as a result."[28]

In addition to adult education programs and community activism, Randolph, Crosswaith, and other black labor leaders in Harlem in the 1930s also tried to draw upon the community's strong sense of racial pride in linking social justice to industrial organization. Though the Harlem Renaissance had largely faded away by the mid-1930s and Marcus Garvey's Universal Negro Improvement Association was no longer what it once was, the deep sense of racial pride that they represented lingered on in African Americans' collective consciousness. As Randolph, Crosswaith, and others continued to push trade unionism as an effective means for achieving equal rights, they challenged black workers to demonstrate to "the white world" that they could "deliberately, soberly, coolly, and dispassionately adopt a course of action which is calculated to protect and advance their social, economic, and political interests." Similarly, in exhorting porters to remain steadfast as the Brotherhood's fight with Pullman intensified, Randolph insisted that the company "must be given to understand" that, just as the entire black population had changed, its porters and maids were "as different from the porter of fifty years ago as the Pullman Company of today is different from the Company fifty years ago." Instead of "servile porters" and "childish maids," Pullman's current black service staff was composed of "manly, upright standing, intelligent men."[29] In linking the porter's movement with the revolutionary legacy of black abolitionism and greater racial militancy, Randolph hoped to create a sense that not only was the Brotherhood's fight with Pullman just, but that it was also a vital part of the broader struggle to secure equal justice for African Americans.

This interpretation certainly explains Crosswaith's proclamation that "NEGRO LABOR MUST ORGANIZE for ECONOMIC AND SOCIAL JUSTICE!" In a pamphlet titled "A Message to Harlem Theater Patrons from the Harlem Labor Committee," Crosswaith insisted that it was in the "interest of our community to support the organized Negro motion picture operators by patronizing only those theaters that are willing to be fair to union labor and treat Negro labor on a basis of equality with other labor!" Only by standing with these organized workers could the community demonstrate that it was no longer willing to accept the "grossly unfair dictum of tradition" that African Americans should "work harder and longer and receive less wages than white workers." In promoting this variation of the "Don't Buy Where You Can't Work" campaign that swept through black communities in the urban North well into the 1940s,[30] Crosswaith hoped to generate community support for the proposition that "a Negro worker is entitled to the same advantages, wages, and treatment accorded a white worker." In pointing out to African Americans in Harlem that the fight of organized black workers was their fight, Crosswaith hoped to convince them that "their victory will be your victory" as well.[31]

As the Great Depression deepened, Randolph, Crosswaith, and others in Harlem stepped up their efforts to connect industrial democracy, economic justice, and social equality. In notes for a developing editorial on the "unusual ferocity" of the Depression's impact on the "great army of black workers," Crosswaith pointed out that "the importance of the Negro worker to the entire super-structure of Negro life" became readily apparent "when it is understood that all Negro institutions—business, religious, fraternal, et al.—depend for their strength and durability upon the earnings of the Negro worker." Crosswaith insisted that even to casual observers of the current "industrial cyclone through which we are passing," it must be clear that the "alarming weakness and instability of Negro economic and cultural life" were directly tied to the social and economic conditions created by racial discrimination. In responding to this "serious racio-economic situation," Crosswaith argued that African Americans needed to follow the lead of other working-class groups and organize into unions. Surely, he insisted, "the hopes of our race" lay along this course of action in that "organized Negro labor will also give strength and relative security to the church, to business, to our professionals, to the whole stream of our social and cultural life."[32]

For Randolph as well, the connection between organizing black workers and broader issues of equal justice became even more concrete as events in Harlem in the 1930s became more unstable. In many ways, this view was further reinforced by his appointment to the Mayor's Commission on Conditions in Harlem. In March 1935, New York City Mayor Fiorello La Guardia convened this body to study the conditions in Harlem that had caused or contributed to a violent eruption on March 19, 1935, that destroyed property and threatened the safety of Harlem residents.[33] In the course of its investigation, the commission determined that false rumors of the beating death of a Puerto Rican teenager caught shoplifting in a local department store by white police officers had "awakened the deep-seated sense of wrongs and denials and even memories of injustices in the South" and sparked the ensuing violence. Over the course of the afternoon and evening, community tensions rose with more and more African Americans in Harlem turning their resentment against "whites who owned stores and who, while exploiting Negroes, denied them an opportunity to work." In summarizing the events of the day, the commission concluded that "the very susceptibility which the people of the community showed toward this rumor . . . was due to the feeling of insecurity produced by years of unemployment and a deep-seated resentment against the many forms of discrimination which they had suffered as a racial minority."[34]

The Mayor's Commission based these general conclusions about the events of March 19, 1935, on interviews it conducted with key officials from law enforcement, public health and safety, and the Emergency Relief Bureau as well as community leaders in Harlem and the sentiments black residents expressed through a series of open forums on the conditions and causes of the violence. While it was immediately apparent to members of the commission that years of negative experiences with white police officers had created a fundamental lack of confidence in law enforcement that was "evident at every stage of the riot," it was equally clear that there was a feeling among black Harlemites that the outburst "was justified and that it represented a protest against discrimination and privations resulting from unemployment." Even those Harlem residents who had never before committed a criminal act "seized" upon the March riot as an "opportunity to express their resentment against discrimination in employment and the exclusive rights of property." The commission determined that only in an economic and social atmosphere entirely shaped by long-standing racial discrimination could an explosion like that of March 19, 1935, be ignited by the "trifling" circumstances uncovered by the commission.[35]

The conclusion that the 1935 Harlem riot drew participants from all segments of Harlem's black community directly contradicts a key element of the typical analysis of race riots of the late nineteenth and early twentieth centuries. Beginning with the New York Draft Riots of 1863 through the Red Summer of 1919, scholars have generally linked urban rioters with the underclass. Yet, this analysis falls apart when applied to Harlem in the 1930s. In this instance, riot participants from all segments of the community directed their anger and frustration at key sources of their discontent—the property and businesses of white merchants who exploited the community through rents, prices, and discriminatory employment.[36] In their examination of events in Harlem, Randolph and the commission concluded that looters mostly targeted those businesses in the community that discriminated against black residents. In this way, even the riot's criminal features were acts of protest against racial discrimination.

The deep-seated discontent reported on by the Mayor's Commission on Conditions in Harlem contributed to Randolph's increasing racial emphasis in organizing black workers because it illustrated that this transition in his thinking did not take place in a vacuum. Instead, Randolph's push to connect the industrial organization of black workers to broader concerns about equal justice for African Americans fit squarely with much of the sentiment running through urban black communities like Harlem during this period. As the disproportionate impact of the Depression on black workers continued throughout the late 1930s, Randolph and others began to insist that unionization was not only central to protecting black workers but also key to ensuring the overall stability of black communities and an important step toward broader economic and social justice. Certainly, it was this understanding that led the Brotherhood to take an active part in protesting the dismissal of black case workers from the New York Department of Public Welfare in the early 1930s. Likewise, Brotherhood officials like Ashley Totten played leading roles in pressing the New York Board of Transportation to adopt an equal employment policy in hiring subway conductors.[37] In fact, as the commission turned its attention more specifically to the problem of employment in Harlem, it became more and more clear why Randolph's increasingly racial emphasis in pushing industrial organization among black workers resonated so strongly in key porter cities like New York, Chicago, and St. Louis.

Though "confronted at all times with the problem of securing suitable homes and free access to the institutions which were intended to serve the needs of the community," the Mayor's Commission nonetheless determined that "the problem of primary importance to the Harlem Negro has been that of securing employment." Even when African Americans managed to find steady employment, the commission's report explained, it generally did not represent significant upward movement in the economic structure. The commission pointed out that while a growing number of African Americans had found jobs in manufacturing and mechanical industries since 1910, occupational figures demonstrate that they were "still in the lowest paid and unskilled occupations." While it might have been somewhat natural to find that "a large proportion of Negroes who have had little experience in industry and trade" were in the lowest paid and least skilled jobs, it was clear to commission investigators that "discrimination and non-economic factors are responsible to a large extent" for relegating African Americans to the lowest rung on the economic ladder. The commission noted that while African Americans are dependent upon the industries, trading establishments, and other economic institutions of the city for earning a living, the biased racial policies of these institutions could not be ignored in explaining the employment woes of African Americans in Harlem.[38]

In its investigation, the commission discovered that employers used the same excuses that "have been used for nearly a century to prevent the Negro from competing on an equal basis with whites." Randolph and his colleagues pointed out that in both the public and private sectors of the city's economy company executives and managers still relied on customary excuses for discrimination, such as black workers' supposed inefficiency and the contention that blacks and whites could not work together. These factors disqualified African Americans from higher-paying skilled jobs and restricted them to "positions symbolic of their inferior status" in society. The commission concluded that though they were willing to accept such "discrimination outside of Harlem with resignation," black Harlemites were especially frustrated by the adamant refusal of public utility companies and other enterprises that relied upon Harlem for economic survival to employ African Americans in any position beyond the most menial of occupations. In fact, many in Harlem, the commission explained, specifically viewed public utilities as "chiefly agencies for exploiting Negroes." A black resident in Harlem had no choice but to use the services of these companies while they "autocratically deny him all opportunity to share in the employment which he helps to provide other workers." As rumors spread that white police officers had beat a black teenager to death in the basement of a local department store, "the pent up resentment of the Negro against exclusion from all but the most menial of jobs in the establishments which he supported" burst forth in a riot. [39]

In concluding that the events of March 19, 1935, reflected black Harlem's deep-seated discontent with racial discrimination in employment, Randolph and his fellow commissioners pointed out that African Americans were more determined than ever to fight economic discrimination in their own community. "As the economic crisis became more acute," the commission explained, "various groups began agitation for jobs in the different enterprises that drew their support from Negroes." Crosswaith's Harlem Labor Committee was a good example of this new kind of community initiative. In addition to promoting unionization among black workers, Crosswaith continually encouraged Harlem residents to patronize only those businesses that treated black workers fairly. Despite the severe financial hardships most African Americans faced during the Depression years, he and others insisted that the community could bring its collective economic clout to bear on the treatment of black workers and consumers by local businesses.[40] In terms of the commission's findings, Crosswaith's Harlem Labor Committee was certainly one of those groups pushing "not simply for the menial jobs which have been traditionally given to Negroes but for the so-called white collar jobs and other positions where intelligence and a high degree of responsibility were required."[41] It was the community's intense resentment against exclusion from this kind of employment that surfaced in March 1935.

While Randolph's role in drafting the commission's final report is unclear, the findings on employment outlined therein were remarkably close to the point of view that he began to develop as tensions between Pullman and the Brotherhood intensified in the same period. Just as he and Crosswaith had argued earlier that the well being of the black community was fundamentally tied to the livelihood of black workers, the commissioners charged with investigating the 1935 Harlem riot concluded that "the low economic status of the Negro in Harlem is basic to every other problem in the community." In a business climate that employed African Americans only in menial positions or not at all, they continued, "no amount of charity, good will, social privileges, or political freedom can compensate for the enforced idleness and poverty" that African Americans experienced in Harlem. In the commissioners' view, it made little sense to raise other vital issues like adequate housing and crime while African Americans were denied "the right to work at lawful occupations."[42]

The extensive interviews Randolph and his co-investigators conducted with Harlem community leaders and residents, city public safety and health officials, and local employers left the commissioners with little doubt that "this spontaneous outbreak, the immediate cause of which was a mere rumor concerning the mistreatment of a Negro boy, was symptomatic of pent-up feelings of resentment and insecurity" among African Americans in Harlem. As they explained, even though the "current economic crisis" was responsible for creating an "appalling amount of unemployment and dependency in Harlem," the majority of African Americans in the community "live even during normal times close to the subsistence level" as a direct result of "certain social factors which keep the Negro worker in the ranks of unskilled laborers and in a state of perpetual dependency." The commission concluded that "more than any other factor," it was the conditions created by such racial discrimination in employment "that arouses so much resentment in the Negro worker." Moreover, when employers barred African Americans from employment or hired them only for menial jobs, it only served to alienate further a large portion of the black "urban proletariat" who increasingly viewed employers as "mere exploiters." Randolph and his fellow commissioners noted that as the black worker was systematically denied the "right to compete on equal terms with other workers for a decent standard of living," he was "slowly but surely" learning the lesson "that only through collective or public ownership of the public utilities can he enforce his right to employment on the same basis as other races."[43]

This report on conditions in Harlem during the Depression era was significant because it highlighted many of the underlying reasons why Randolph's evolving message about the connection between the organization of black workers and broader issues of social justice resonated so strongly in urban black communities. By insisting that the first step toward social justice was ensuring fair employment and equal access to decent living standards for all citizens, Randolph tapped into the deep well of racial feeling among African Americans that had repeatedly spilled over into racial violence throughout this period. In linking the porters' fight with Pullman with a broad-based commentary on the "fallacious" notion that "Negroes are inferior beings" who "cannot do the things which are recognized as a matter of course among white men," Randolph set out to build public support for the porters' cause. He also hoped to direct the resentment over discrimination simmering in black communities across the country against the racist infrastructures that relegated African Americans to second-class status.[44] As he and others increasingly began to emphasize unionization, even black unionism, as a central means of securing social justice, the deep-seated community sentiment uncovered by the Mayor's Commission on Conditions in Harlem helps to explain in part the appeal of their message.

Another aspect of the commission's report that warrants comment was its portrayal of communists in Harlem during this period. Though Randolph and his co-investigators made a point of crediting the young white men who "took the part of the indignant Negro crowds" with preventing an all-out race riot by literally changing "the complexion of the outbreak," the commission nonetheless conveyed the impression of communists in Harlem as outsiders and simple opportunists. Unlike the Young Liberators, a community group consisting mostly of African Americans who sought to protect black rights and who attempted to verify the facts surrounding the police incident before organizing protest meetings during the March riot, the commission criticized the Young Communist League for making no attempt to substantiate the rumored beating death of a black teen by white officers before circulating leaflets and organizing demonstrations against police brutality. By moving into the community without corroborating any part of the story, the report contended that communists exhibited a fundamental "lack of due regard for the possibly serious consequences of acting on mere rumor." Randolph and the commission concluded that although this degree of recklessness ultimately was not "responsible for the disorder and attacks on property which were already in full swing," comparing the behavior of communists in Harlem to other community groups suggests that the commission felt a clear need to distinguish the protest activities of communist organizers from the legitimate complaints raised by Harlem residents.[45]

This depiction of communists in many ways complemented the essence of Randolph's anticommunist sentiment. Despite his initial enthusiasm for the Bolshevik Revolution, he became an ardent anticommunist shortly after the founding of the American Communist Party. In fact, as early as 1923 the *Messenger* began describing communists as "disruptionists" intent upon breaking down the morale and confusing the aims and ideals of the New Negro Liberation Movement. In an August article titled "The Menace of Negro Communists," Randolph's *Messenger* insisted that "communism can be of no earthly benefit to either white or Negro workers in America" because ultimately it sought simply "to wreck all constructive, progressive, non-communist programs." According to the *Messenger,* black communists were a particular menace because they helped to lure African Americans to "doctrines of extremism" that were, in fact, "so inane and childish that they would be amusing were they not so tragically disastrous to aggressive, independent, and rationally radical manhood efforts." It was in this light, then, that Randolph determined very early on that communists were a "menace to the workers, themselves, and the race."[46]

Randolph's opposition to communists stemmed from his belief that they were utterly "committed to an anti-democratic program." In an essay titled "Are Communists a Threat to Democratic Organizations?" written in the mid-1930s, Randolph outlined several characteristics to illustrate his point. First and foremost, he insisted that the "sole intent" of the communist program was to infiltrate radical organizations. Communists sought to "bore from within and capture and control democratic movements" for the purpose of glorifying Soviet Russia "as the promised land of the workers and the hope and salvation of the oppressed people of the world." This strategy, Randolph noted, called for communists to "simulate democratic behavior" strictly as a means of establishing a useful presence within radical groups. "Once they establish a base in a democratic organization," he continued, communists employed "the most ruthless and dictatorial tactics in utter disregard of democratic principles and traditions" to advance and consolidate their "conspiratorial world policy."[47] In this way, Randolph warned, legitimate radical and progressive reform efforts were subverted to serve foreign and, in many ways, alien interests.

Randolph was equally concerned about the way in which communists executed this strategy of subversion. He maintained that instead of operating from some sense of shared interest or concern, communists organized cells within democratic organizations and used "caucus tactics" to redirect group policy toward Soviet Russia. "In other words," he explained, "the direction and voting of communists in a democratic organization do not result from reasons and facts that are developed concerning a [group's] given program, but are the result of instructions and orders they receive from the Communist Party whose single aim is to establish dominion over every democratic movement possible." For Randolph, it was the insidiousness of this effort to corrupt democratic processes that was the most threatening aspect of communism. It directly threatened the essence of the open, participatory democracy central to his understanding of genuine social justice. When the agenda of a democratic organization could be hijacked by members whose positions "cannot be changed by logic, reason, and facts" but are directed by "a caucus under the control of an outside organization," then, he insisted, "they are a definite menace to democracy." Randolph certainly believed that this critique accurately described communists in America.[48]

In the specific case of black workers, Randolph maintained that "totalitarian communism must be ruled out as a solution of the Negro problem or way of life for the Negro people." Any political system, he explained, that does not guarantee individual civil liberties "cannot solve the problem of the Negro, for without civil liberties, Negroes cannot even present their problem."[49] Even when confronting racial discrimination from every direction, it was clear to Randolph that African Americans could hope to achieve equality, freedom, and dignity only within the framework of an open, participatory democracy where political institutions and traditions protected civil and human rights. Throughout this period, he insisted that, though "American democracy is no lily of purity," African Americans nonetheless "have the right to fight for their rights" and this was "more important than all the other rights for which Negroes . . . are fighting." As long as African Americans had the right to fight for justice and equality, he explained, they could always hope to improve democracy. While the "American democratic system needs much cleansing of its sins against minorities," Randolph adamantly believed that African Americans were better off taking their chances with it "with a view to eliminating these things" than turning toward totalitarian communism.[50]

This view ultimately dictated Brotherhood policy toward communists. In addition to waging a "consistent and relentless struggle for material benefits for the porters," Randolph pointed out that the Brotherhood was also in the forefront of "the fight among Negro workers on and off the railroads against the communist menace." Despite early and persistent communist efforts to "rule or ruin trade unions," Randolph insisted that they "never constituted a serious internal threat" to the Brotherhood because of a "comprehensive, persistent, and systematic exposé of communist tactics, trickery, and treachery."[51] Throughout this period, Randolph maintained that African Americans could "only hope to achieve a status of equality, freedom, and dignity within the framework of democracy" and that by "striking at the heart" of American democratic institutions and traditions, communists were ultimately "endangering the progress and hope of the Negro, minorities, and labor." In a Brotherhood press release publicizing a speech on why African Americans should stand with the United States against Soviet Russia, Randolph insisted that despite the injustices and wrongs perpetrated against African Americans in America, African Americans nonetheless "have the right to hire a hall or stand upon a soap box . . . and tell their story to the American public and the world." No communist in Soviet Russia, he noted, could lay claim to "a comparable right" of free expression. Consequently, Randolph concluded, it made no "sense to add to the handicap of being black the handicap of being red" when the wholesale lack of human freedom under communism was the "kiss of death" to the principles of democracy central to winning first-class citizenship.[52]

This idea that democratic institutions and traditions were central to African Americans' push for equal justice also served to connect Randolph's anticommunist sentiment to his evolving views about the link between race and class. Whereas he warned against communists who sought to use caucus tactics to co-opt labor organizations, Randolph routinely urged black and white workers to set aside long-standing racial differences and build the kind of economic and political strength necessary to reform industrial capitalism. Unlike communists whose actions and positions were dictated by outside forces, Randolph insisted that workers who joined together to create political majorities undertook a rational course of action to further their specific class interests. Moreover, he firmly believed that social justice for African Americans would occur only within a framework of genuine industrial democracy. Without a capitalist elite to benefit materially from racial discrimination, the social inequities that had plagued African Americans for generations could be permanently resolved. As the porters' struggle moved toward a final conclusion in the mid-1930s, Randolph again began to rearrange his views about race and class.

Randolph asserted throughout this period that "more than any other group in America," African Americans needed "to develop economic strength and organize with white workers to fight and abolish all forms and forces that attack their rights as workers." He pointed out that African Americans were already victims of exploitation and oppression in the South and that across the nation they faced a "doubly serious period" of economic upheaval as the decline of modern capitalism served to extend conditions that have "existed for Negroes ever since the passing of the slave system" to all workers. In a floor speech to the first Negro Labor Conference in 1935, Randolph insisted that labor solidarity was central to resolving the economic crisis that all workers faced. "Unless workers develop organized power to fight militantly for their rights," he assured his audience, "all workers will be treated like the black laborer in Georgia and other sections of the South." He concluded that white organized labor needed to capitalize on the radical potential of black workers in the South and across the nation because, without them, "there will be no enduring labor movement." At the same time, African Americans needed to recognize that "their class interests are with workers wherever they are—even those that discriminate against you."[53]

The symbiotic relationship between black and white workers stressed here represented a significant transformation in Randolph's thinking about African Americans and industrial organization. Prior to his involvement with the Brotherhood, he had framed his discussions of labor unions almost exclusively around issues of class. Despite a racially militant tone, the *Messenger* throughout the late 1910s and early 1920s routinely downplayed issues of race in favor of issues of class. As his experiences with the Brotherhood and the onset of the Depression demonstrated that racial discrimination created unique challenges for African Americans and that white labor unions were as much a part of the problem as they were a part of the solution, Randolph de-emphasized the straightforward class rhetoric of the Socialist Party in favor of the more racially conscious self-help initiatives embodied in groups like the Trade Union Committee for Organizing Negro Workers or Crosswaith's Harlem Labor Committee. By the mid-1930s, however, Randolph was staking out the middle ground position outlined in his floor speech to the 1935 Negro Labor Conference. Having weathered the Pullman onslaughts of the late 1920s and early 1930s with the tepid support of William Green and the American Federation of Labor and having witnessed the far-reaching impact of the Depression on both black and white workers, Randolph became convinced that the success of any race or class movement depended upon the ability to mobilize workers, both black and white, around a progressive agenda. It was this understanding that led Randolph to exalt the Southern Tenant Farmers Union, where blacks and whites were "fighting against their common enemy capitalism and landlordism," as "one of the most significant movements in America."[54]

Randolph's emphasis on the symbiotic nature of black and white labor in pushing for social and economic reform certainly captured the essence of the founding mission of the Negro Labor Conference. As Crosswaith's preface to the conference proceedings explained, just as African Americans were "becoming conscious of the importance of trade union action as the most effective means of attacking his problem," more and more labor leaders were "coming to appreciate the truism that white labor cannot release itself from the coils of exploitation and industrial slavery unless Negro labor is also saved." And though this point of view certainly overstated the degree to which the average black and white workers were prepared to cooperate with each other in pushing for reform, the notion of mutual need that framed Crosswaith's declaration also outlined the shift in Randolph's thinking about the connection between issues of race and class. While his position as president of the Brotherhood of Sleeping Car Porters, the only all-black trade union affiliated with the AFL, gave Randolph a national platform for explaining the fundamental connections between race and class, he was by no means the only person considering such ideas.

In fact, in its call to local unions affiliated with the AFL, signed by both Randolph and Crosswaith, the 1935 Negro Labor Conference explicitly acknowledged the "invaluable service" that the Hebrew Trades and the Women's Trade Union League were rendering to labor in drawing workers largely excluded from AFL brotherhoods into the labor movement. By promoting class consciousness among these groups of disenfranchised workers, conference organizers pointed to the Hebrew Trades and the Women's Trade Union League as good models for what "may be duplicated among Negro workers with equal advantage to the organized labor movement." Crosswaith, in particular, noted that labor needed the support of women and other minority groups, and he was "convinced that white workers never will and never can be free until and unless Negro workers also are free." In accepting the nomination as chairman of the Negro Labor Conference, he pointed out that no matter how "narrow-minded and bigoted and blind" organized labor might be, the Negro Labor Conference was determined "to teach Negro workers that they must not be shunted off on some grounds and hope to battle effectively in this modern industrial hell without the aid of the organized white working-class."[55]

Though, in general, Randolph concurred with Crosswaith's assertion that the fortunes of black and white workers were inextricably linked, he nonetheless continued to insist that "the task of realizing full citizenship for the Negro people is largely in the hands of the Negro people themselves." As the lessons of the porters' struggle with the Pullman Company demonstrated, with or without the support of organized labor, African Americans needed to be in the forefront of any push for social and economic justice because "neither freedom nor justice is ever a final and complete fact."[56] He had come to understand that there would always be "forces that seek to nullify and destroy the civil, political, economic, and social rights of the Negro."[57] Instead,

Randolph insisted that the process of maintaining freedom and justice was an ongoing struggle. And while it was indeed the "task of labor and the progressive and liberal forces of the nation" to help secure full citizenship for African Americans, Randolph had come to see that in the case of black workers, "true liberation can be acquired and maintained only when the Negro people possess power." The Brotherhood's experience proved unequivocally that "power is the product and flower of organization." The building of such power through mass organization served as an essential motivation for Randolph to link black protest activity to the evolving labor movement.

Crosswaith and others involved in the 1935 Negro Labor Conference to some extent de-emphasized racial distinction within the labor movement, but Randolph found new meaning in racial identity for black workers within the labor movement as the porters' struggle with Pullman came to an end. Though he recognized that "Negro people are an integral part of the American commonwealth" and that "theirs is the task of consolidating their interests with the interest of the progressive forces of the nation," he also understood that African Americans alone faced the problems of "Jim-Crowism, segregation, disfranchisement through grandfather clauses and lily white primaries, and the terror of the Ku Klux Klan." Thus, as the first president of the National Negro Congress, an association that emerged out of the Negro Labor Conference in 1936, Randolph maintained that the "primary program" before black activists was not organizing African Americans into trade unions and civil rights movements, but rather "to integrate and coordinate the existing Negro organizations into one federated and collective agency so as to develop greater and more effective power." For Randolph, the porters' victory over Pullman demonstrated the absolute necessity for African Americans to develop their own internal organizational structures before joining in broader initiatives for social and industrial reform. Only with a clear sense of identity and organizational cohesion could African Americans ensure that their specific racial needs were not pushed aside by broader class concerns.[58]

Randolph reiterated this point in his presidential message announcing the 1937 National Negro Congress. Explaining the "birth and conception of the Congress," he pointed out that the "distressing weakness of Negro people" resulted from the lack of "integration, federation, and coordination" among black organizations that was vital "to creating more effective power." Despite the fact that "Negro organizations are numerous and far-flung" and "possess high purposes and aims for the advancement and defense of the rights and opportunities of the Negro," Randolph understood that "as separate units, they are weak." He maintained that it was only through the "common convocation of the Negro leaders and workers of thought and action" that African Americans could build the power base necessary to seek effective "fellowship and alliance with white workers . . . for protection and advancement in industry and government." While he continued to believe that interracial class cooperation was key to any program of social or industrial reform, black organizations like the Brotherhood of Sleeping Car Porters or the National Association for the Advancement of Colored People "must and ever will be the vanguard and the basis of fundamental Negro economic hope and progress."[59]

In the twelve years between the founding of the Brotherhood of Sleeping Car Porters and the signing of the porters' first wage contract with Pullman in 1937, Randolph's ideas about race and class issues changed significantly. While it was the radical economic views primarily shaped by the class theories of the Socialist Party and persuasively outlined in the *Messenger* that brought him to the attention of the porters, the clear-cut racial discrimination that the Brotherhood encountered in pushing forward the porters' case fundamentally undercut this straightforward class orientation. Randolph quickly discovered that the Pullman board of directors, the executive council of the American Federation of Labor, and federal agencies charged with overseeing labor disputes routinely dismissed the concerns and needs of African Americans. It was in searching for new ways to advance the porters' cause that Randolph began to fashion an understanding of the importance of a dual awareness of race and class consciousness. He increasingly encouraged African Americans to pursue their general class interests without ignoring their special racial needs. As the impact of the Great Depression continued to affect the lives and livelihoods of African Americans into the late 1930s, more and more Randolph placed racial awareness at the center of his push to organize black workers into labor unions and moved beyond the long-standing dichotomy between self-help and interracialism that confounded many of his contemporaries.

9

Marching Toward
Fair Employment

*Randolph, the Race/Class
Connection, and the March
on Washington Movement*

Even before the final resolution of the Brotherhood's dispute with Pullman, Randolph had concluded that the race and class issues confronting black workers were inseparable. He realized that as industrialization continued to transform the nation's economy in the war years, the central problem facing African Americans was no longer just one of civil rights but of economic rights as well. By the time the Brotherhood and Pullman signed their first wage contract, Randolph was persistently pressing the point that civil rights without economic rights lacked any real social substance.[1] Even after the threatened march on Washington was cancelled, this idea remained central to his later organizing efforts. In his keynote address to the 1942 policy conference of the March on Washington Movement (MOWM), Randolph set goals and formulated strategies for establishing a permanent Fair Employment Practice Commission. He insisted that while "equality is the heart and essence of democracy, freedom, and justice," without "equality of opportunity in industry, in labor unions, schools and colleges, government, politics, and before the law" Negroes were certain to be consigned to a state of second-class citizenship.[2] This recognition of the interrelated character of civil, political, and economic rights in securing genuine social justice harkened back to Du Bois's recognition of the interrelatedness of civil and social rights and ultimately shaped Randolph's actions in the years leading up to and following World War II.[3]

In the wake of the struggle to establish the Brotherhood of Sleeping Car Porters as the bona fide collective bargaining agent for Pullman porters and maids, Randolph entered the prewar years with very definite ideas about the deep connection between issues of race and class. His conviction that "the fight for justice and freedom for minorities and labor is indivisible because freedom and justice are indivisible" took clear shape in these years. Randolph elaborated on this point in a speech at a Brotherhood-sponsored banquet for AFL president William Green held shortly after the signing of the porters' first wage contract with Pullman. Randolph used the occasion to explain that even "a cursory examination of the problems of minorities and labor will reveal that the struggle to exterminate racial and religious discrimination cannot be separated from the fight against [economic] inequality and insecurity." Discrimination in any form, Randolph continued, simply served to weaken "the labor movement and disarms it in its fight to achieve higher wage rates, improved working conditions, shorter hours of work, democracy, and peace."[4]

To illustrate his point that "the interests of labor and the interests of the Negro and other minority groups are tied up together," Randolph highlighted the fact that "the same forces that attack Negroes' struggle for their rights, attacks the struggles of labor for its rights." For Randolph, these common foes of social and industrial reform and the ferocity with which they set out to protect the social and economic status quo came to define his understanding of the connection between race and class. In a wartime speech in Memphis on the virtues of free speech and free association, Randolph explained, "organized labor more than any other single group in America can least afford to follow the dreadful, dismal, and disastrous doctrines of racism." Instead, he continued, "true and sound friendly relations [between labor unions and African Americans] can only grow out of justice and fair play. And the justice and fair play must be based upon equality, otherwise it isn't worth a tinker's dam. Justice is not qualified. Freedom is not limited. Citizenship cannot exist in degrees. It must be full and complete. All or none." He argued that unless organized labor successfully addressed the problem of discrimination and recognized that "Negroes today want every right, privilege, and immunity enjoyed by any other citizen," labor had little chance of standing against the "forces of anti-labor and fascism" intent upon crushing all progressive change.[5]

He argued that unions had to reconcile effectively the basic racial tensions that had plagued the AFL for so long before the labor movement could successfully reform industrial capitalism. This outlook defined Randolph's understanding of race and class issues.[6] He had previously emphasized the need for effective, independent black organization and action before seeking broader class collaborations in pushing for industrial and social reform.

However, in the last years of the 1930s, he increasingly came to view organized labor "as an effective movement for hastening the achievement of complete civil rights and the elimination of second class citizenship of the American Negro." Despite the early roadblocks that the porters encountered in the AFL, Randolph became much more optimistic about the collaboration between black civil rights and the labor movement after signing the porters' wage contract with Pullman and after the AFL issued the Brotherhood a full international charter in 1938. As Theodore E. Brown, the Brotherhood's director of research and education, explained, both events assured African Americans a strong position in the future course of the American labor movement and led Randolph to feel more confident about "the free trade union as a means for fighting to eliminate Jim Crow from every area of American life."[7]

Though he continued to criticize AFL executives and rank-and-file members for their slow pace in addressing racial discrimination within the organization, more and more in the years leading up to World War II Randolph connected a general civil rights agenda for African Americans and other racial minorities to the broader reform of industrial capitalism. He came to recognize that "since jobs for minorities are tied up with discrimination against them," it was "important that something be done about the basic question of race relations if we are to do anything about solving the problem of jobs in the postwar world." This understanding was directly related to his revised opinion of organized labor as an effective pathway for pursuing both a racial program of social reform and a class program of industrial reform. In a speech titled "Negroes and Race Riots" explaining the outbreak of racial violence across the country during World War II, Randolph concluded that "it is not a particular race which is responsible for the conditions of any other race, but . . . our social and economic system" that "has, up-to-date, failed to provide for freedom, peace, and plenty" for either black or white workers. In this speech, most likely delivered around 1939 when American manufacturing expanded to meet growing demand in Europe, Randolph insisted that regardless of race "the whole job question goes deeper" than which group of workers, black or white, got hired. Indeed, the job question was thoroughly "tied up with many social, economic, and political factors that result in periodic conditions of job scarcity."[8]

In promoting industrial reform as a catalyst for social reform, however, Randolph remained focused on the particular ways in which racial discrimination hampered African Americans. He clearly believed that "the needs of all poor people—black and white" were routinely ignored by industrial capitalism, but he maintained that African Americans were hurt "most severely" because they made up such a disproportionately large segment of the nation's poor. In the war years he continued to focus on solutions that addressed issues of both race and class. He began to insist that "in thinking of a solution to the problem" of racial discrimination, African Americans "must avoid at all costs the idea of a black solution" or "that a separate black economy is a realistic or desirable alternative." In an essay titled "The Economics of Black America," he explained that "separatism will only aggravate the problems from which blacks suffer because it will isolate them from the mainstream of the economy where the best jobs are to be found." The solution to the problems that African Americans faced, Randolph continued, was "a full employment economy" that, along with the end of racial discrimination, "will bring with it expanding employment opportunities" for everyone.[9]

Though this view was distinctly different from the more racially focused point of view he adopted in the early 1930s, his emphasis on the connection between issues of race and class in pushing for genuine social justice firmly shaped Randolph's course in the war years. As he explained in a news release for the *Amsterdam News* titled "The Negro and the Next Five Years," he sincerely believed that African Americans' future was directly "bound up" with the "continued militant and uncompromising struggle for civil rights" and "active participation by Negro workers in the trade union movement." As it became clear to him that labor's efforts to reform industrial capitalism could effectively serve a racial program of social change, Randolph became more committed to increasing black participation in the AFL. As "a minority which is exploited and oppressed," he pointed out, African Americans needed to be "fighting for complete, full, first-class citizenship in the labor movement by the elimination of all forms of discrimination and segregation."[10] Only then could African Americans ensure that the industrial democracy for which organized labor was fighting fulfilled completely the promise of genuine social justice for all. As the nation moved closer to war around 1940, Randolph moved closer to the conviction that African Americans' struggle for civil rights and labor's fight for industrial reform were inseparable.

Though he had argued for years that black and white workers needed to work together in pushing forward a program of progressive reform, Randolph's understanding of the important ways in which industrial reform could be directed toward the special needs of African Americans fundamentally recast his thinking about interracial class collaboration in the late 1930s. With the signing of the Brotherhood's first wage contract with the Pullman Company and continuing through the 1960s, he insisted that black workers had a "responsibility" to move organized labor "in the direction for which it was formed." That meant, he argued, that "in the field of labor," African Americans had to push trade unions to "develop and use the struggles of workers for economic, racial, and social justice." In a subsequent speech titled "The Role of the Negro Worker in the American Trade Union Movement and the Problem of Racial Discrimination," he announced that African Americans must "build and join trade unions for their own economic salvation" and also to ensure that industrial reform helped to "advance the improvement of all communities," regardless of race.[11] Just as the Brotherhood's struggle led him to recast his views about independent black organization and action, Randolph revised his previous ideas about interracial class collaboration during the war years and beyond by insisting that union membership for African Americans was more than just a simple class obligation.

It seems likely that in addition to these realizations about the special conditions racial discrimination imposed on black workers as a result of the Brotherhood's struggle, the impending war also factored significantly in changing Randolph's view of the relationship between industrial and social reform. As international tensions intensified in the late 1930s, Randolph certainly understood that the success of all progressive reform, whether racial or economic, was "tied up with the hope, future, and destiny of American democracy." He understood that neither African Americans nor organized labor would fare well under totalitarianism. As he explained, there would be "no rights for freedom of assembly and the press, trial by jury, right[s] of petition and freedom of worship" under fascism. He elaborated on this point in a wartime editorial titled "The Negro, the War, and the Future of Democracy." He underscored the point that the future of both the Negro and the labor movement depended on the triumph of the world's democratic powers. "If America goes down," Randolph predicted, "the Negro goes down." And in this instance, "what is true with respect to the Negro, is true with respect to organized labor."[12] The threat of war further clarified for Randolph that in some important ways African Americans and organized labor were in similar straits. As the nation headed toward war, it became more important than ever for him to craft a program that actively drew African Americans into labor unions while simultaneously advancing their specific racial goals.

Recognition of the threat that totalitarianism posed to both social and economic reform also reshaped Randolph's criticism of discrimination in organized labor. He used the new platform created by the Brotherhood's affiliation with the AFL to argue vigorously that organized labor could not "mobilize the complete strength of American labor or develop a healthy and sound progressive existence" until it "realistically" attacked "the question of racial discrimination." He had previously attacked racial discrimination in organized labor as unsound labor practice, but from the late 1930s through the 1950s he began to insist that continued racial discrimination jeopardized the basic progressive tenets that gave the labor movement substance. As the war spread and the nation's industrial capacity became a factor in it, Randolph argued vigorously that unless labor acted "to square its practices with its principles," it would "forfeit and lose the confidence and faith of the enlightened and liberal people of America and the world." Until the AFL acted "to cleanse" itself "of the poisons of discrimination on account of race, color, religion, or national origin," it would be unable, "despite its material and economic power," to "justify its existence as a symbol and expression of the age-old struggle of the working people in particular and mankind in general to achieve justice, freedom, and equality."[13]

Throughout the war years, Randolph certainly seized any opportunity to drive home this point. In a floor speech at the 1943 AFL convention in Boston, he lectured convention delegates on the dangers of continued discrimination. Explaining that two-thirds of the world's population was made up of people of color, he cautioned convention delegates against ignoring issues of equality at home and abroad. African Americans, he added, were persistently raising "the question of their freedom and independence to a major world political issue," and lingering racial divisions within the labor movement would be "fatal" to labor's "existence and future." Not only did discrimination undercut trade unions' progressive credentials, but if the AFL was to capitalize on the radical spirit of the working poor in developing countries as well as the increasingly militant drive of African Americans for equal justice, it could no longer overlook the corrosive effects of discrimination on class unity. "The race problem" was the "number one problem" facing organized labor, he concluded, and "the American Federation of Labor cannot continue to exist with a part of its members who are white as first-class union men and another part who are colored as second-class union men." Racial discrimination, he explained, "should be abolished" for the benefit of Negroes and other minorities and to ensure the AFL's continued viability. It should be clear to all, Randolph concluded, that "the rights of no white union workers are secure as long as the rights of a black worker are insecure."[14]

In casting continued racial discrimination as a fundamental threat to the viability of labor's leadership of progressive reform at home and abroad, Randolph modified his critique of the AFL's racial practices somewhat. Though he continued to stress his uncompromising commitment to ensuring that "the same reverence and respect for the dignity of the personality of the white worker shall be accorded to the black worker," between the late 1930s and the 1950s he increasingly tied such statements to world affairs where people of color, especially in Asia and Africa, were increasingly threatened by totalitarianism.[15] He explained in an essay titled "Racially Segregated Unions" that while "it is well-nigh axiomatic that labor in a white skin can never be fully free while labor in a black skin lives in the slavery of segregation," it was nonetheless "utterly impossible" for organized labor "to build and maintain prestige among the African and Asian, or even European workers, so long as the house of labor is defiled by the curse of color caste."[16] He analogized continued racial discrimination against African Americans in organized labor as similar to Hitler in Europe, Mussolini in Africa, and Hirohito in China. Though he remained primarily focused on articulating the important connections between issues of race and class and drawing African Americans into the labor movement, his wartime emphasis on the broader consequences of continued discrimination on progressive reform at home and abroad was significant. By internationalizing the discrimination issue and outlining the possibly dire consequences that labor faced abroad if it did not change its ways at home, Randolph hoped to give new momentum to his efforts to break down the racial barriers that black workers faced.

Though his view of the connection between issues of race and class continued to evolve in these years, the basic premise that race complicated class concerns that he first began to formulate in the late 1920s and early 1930s remained a guiding principle for Randolph in the war years and beyond. In both the 1940s and 1950s, this basic recognition helped to shape key features of Randolph's activism. With a signed wage contract with Pullman and an international charter in the American Federation of Labor, Randolph turned his attention more intently to government-sanctioned discrimination in this period. He reasoned that as the "largest single enterprise in our national society maintaining a policy of racial discrimination," the federal government's racial practices went a long way toward setting "the pace for the semi-private and private industries throughout the nation."[17] He believed that ending government-sponsored discrimination, especially in heavy manufacturing, would undercut the racial barriers that African Americans faced in other sectors of the economy. In the war years especially he began to insist that the "problem of minorities and jobs" required a "national policy" promoting fair employment to "deal with the question of discrimination on account of race, creed, religion, or national origin on a national scale."[18] In reflecting back on his threat to lead a hundred thousand African Americans in a march on the nation's capital in Washington, D.C., to protest racial discrimination in war industry jobs, this conception of the crucial connection between race and class that first took shape in the late 1920s and early 1930s found new expression in the war years.[19]

Though the New Deal in general did not substantially change the material conditions of black workers, the effort to reorganize the national economy to create job opportunities for the working poor revolutionized African American expectations.[20] When the nation's defense industries began to boom in late 1940 and early 1941, African Americans fully expected to participate in the revitalization. Randolph and the Brotherhood set out to transform these expectations into concrete results. Throughout these years, he and the porters' union issued statements and passed convention resolutions decrying continued racial discrimination in the area of national defense. In the summer of 1940 he joined forces with Walter White of the National Association for the Advancement of Colored People (NAACP) and T. Arnold Hill of the National Urban League (NUL) to call for a cabinet-level meeting with the Roosevelt administration to discuss the question of discrimination in the armed services. In September 1940 Randolph, White, and Hill met with White House officials and submitted a forceful memorandum calling for the immediate and complete integration of all defense preparations. The White House, however, chose to ignore their petition and released a press statement that not only reaffirmed the War Department's practice of segregating African Americans but also suggested that Randolph, White, and Hill fully endorsed this policy.[21]

The outcome of this September meeting at the White House left Randolph thoroughly disillusioned with the strategy of negotiation that characterized most black civil rights efforts of the day.[22] As he explained in a 1970 interview with John Slawson of the American Jewish Committee, Randolph "came to realize that mere statements by Negro leaders, while useful and necessary and proper, were not sufficient." His September meeting with the president and other administration officials also led Randolph to conclude that even though they had met with "top representatives in government who could do something about the problem of racial bias . . . nothing definitive was done about many of the basic problems."[23] He set his mind toward devising a new strategy for expressing African Americans' concerns that could not be co-opted or twisted by those who had no intention of willingly meeting their needs. In December 1940, while touring Brotherhood divisions in the South with Milton Webster, Randolph began tinkering with the idea of convening a large number of black workers in Washington to voice their discontent with continued racial discrimination. On their first stop in Savannah, Georgia, Randolph first publicly proposed the idea of gathering thousands of African

Americans in the nation's capital to demand jobs in the defense industry, and the idea quickly took on a life of its own. By March of the following year, a national March on Washington Committee (MOWC) was in place with Randolph as its director, and a separate Sponsoring Committee was formed that included Walter White, Lester Granger of the NUL, and other black and white civil rights leaders.

Randolph's March on Washington Movement captured the imagination of African Americans all across the country and created an outlet for venting their growing despair over the shift of federal resources away from New Deal relief to war production.[24] As the NAACP and the NUL struggled to keep the interests and issues of importance to African Americans before the nation, the sheer desperation that gripped most black communities seemed to mandate more radical protest strategies.[25] To a significant degree, Randolph's march plans became a vital lightning rod for the deepening disillusionment that engulfed African Americans in these years.[26]

As a vehicle for expressing African American discontent, the MOWM illustrated how the tactics of mass direct action began to take shape. Blending the high moral purpose of equal justice with the sit-down strike tactics of industrial unionism, the MOWM gave concrete form to the philosophy, strategy, and organization that in many ways prefaced the promise and problems of the civil rights movement of the 1950s and 1960s.[27] One can certainly look back and see the roots of the MOWM in mass protests like Coxey's Army in 1894 or the bonus march of 1932 that brought thousands of demonstrators to Washington, D.C., demanding war pensions.[28] But it is perhaps more important to recognize the ways in which Randolph's MOWM both foreshadowed the 1963 March on Washington and created the foundation on which the 1963 march was built.[29]

Randolph's proposed 1941 march also fit directly into his overall scheme for pursuing equal justice for African Americans. Since the early 1920s he had been actively engaged in organizing protest groups around issues of race and class, and the MOWM was part of his continuing effort to transform the "socio-economic racial milieu." More specifically, though, Randolph clearly saw the booming wartime defense industry as an opportunity to extend the gains achieved with the Brotherhood's stronger position within organized labor. As he later explained in a keynote address to the Policy Conference of the March on Washington Movement convened in Detroit in 1942, one of the broad goals of the movement was to ensure "the dispersal of equality and power among citizen-workers in an economic democracy" without regard to race, creed, or national origins.[30] In emphasizing concepts like citizen workers and economic democracy that linked civic participation and economic opportunity in the context of this effort to end racial discrimination in defense industries, Randolph firmly connected the MOWM with his earlier ideas about the interrelatedness of race, class, and social justice. While it is important to understand the historical precedents to Randolph's march initiative, looking at the MOWM in this framework clearly distinguishes it as the culmination of a long and steady push to address African Americans' race-based and class-based needs.

Just as Randolph viewed the Brotherhood as the advance guard in breaking down discrimination in labor unions and the private sector of the economy, he envisioned the MOWM as the vanguard in challenging government-sponsored racial discrimination. He believed that "the Negro must assume the major responsibility for the solution of his problems" and demand a greater role in the nation's wartime defense effort. Jews, the working class, and women have relied on their own interest groups to address problems specific to them, and in this case, the black worker needed "an all-Negro movement to fight to solve his specific problem." Speaking before a large audience at the Chicago Coliseum in 1942, Randolph encouraged African Americans to "join in common civic movements" with other progressive groups "on general problems" like war and peace, workmen's compensation, and better schools. But, he insisted that such cooperation did not negate the fact that Negroes must first "depend on Negroes to fight the battles of Negroes." Progressive interracial organization was "necessary, valuable, and sound," but it should supplement, not supplant, black protest activity.[31]

Again, the rationale that Randolph used to justify his insistence that the MOWM should be an all-Negro protest movement followed the reasoning he crafted in organizing the porters' union. Previously he had emphasized the all-black character of the Brotherhood and deemed its success as vital to demonstrating to whites that "Negroes have reached the point in their development . . . where they will deliberately, soberly, coolly, and dispassionately adopt a course of action which is calculated to protect and advance their social, economic, and political interests."[32] He viewed the MOWM in much the same way. In an essay titled "Weeping for Poor White Folks," Randolph responded to critics of his. He wrote that a "primary condition" for building up "the status of equality for the Negro in our American economy" was for Negroes to become conscious "of their historical mission, moral obligation, and responsibility to take the initiative and make the fight and sacrifice to free themselves." It would be difficult to develop such consciousness in an interracial framework, but, Randolph explained, "it can and will be awakened and nurtured in an all-Negro movement."[33]

Responding to charges that excluding sympathetic whites from the MOWM was akin to the exclusionary practices of white primaries in the South, Randolph countered that since it was the white primaries that decided elections in the South, "the exclusion of Negroes from membership in the Democratic Party restricts and negates their ability to exercise their constitutional right to vote as American citizens." African Americans had to fight to participate in white primaries in the South "because they have an economic and political stake involved." Conversely, there was no comparison between the cases of African Americans seeking to join the Democratic Party in the South and whites seeking to join the MOWM. The exclusion of sympathetic whites from the planned protest march had no real consequences for them in exercising their rights as citizens. "If a white person was allowed to join the MOWM," Randolph explained, "he would gain no right he did not already possess before he joined." This was not true for a Negro who tried to join a trade union that excluded African Americans. "When a black machinist joins the Machinists' Union," Randolph explained, "he gains the right to work which he did not already possess." Since membership in the MOWM would not confer on whites any civil, social, or economic right that they did not already possess, he concluded, contentions that "the denial of the right to join [the] M.O.W.M. to white people is undemocratic, is naive, silly, and ridiculous."[34]

In Randolph's view the material benefits that African Americans stood to gain if the MOWM proved successful reinforced the need for the organization to be all black. Just as in organizing sleeping car porters, Randolph "pointed out to Negroes that, before we go to our friends for help in this fight for fair employment practice, we must demonstrate that we are committed to this principle and are determined to fight for it ourselves." While the emphasis he placed on this racial aspect of the movement overshadowed to a degree the class aspects of fair employment, Randolph felt compelled to push forward in mobilizing African Americans behind the MOWM. As he explained in his later reflections on this period, he fully expected to hold a conference with President Roosevelt on the question of defense industry jobs and wanted to be able to state unequivocally "that Negroes would not stand idly by and be turned away from defense industries where jobs were being given to white workers every day and fail to do anything about it."[35] In this instance, he correctly recognized that an all-black organization financed and led exclusively by African Americans would immeasurably strengthen his claim.[36]

Despite this racial emphasis in organizing the March on Washington Movement, Randolph's push for fair employment in defense industries fit squarely within the race/class framework he established in organizing the porters. Acknowledging the unique challenges that racial discrimination created for black workers, he insisted throughout the 1930s that porters doggedly pursue their special racial needs even while they looked to address broader class interests through organized labor unions. As New Deal reforms transformed the workplace and wartime defense spending both revived the economy and fundamentally changed the fortunes of the white working class, Randolph once again looked to racial organization to secure a fair share of the resulting prosperity for African Americans. "The March on Washington," Randolph wrote in 1941 in the *Black Worker,* the official organ of the Brotherhood of Sleeping Car Porters, "was the last resort of a desperate people who had failed to get decisive results in the form of jobs in national defense through conference, petitions, and appeals to leaders of government and private industry."[37] As the idea of a large-scale protest in the nation's capital took deeper root through the spring and early summer, Randolph's reasoning in promoting the march on Washington followed even more closely the lines he established in forming the porters' union.

With the porters' union, Randolph developed clear ideas about the relationship between effective organization and political power.[38] His experience led him to believe that "true liberation can be acquired and maintained" only when African Americans developed the kind of political leverage that was "the product and flower of organization."[39] This outlook shaped his threatened march on Washington more than ten years later. In a May 1941 editorial in the *Black Worker* titled "Call to Negro America to March on Washington for Jobs and Equal Participation in National Defense," he noted that "in this period of power politics, nothing but pressure, more pressure, and still more pressure, through the tactic and strategy of broad, organized, aggressive mass action behind the vital and important issues of the Negro" will be effective in undermining government-sanctioned racial discrimination. "With faith and confidence of the Negro people in their own power for self-liberation," Randolph explained, "Negroes can break down the barriers of discrimination against employment in national defense . . . and smash and blast through the government, business, and labor union red tape to win the right to equal opportunity in vocational training and re-training in defense employment." The Brotherhood was a first effort at marshaling the collective resources of black workers to challenge Pullman and the AFL. Randolph hoped to extend those gains by organizing the 1941 march on

Washington and the subsequent MOWM with very clear ideas about the use of mass action in pushing for equal justice.[40]

Another aspect of Randolph's campaign for fair employment that paralleled his organization of the porters was his recognition of the disconnection between the American creed of liberty and justice for all and racial discrimination. With black soldiers dying abroad, Randolph poignantly asserted that "if American democracy will not defend its defenders; if American democracy will not protect its protectors; if American democracy will not give jobs to its toilers because of race or color; if American democracy will not insure equality of opportunity, freedom, and justice to its citizens, black and white, it is a hollow mockery and belies the principles for which it is supposed to stand." In calling on President Roosevelt to "free American Negro citizens of the stigma, humiliation, and insult of discrimination and Jim Crowism in government departments and national defense," Randolph insisted that the government could not with "clear conscience call upon private industry and labor unions to abolish discrimination based upon race and color as long as it practices discrimination itself against Negro Americans."[41]

In fact, the recognition that government-sponsored discrimination in many ways set the tone for both the employment practices of private industry and racial prejudice in labor unions was a central factor in Randolph's conception of the MOWM. Writing about Roosevelt's executive order banning racial discrimination in national defense in the *Black Worker,* Randolph maintained that it was the "firm and reasoned judgment" of MOWM leaders that "the inexcusable practice of discrimination against persons because of race, color, creed, and national origin by the government itself" served as an important "cue to and pattern for private employers to commit un-American and undemocratic offenses of discrimination also."[42] By specifically forcing the administration to adopt a general nondiscrimination policy in national defense contracting, Randolph hoped to affect the racial practices of companies and unions by denying firms that discriminated against African Americans lucrative government contracts. The implementation of this strategy led him to insist on an executive order "with teeth in it" that could "compel all concerns that have government contracts or that will receive government contracts to put Negroes to work."[43]

Building upon the successes and learning from the mistakes of organizing the Brotherhood, Randolph approached the MOWM intent on creating a mass movement with enough political power to demand firm guarantees from government officials that black workers would have a meaningful role in defense industries. Unlike Booker T. Washington and his Tuskegee Machine that in the past had depended heavily on personal appeals and persuasion to improve conditions for African Americans, the porters' experience convinced Randolph that whites were prepared to treat African Americans fairly only when forced to do so.[44] This conviction was reinforced by the fact that despite his numerous conferences with high-level government officials—even President Roosevelt, who Randolph believed was "quite definite in his own condemnation of discrimination," black workers still found themselves left out of the expanding industrial production. In a June 1941 speech before the Thirty-Second Annual Conference of the NAACP, Randolph pointed to this experience as a motivating factor in proposing the march on Washington strategy. "As a result of my experiences in these conferences," he explained, "I told Walter White and a number of others that I did not believe we were going to get very far and that I thought we needed to develop and work up some other technique of action."[45] As the threatened march date drew nearer and administration efforts to forestall it intensified, Randolph's resolve to secure an executive order guaranteeing African Americans a role in national defense hardened.

This determination was a central feature of Randolph's negotiations with official and unofficial emissaries from the Roosevelt administration. In the days following the organization of the national March on Washington Committee, Randolph and Walter White met with Eleanor Roosevelt and Fiorello La Guardia, the mayor of New York City.[46] As Randolph recalled, "the burden of the talk by Mrs. Roosevelt and the Mayor was that this march on Washington must not be had." The First Lady explained that the president was "greatly wrought up" over it and hoped that there was still a way to call the demonstration off. She explained the administration's view that the march was "too drastic" because it targeted allies as well as enemies of the Negro in equal measure. "The Negroes have friends in America," she insisted, "and they must recognize that fact." Randolph's response to the First Lady's appeal was firm. Despite his genuinely warm feelings toward her and his belief that the president was not "indifferent" to the plight of African Americans, Randolph remained convinced that the barriers that black workers faced in getting jobs in munitions factories and other areas of national defense continued to be a "pressing question" that required immediate attention.[47]

Randolph's determination to proceed with the march, despite increasing political pressure to call it off, was not surprising given his experience with the problem of racial discrimination in defense industries. In recounting the details of this meeting with the First Lady, he explained that African Americans had "reached a point in their history" where it was necessary to make independent decisions regarding their social, economic, and political interests "even when their judgment is at variance with the judgment of their very best white friends." In this and subsequent meetings with Roosevelt's inner circle, he consistently held to this view, "not merely for the purpose of differing" with the president; he fervently believed that it would be sheer "folly" for Negroes to fall back on the "old technique" of a conference and to abandon "the weapon of Negro mass power . . . unless something definite, tangible, [and] concrete was done in the interest of jobs for Negroes in national defense." While he agreed in general that it was proper to show some deference to the position of white allies who express an opinion on questions affecting the interests of African Americans, in this instance he explained the March on Washington Committee was determined to press march "demands until we achieved some concrete and definite concessions in the interest of abolishing racial discrimination in industry, labor unions, and government as a whole."[48]

Randolph's resolve to proceed with the march regardless of the political pressures to call it off cannot be separated from his experience in organizing the porters' union. One of the central insights that he gained from working with the Brotherhood of Sleeping Car Porters was that despite the intentions of some sympathetic whites, American society was generally only willing to treat African Americans fairly when compelled to do so. This realization fundamentally shaped Randolph's conception of mass direct action. He hoped that in pushing forward with the March on Washington despite strong opposition from the White House the MOWM could create the necessary leverage to extract some concrete gains for black workers. As he made clear in a May 1941 editorial in the *Black Worker*, he believed that "Negroes by the mobilization and coordination of their mass power can cause President Roosevelt to issue an executive order abolishing discrimination in all government departments, Army, Navy, Air Corps and national defense jobs."[49] In fact, Roosevelt's unspoken but real concern that the protest march would lead to widespread racial violence in the nation's capital worked in Randolph's favor. By holding firm on proceeding with the march unless the president issued an executive order banning racial discrimination in national defense, the March on Washington Movement trapped the president between giving in to the demands of African Americans and the prospect of a catastrophic racial explosion as the nation prepared for war.

In the days following the New York conference with the First Lady and Mayor La Guardia, Randolph and Walter White were summoned to Washington to meet with the president and key members of his cabinet. Though cordial in receiving Randolph and White, President Roosevelt refused to commit to any firm agreements regarding Negroes in defense work. As Randolph recalled, the president insisted that he would not sign any executive order on the matter because he would then "be required to sign it for other groups" as well. Instead, he sought to assure Randolph and White that he intended to do "something about this matter of racial discrimination with respect to defense jobs," but their insistence on immediate action only served to "block his efforts in this respect." The president explained that, in his view, the problem African Americans faced in securing employment in national defense arose from the fact that there was no authority to which they could present their complaints. In due time, he promised, he would establish a board that would have the power to investigate allegations of discrimination and carry out measures of redress. Negroes, the president insisted, simply "must be patient."[50]

In response, Randolph and White pointed out that African Americans "had been very patient since the beginning of national defense," yet they still "had not gotten any jobs of any consequence." While the president and his staff maintained that African Americans had made some gains since the war began, Randolph replied that any such gains "were too fragmentary" to constitute any significant material improvement in black workers' conditions. As an example, Randolph and White cited case after case of qualified African Americans being turned down for jobs despite clear manpower needs. They described the case of an African American graduate of New York University's aeronautical engineering program who had applied for jobs with twelve different aircraft manufacturers. All of his white classmates found jobs, Randolph explained, but six of the firms that the African American contacted refused to hire him, and the other six simply ignored his inquiry. Such blatant discrimination required immediate redress, and Randolph refused to call off the march unless Roosevelt issued an executive order specifically banning such behavior.[51]

Following this exchange the president adjourned the meeting but requested that Randolph and White continue their discussions with key members of his cabinet as well as Mayor La Guardia and Sidney Hillman, president of the Amalgamated Clothing Workers Union and director of the wartime Office of Production Management. Randolph recalled that from the outset of this second meeting the president's aides "attempted to make it definitely clear that they had no intention of going against the president's wishes." Secretary of the Navy Frank Knox was particularly incredulous about achieving racial equality in the armed services. At one point during the discussion, Randolph remembered, Secretary Knox heatedly stated his clear opposition to forced integration and asked if Randolph actually believed that "Negroes and whites should be compelled to live together on the same ship." Not only was it "perfectly fantastic" for anyone to assume that Negroes and whites could not get along and work together in the Navy, Randolph replied, but there was "no good reason" for assuming otherwise. He referenced numerous instances in which blacks and whites worked together effectively to achieve common goals and insisted that the two could be equally successful in the area of national defense if given the chance.[52]

Moreover, Randolph recalled, "it was utterly impossible for me to change my position on this matter because I was simply reflecting the spirit of the masses of Negroes throughout the nation on this question." He pointed out that he and others had traveled around the country telling people about the nature and magnitude of the problem of discrimination in war jobs and that "the colored people of the country were looking forward to some action with respect to the opportunity of Negroes to get employment in defense industries." Randolph conveyed that African Americans fully expected Roosevelt to live up to the standards of justice and fairness underlining his Four Freedoms, the core values justifying the nation's entry into World War II, and were prepared to make sure that he did. The president would have to take some unambiguous federal action before Randolph would consider calling off the march. As Randolph recalled, he told Secretary Knox, Mayor La Guardia, and other administration officials present that he "neither had the right or the power" to alter plans for the demonstration unless the president "issued an executive order banning racial bias in the employment of Negroes in defense industries and government." This declaration convinced Mayor La Guardia, a longtime acquaintance of Randolph's, that the administration "would get nowhere" in trying to change Randolph's mind without an executive order.[53]

La Guardia's stance seemed to break the impasse.[54] Pointing to his longtime association with Randolph, La Guardia explained to Secretary Knox and other administration officials that he was "rather confident" that Randolph would not be dissuaded from his position and suggested instead that the group "work out something definite and specific . . . to deal effectively with this problem." Under La Guardia's guidance a group of administration officials drafted an executive order that they thought would satisfy Randolph's concerns. When presented with this proposed order, Randolph immediately indicated that it failed to cover discriminatory acts by the government and, therefore, was unacceptable. "We want an executive order which applies to the government," Randolph explained, "because the government is guilty of racial discrimination itself with respect to jobs for persons of color." In fact, Randolph continued, "racial discrimination is in practically all departments of the government." Though skeptical of this assertion, the president put aside his reservations and in June 1941 issued executive order 8802 banning racial discrimination in all government agencies and departments concerned with vocational and training programs for defense production, mandated non-discrimination provisions in all government defense contracts, and created within the government's Office of Production Management (OPM) a committee on fair employment practices to receive and investigate complaints of discrimination.[55]

In many ways, the strategy that Randolph pursued in pushing for an executive order banning discrimination in national defense mirrors aspects of the tactics behind the Brotherhood's threatened 1928 strike against Pullman. In both instances, Randolph ultimately hoped to challenge the racial status quo through mass direct action. Also, just as in 1928 where it was unclear exactly how much popular support Randolph's strike plan enjoyed among porters, it is not exactly clear how many African Americans were prepared to heed Randolph's call to march on Washington. Though Randolph had traveled the country promoting the march, no one knew for sure what the response would be. The key feature of both initiatives, however, was Randolph's recognition of the potential of collective action in creating pressure for change. The porters lacked sufficient force to extract concessions from Pullman in 1928, but the prospect of a hundred thousand or more African Americans arriving in Washington, D.C., to protest racial discrimination was more than enough to convince the president to take Randolph's demands seriously. As Randolph pointed out to the Thirty-second Annual Conference of the NAACP in Houston, he and other Negro leaders encountered great difficulty getting anyone in government to heed their concerns prior to organizing the march. But when faced with a broad-based committee working to integrate, coordinate, and connect the activities of various African Americans from all over the country, "even the president of the United States began seeking a conference with Negro leaders."[56]

Almost from the moment that Roosevelt signed the executive order banning discrimination in national defense and creating the Fair Employment Practice Committee (FEPC), challenges to its implementation arose. A major question involved the composition of the five-member panel to be appointed to investigate allegations of discrimination. Sidney Hillman, director of the Office of Production Management, insisted that two members of the FEPC should come from organized labor—one from the AFL and one from the

Congress of Industrial Organizations (CIO). His view was that since the whole question involved labor, "it could not be properly handled without representatives from these two bodies." Randolph certainly agreed that labor should be represented, but his concern about Hillman's plan was that it gave organized labor too much influence over the committee's direction. Given the labor movement's historical antipathy toward black workers, Randolph's apprehension was justified. In a July letter to Anna Rosenberg, coordinator of the Social Security Board and a key facilitator of the June meeting between Randolph and the president, Randolph explained that Hillman's proposal "will give organized labor two-fifths of the members of the Committee which is an unduly large proportion in any quorum of three." Though Randolph agreed that labor should be prominently represented on the committee, he sought to temper its influence by pushing for a strong African American presence as well.[57]

He explained to Mrs. Rosenberg that "it is the firm and insistent opinion" of the National March on Washington Committee that two of the five FEPC members should be African Americans since "the committee is primarily concerned with the problems of Negro workers." While some opponents might charge that such a strong African American presence "will tend to make it a Negro committee and lessen its influence and value," Randolph wrote that this view simply catered to the very race prejudice that the March on Washington was intended to combat. Not only would the American people as a whole welcome African American appointees to the FEPC, he added, but "it certainly would not meet with the approval of the National Negro March on Washington Committee or the Negroes throughout the country" to exclude African Americans from decision-making positions. He contended that appointing African Americans to the committee was "absolutely necessary." The president, moreover, should go beyond the usual cast of characters in identifying suitable African American appointees. Randolph explained that government officials routinely turn to black lawyers, social workers, teachers, and ministers to represent the interests of African Americans on various committees. In the case of the FEPC, however, such a choice would be a mistake. The March on Washington Movement, Randolph emphasized, was a mass demonstration that "can only be represented adequately and effectively from a moral and spiritual point of view by someone who reflects and expresses the aspirations and hopes of the Negro masses."[58]

In a separate letter drafted to the president, Randolph and the MOWC raised questions about the size and strength of the FEPC. Given Hillman's view that both the AFL and CIO should be individually represented and the

MOWC's insistence that two members of the panel be African American, Randolph suggested that the FEPC should be increased from five to seven members. Such a change would ensure that no one factor could exercise "disproportionate power . . . in the event that the board should establish a ruling that three shall constitute a quorum." Randolph explained that it was "of the utmost importance . . . that the board be made up of persons of national reputation" to "assure the respect of the public." A committee that did not command broad public respect would undercut its authority as an investigative body and "negate" a key feature of the executive order. It was "imperative," Randolph continued, that panel members be of such "national standing" as to be able to "deal firmly" with employers, labor unions, and "responsible government heads" in Washington "if the objectives of your executive order are to be carried out."[59]

In raising such concerns about the ability of the FEPC to deal effectively with obstinate government officials and others resistant to change, Randolph addressed one of the major challenges that the committee faced. In addition to congressional opponents as well as strong resistance from private industry, the nondiscrimination features of the president's order were questioned even by key members of his administration. In a November 1943 letter to Attorney General Francis Biddle that addressed the opinion of the comptroller general that the nondiscrimination feature of Executive Order 8802 was "directive only and not mandatory in requiring insertion in all government contracts," the president restated the objectives of his executive order in no uncertain terms: "there is no need for me to reiterate the fundamental principles underlying the promulgation of the executive order, namely, that the prosecution of the war demands that we utilize fully all available manpower and that the discrimination by war industries against persons for any of the reasons named in the order is detrimental to the prosecution of the war and is opposed to our national democratic purpose."[60]

While acknowledging the understandable hesitancy of letting government contracts not in compliance with this nondiscrimination policy go unpaid, Roosevelt nonetheless explained his "wish to make it perfectly clear that these provisions are mandatory and should be incorporated in all government contracts."[61] It was just this sort of opposition that prompted Randolph to call for a larger FEPC and the appointment of board members of "the stature that a presidential committee ought to have."[62]

Another early concern that Randolph and the MOWC raised about the FEPC dealt with the extent of the committee's autonomy from outside influences. Randolph and White wrote in an August 1941 letter to committee chairman Mark Ethridge about the "desirability and necessity" of a "completely independent" administrative staff for the committee. "It appears to us imperative," they argued, "that there be no basis or any suspicion" that the FEPC "is influenced or may be influenced in the future to any degree by any bureau or agency of the federal government." With such widespread ambivalence in the administration over enforcing the president's order, Randolph and White were "firmly convinced" that the independence of the committee be beyond question. "Neither the OPM or any other governmental agency," they suggested, "should have a budgetary veto over your committee," nor should any government agency "in any wise attempt to insist that your committee employ any particular person nor follow any procedure save the ones which you independently agree upon." Establishing this degree of independence, they insisted, would "greatly contribute" to the committee's success by ensuring its "freedom from any suspicion or implication of undue influence" on its "deliberations by any group of employers, unions, or governmental bureaus."[63]

Despite these early logistical challenges to setting up the FEPC, the strategy Randolph employed in persuading the president to issue this executive order set the tone for his subsequent efforts to pressure the federal government into addressing African Americans' concerns. As African Americans streamed into the Democratic Party in the 1930s, Randolph increasingly looked to exploit the political leverage that came with the emerging political coalition of African Americans, urban workers, and immigrants that emerged out of Roosevelt's New Deal. Even as the FEPC began holding its first public hearings in October 1941, Randolph made clear that he and the MOWM would continue the work of "creating the force and bringing pressure to bear" on the president and other administration officials to fight racial discrimination in government departments and in war industries. "I think that the most important and significant thing that has come out of this whole struggle," Randolph explained to a NAACP audience in June 1941, "is the lesson that Negro people have learned" about the power they possess.[64] Certainly the tactic of mass organization and pressure politics became a central feature of Randolph's emerging strategy of direct mass action. Nonetheless increasing opposition to the FEPC among southern Democrats in Congress and industrial manufacturers eventually handicapped the committee's operation.

Under pressure from Congress and with the war demanding his full attention, Roosevelt transferred the FEPC to the War Manpower Commission (WMC), where it found less freedom to investigate discrimination. Initially organized as part of the president's executive office, where it reported directly to Roosevelt and could draw directly on the prestige that came with being a presidential commission, this reorganization now placed the FEPC under the supervision of War Manpower Commissioner Paul V. McNutt and drastically reduced its political profile. Though both the president and McNutt insisted that the shift was intended to strengthen the FEPC, Randolph clearly believed that the change reduced the capacity of the committee to root out racial bias. Under the WMC the FEPC now fell under the immediate budgetary scrutiny of a Congress dominated by southern Democrats. Also, as part of the WMC, the FEPC found itself in the awkward position of investigating government departments of which it was now a part. And, lastly, the shift created a significant conflict of interest for the WMC in that any sanctions the FEPC might recommend would have to be implemented through an agency whose primary goal involved working with manufacturers to speed up wartime production.

The early concerns that Randolph and others raised about the reorganization of the FEPC took concrete shape at the end of 1942 when Commissioner McNutt unilaterally suspended planned hearings into the hiring and promotion practices of the railroads—an industry vital to wartime production but also notorious for its unfair treatment of black workers. The principle of fair employment and the integrity of the committee's investigations fared better in other industries. In hearings conducted in Los Angeles, Chicago, and New York in the first months of 1942, the FEPC exposed significant racial discrimination throughout the West, Midwest, and Northeast in the agencies and industries involved in the wartime buildup. But as the committee turned its attention south with hearings in Birmingham, Alabama, in June 1942, opposition to the committee climaxed. Reaction from southern Democrats, northern industrial interests, and some government officials alienated by the FEPC's effort to end discrimination in their agencies came together to pressure the president to rein in the committee at a time when he was least prepared to resist it. Still shaken by the Japanese attack at Pearl Harbor in December 1941, the president had turned his full attention abroad and was prepared to let subordinates manage manpower and, in the case of African Americans, ignore discrimination issues. Without the full weight of the president's attention, there was little counterpressure on McNutt to push ahead with discrimination hearings in the face of powerful opposition from key members of Congress and business leaders.

For Randolph and other leaders of the MOWM, the abrupt and unilateral postponement of the FEPC's railroad hearings was a serious "moral and psychological" blow. In a wartime testimonial addressed to the president, Randolph explained that, despite the "necessities of adjustment and compromise" required of any political leader, "some issues cannot be compromised." He insisted that in the context of the nation's defense of freedom abroad, "the principle that there can be no second-class citizenship, no ceiling of color or creed in the defense of democracy" was as basic as freedom of speech, freedom of religion, freedom from want, or freedom from fear. Randolph added that the principle of fair employment was central to the "system of moral, ethical, and social values which we call civilization and with which we oppose the vicious, lying dogma of totalitarian racism." Pointing to the "profoundly salutary" work of the FEPC as a "new Emancipation Proclamation" and "Bill of Economic Rights for racial minorities," Randolph argued that people of color the world over were looking for affirmation that such basic principles as Roosevelt's Four Freedoms, "when dipped in the acid test of present political and military realities," still emerged as "edged and shining" weapons in the "battle for human honor and justice." By allowing the FEPC to flounder in the hands of ambivalent subordinates, Randolph concluded, the president helped to undermine "the faith and hope of democracy in the modern world."[65]

As a backdrop for his criticism of the War Manpower Commission's handling of the FEPC, the war was an important feature in Randolph's argument. Not only did he draw poignant distinctions between American rhetoric of freedom and democracy and the treatment of African Americans, but in opposing fascism abroad and its merciless persecution of Jews in Europe the war gave Randolph's viewpoint new traction at home. In these years, Randolph and the March on Washington Movement collected numerous editorials from mainstream newspapers from across the country supporting their protest of McNutt's suspension of the railroad hearings. Randolph and the MOWM undoubtedly concurred with the *Philadelphia Inquirer*'s view that "to deprive anyone of his livelihood or to bar him from job opportunities because of his race, his religious beliefs, his color or his national origin is not only unfair, it is un-American." The *Washington Post,* too, echoed the basic sentiment underlying Randolph's position in a March 1944 editorial insisting that "the FEPC is simply trying to bring about a fuller mobilization of the nation's manpower for war and a fuller realization of the principle of human equality on which the nation is founded." To renounce the FEPC, the *Post* continued, "would be to slam a door upon the legitimate hopes which our own American litany has engendered and encouraged." Similarly, the *Pittsburgh Post-Gazette* editorialized that in "taking due note of the whole spirit of our democratic laws, it is hard to see how any member of Congress can argue that fair employment practices are either unconstitutional or un-

American" when "our government can draft Negroes to fight with white men for their common safety and security but cannot insist that Negroes as well as white men be used in maintaining maximum production on the home front." Such reasoning, the *Post-Gazette* wrote, split hairs "too thin for logic."[66]

While these editorials were unquestionably far in front of the general opinion of most Americans on the issue of fair employment, they nonetheless bolstered Randolph's criticism of the War Manpower Commission's oversight of the FEPC. In his defense of the principle of fair employment, the war, and the fundamental democratic principles attached to it, the contradiction between Roosevelt's war rationale and the treatment of black workers certainly became a powerful rhetorical tool for Randolph to attack discrimination in national defense.[67] As the *Bismarck Tribune* observed in October 1944, "no war agency is more American in the finest sense and more absolutely expressive of the ideals for which we are fighting in this war than the Fair Employment Practices Committee."[68] For Randolph, reactivating the FEPC was a dire necessity not only because the suspension of the railroad hearings "greatly lowered" the morale of African Americans, but also because it encouraged the forces of racial discrimination to "become more arrogant, intolerant, and aggressive" in disregarding the rights of racial minorities seeking employment and better job opportunities in defense industries and the government.[69]

To address the criticism leveled at him and his agency's handling of the fair employment issue, Commissioner McNutt convened a Washington conference in February 1943 to examine the scope and powers of the FEPC. With Attorney General Francis Biddle and other key War Manpower Commission aides by his side, McNutt attempted to reassure representatives of a wide range of minority groups including Randolph, Walter White, and Lester Granger, that despite the suspension of hearings there was no change in the status of the FEPC and that the president's executive order banning discrimination still stood. In fact, he explained, the purpose of this meeting was to give Randolph and others "ample opportunity" to express their opinions on how best to handle the "very vital problem" of reviving the committee. He insisted, moreover, that "no commitments have been made of any kind" as to the future direction of the FEPC and that Randolph and the others attending the meeting did not have to limit their discussion in any way.

Despite McNutt's assurances of an open and free-flowing discussion rather than a "Quaker meeting," Randolph and the other conference attendees continued to doubt the commissioner's interest in conducting hearings that genuinely probed employment discrimination. "The feeling among the Negro people," Randolph began, was that the initial FEPC hearings into the employment practices of railroads were called off principally to appease "the powerful interests" of key railroad brotherhoods and carriers. Both railroad unions and carriers, Randolph maintained, were determined to prevent further hearings that might "expose a secret agreement made between the Southern Carriers Committee and the Brotherhood of Locomotive Firemen and Engineers limiting the right of Negroes to serve as firemen in the railroad industry." He argued that these kinds of secret "non-promotability" agreements prevented African Americans from working as firemen. Such blatant discrimination made the reconstitution of the railroad hearings absolutely vital. He went on to point out that African Americans had so "very little faith" in the "spirit of the administration on this particular issue" precisely because, in the face of such blatant racial discrimination, "they feel that the administration should not have surrendered to the clamor and the general propaganda that brought about the cancellation of the railroad hearings" in the first place. [70]

In presenting his assessment of the War Manpower Commission's handling of FEPC hearings, Randolph maintained that "Negroes are in a position different from that of any other section of the population." Other minority groups undoubtedly faced various kinds of discrimination, but he contended only "Negroes are in the position of having to fight their own government." "As a matter of fact," he added, the U.S. government "is the only government in the world . . . that segregates its own citizens." In many ways, Randolph suggested, the government has become "the primary factor . . . in propagating discrimination against Negroes." Because of the government's historical role in "perpetuating and freezing an inferior status of second-class citizenship" on Negroes in America, Randolph explained that the FEPC needed to be independent and invested with the appropriate authority to examine all agencies and industries without interference. To reorganize the FEPC in any other way would simply result in an agency susceptible to the same kind of forces that shut down the railroad hearings.[71]

Randolph's position on the need for a strong, more independent FEPC received wide support from the assembled civil rights, minority group, and labor organizations attending McNutt's conference. Though he disagreed with Randolph's assertion that Negroes were "in the position of fighting with their own government," Lester Granger of the National Urban League nonetheless concurred with Randolph's assessment of the War Manpower Commission's handling of the FEPC. He explained the Urban League's view that the clear reluctance of top administration officials to take "prompt action" against racial discrimination in employment was principally due to the "administration's fear, as Mr. Randolph has said, of reactionary combines in

Congress and other places of power." Again echoing Randolph, Granger asserted that the FEPC's railroad hearings should be rescheduled immediately "as a means of reestablishing good faith in the government in the minds of colored people."[72]

Walter White, too, reiterated many of Randolph's points. He lamented that it was "most unfortunate that the present administration is apparently afraid of some reactionary forces." Yielding to them was akin to "appeasement," he cautioned, and was "very dangerous" for the cause of fair employment. With such forces in Congress "riding high, wide, and handsome," White argued, it was even more important that the administration "take a more courageous point of view" on the matter of the FEPC. "There are a great many people in the country," he emphasized, "who are anxious and ready to support courageous leadership instead of holding back in the fight for social gains." The president should use his "ample authority" to direct all contracting agencies of the federal government "to recognize the findings of the FEPC and recognize them as binding." The FEPC "is not only an instrument but a symbol of the sincerity and good faith of the government so far as Negroes are concerned," White explained, and the administration had an absolute responsibility "to take an affirmative stand and a very positive position" against the forces of reaction in this matter. Otherwise, he concluded, "all that we are fighting for in this war is going to be lost."[73]

Others present at this conference with McNutt cast the reinstatement of the railroad hearings in moral terms. Morris Milgrim of the Workers' Defense League connected the FEPC fight to the worldwide struggle to preserve liberal democracy from totalitarianism. "It is essential," he counseled, "that the FEPC adhere to the technique of holding public hearings on discrimination" because such transparency is "basic" to American democracy. Rabbi Israel Goldstein of the Synagogue Council of America echoed this sentiment, insisting that fair employment was a "moral priority" that should be practiced at home with as much vigor as it was preached abroad. Only full reinstatement of the FEPC and its canceled hearing, he declared, would "enable us to maintain our enthusiasm and our moral conviction" and "to say wholeheartedly to our people that we are conducting this war in a way that cannot be questioned or indicted."[74]

The point that each of these speakers made about the FEPC, the principle of fair employment, and the nation's moral health paralleled much of what Randolph had said in pushing for the creation of a fair employment committee. Though not in total agreement with his insistence that there was not "one single department in the government which does not practice segregation against Negroes," each organization represented in this conference absolutely accepted Randolph's premise that calling off the FEPC's railroad hearings "was evidence of the utter disrespect and disregard for the Negro people of this country." The participation of such a wide selection of minority groups and religious and labor organizations strengthened Randolph's assertion that there was a "very definite" government policy of segregating Negroes that was "setting the pace and giving the cue to other agencies in the country on discrimination." By participating in this meeting to defend an independent and strengthened FEPC, each represented organization responded to Randolph's call for African Americans and liberals to fight racial discrimination.[75]

The effort to construct a liberal coalition between minority groups and labor organizations around the issue of fair employment extended beyond the immediate problem of reinstating the FEPC. The nearly universal conviction among its supporters that fair employment was a central feature of American democracy became something of a rallying point in Randolph's push to make the FEPC a permanent body. Following a September 1943 conference organized to reinstate hearings into the employment practices of railroads, Randolph and his allies formed the National Council for a Permanent FEPC. They were "keenly aware of the limited powers and transiency of this wartime agency" and, despite strong opposition from southern Democrats in Congress, now "felt it was necessary to give it a permanent legislative base." Randolph, who was elected chairman of the organization, asserted that the group's basic objectives in promoting in every possible way the establishment of equal opportunity in employment and the creation of a permanent federal fair employment committee were "essential not only for the permanent maintenance of the FEPC, but for the permanent maintenance of democracy." The postwar effort to establish a stable peace, he concluded, "cannot be successful unless and until we protect and preserve the pillars of democracy" that uphold such a peace.[76]

In late January 1944, Randolph's new organization convened a two-day national conference to map out a strategy for implementing its objectives. In the process, Randolph and his associates crafted a general statement in support of permanent FEPC legislation that again argued that the principle of fair employment was essential to the postwar peace. As the war in Europe came to an end and success in the Pacific looked ever more likely, Randolph and his fellow conferees pointed out that just as the "urgent necessities of war" required the "fullest possible utilization of all available manpower," the manpower needs of the postwar peace "will be just as urgent." For conference participants, it was clear "that the first and indispensable condition for a lasting peace is an economy of abundance" and, they insisted, that was "synonymous with full employment of all available workers on the basis of

fitness and skill, regardless of their race, color, creed, or national origin."
Without forceful nondiscrimination policies to grant full and equal economic
opportunities to racial and religious minorities, the "formidable" social and
economic problems that confronted the United States at the conclusion of
the war might "prove to be overwhelming and the peace may well prove to
be as upsetting to the nation as has been the war itself."[77]

In their general statement supporting a permanent FEPC, Randolph and
his associates maintained that "precisely because of the great task that still
lies ahead in abolishing discrimination" as part of the transition from war to
peace, "the time has come to make the FEPC a permanent statutory agency."
Not only would attacking racial discrimination serve as a powerful "symbol
to all the oppressed peoples of the world of the sincere and practical determination of the United States to implement the Four Freedoms as quickly
and effectively as possible," but Randolph and the other conference attendees
insisted that the exercise of such freedoms "depend in very large measure on
the freedom of economic opportunity." It was "incontestable," they pointed
out, that if racial and religious minorities are good enough to be drafted to
fight and die for their country, "they are good enough to be protected against
discrimination in job opportunities" by a permanent FEPC. In pursuing a just
peace at home and abroad, conference attendees argued that the nation "must
not allow the forces of reaction to confuse the problem" with racist appeals,
but must recognize that "no other issue is involved but the fundamental human right of all citizens, regardless of race, color, creed, or national origin,
to work in American industry on equal terms, according to their fitness and
ability."[78]

In promoting fair employment, Randolph attempted to fulfill his belief
that civil rights for African Americans without meaningful economic opportunity fell well short of first-class citizenship and genuine social justice.
Just as he insisted in the late 1920s and 1930s that Pullman porters needed to
attend to their specific needs as racial minorities while also pursuing their
broader class interests as part of a revitalized labor movement, Randolph's
push for fair employment focused on the core connection between African
Americans' civil and political rights and economic needs. As he discussed
in a 1948 radio address in support of the National Council for a Permanent
FEPC, "discrimination in employment goes deeper and is far more corrupt-
ing than all of the other discrimination that minorities suffer."[79] As he turned
his attention to challenging various other inequities that constricted black
life in the 1950s and 1960s, the recognition that issues of race and class were
inextricably linked continued to shape him.

Epilogue
A. Philip Randolph's Reconciliation of Race and Class in African American Protest Politics

In pushing the principle of equal job opportunity in establishing the Fair Employment Practice Commission (FEPC), Randolph brought together for the first time all of his core beliefs about improving the lives of African Americans. This initiative clearly highlighted the fact that genuine social justice required fair access to both civil and economic rights, that issues of race and class were inextricably linked, and underscored the political potency of mass action for affecting social change. Though his subsequent efforts to challenge racial discrimination in other facets of American society would continue to refine these key points somewhat, Randolph's basic understanding of these central precepts remained unchanged throughout the rest of his career as a trade unionist and civil rights activist. More importantly, perhaps, the specific combination of ideas that first came together with the FEPC fight and the organization of the National Council for a Permanent FEPC profoundly shaped the course of the civil rights movement in the post–World War II years.[1] As Bayard Rustin, a protégé of Randolph's and a key organizer of the 1963 March on Washington, noted in a 1969 retrospective essay on Randolph's life and career, it was Randolph's "perception of the economic basis of Negro freedom" that enabled him "to grasp the unique significance of the 1963 march on Washington . . . which brought a quarter of a million Americans to the nation's capital to demand 'jobs and freedom' for Negroes."[2]

The FEPC was a monumental step forward for African Americans in the struggle to end discrimination in employment, and Randolph pursued a similar protest strategy in challenging Jim Crow in the armed services in the late 1940s and 1950s. Even before the war ended, he was arguing in essays like his 1943 commentary, "Are Negroes American Citizens?" that since "Negroes have shared in the building of our common country" and shed blood on "the sands of every war in defense of American democracy," they deserved a "democratic army" that did not "discriminate against any person on account of race or color." Certainly, he asserted, in making the world safe for democracy, "race prejudice is obstructing the nation's effort to win the war and plan a real peace."[3] In 1947 he turned these sentiments into the Committee Against Jim Crow in Military Service and Training. Responding to growing postwar pressure for universal military training, Randolph renewed efforts to prohibit "all segregation and discrimination" in military training programs, service branches, and reserve corps. He also proposed bans on Jim Crow in interstate travel for servicemen in uniform, federal laws against attacks on or the lynching of servicemen in uniform, and prohibitions on poll taxes in federal elections for servicemen otherwise eligible to vote.[4] He recognized that the protection of such rights for black servicemen was an important first step to securing first-class citizenship for all African Americans.

The connection between fair employment and desegregating the armed services also became important for Randolph. He wondered how the FEPC would effectively "criticize job discrimination in private industry if the federal government itself were simultaneously discriminating against Negro youth in military installations all over the world." In testimony before the Senate Armed Services Committee in March 1948, Randolph hammered home the point "that Negroes are in no mood to shoulder a gun for democracy abroad so long as they are denied democracy at home." Negroes, he explained, particularly "resent the idea of fighting or being drafted into another Jim Crow army." Wholeheartedly condemning the army as contributing significantly to "the greatest segregation system of all times," he asserted that "the current agitation for civil rights is no longer a mere expression of hope on the part of Negroes" but rather is both "a positive, resolute outreaching for full manhood" and "an equally determined will to stop acquiescing in anything less." The refusal to accept continuing "compulsory military segregation," Randolph assured the committee, was only one indication of "the bitter, angry mood of the Negro in his present determination" to secure full citizenship.[5]

The connection that Randolph drew between federally sanctioned racial discrimination and the discrimination practiced by private industry and regular citizens placed added emphasis on his call for mass action in support of the FEPC and his campaign of civil disobedience to protest segregated military service. Just as segregated military service and training helped to set a tone for racial discrimination in industry and unions, it also helped to sustain

American racism more broadly. Pointing specifically to postwar draft proposals that continued to allow Jim Crow policies in the armed services to be used "as a means to sanction and legalize the concept of a pure Aryan race," he warned the Committee that he had "no alternative but to call upon Negroes and freedom-loving whites in the armed services . . . to consider laying down their guns in protest against further participation in what would be a Ku Klux Klan military establishment."[6] In a co-signed 1947 letter to the editor of the *New York Times,* he and Grant Reynolds, chairman of the Committee Against Jim Crow in Military Service and Training, outlined their intention "to rally Negroes and progressive forces" behind "anti-segregation amendments which even the Pentagon could not circumvent." This committee, they made clear, was "firmly committed" to the proposition that Negroes should no longer "suffer under any permanent Jim Crow draft" and prepared to "take whatever action becomes necessary" to end segregation in the military.[7]

Randolph in particular made clear his personal resolve to challenge racial discrimination in the military by encouraging Negroes to resist draft induction. He vowed to the Armed Services Committee that "so long as the armed services propose to enforce such universally harmful segregation not only here at home but also overseas," he would "advise Negroes to refuse to fight as slaves for a democracy they cannot possess and cannot enjoy." He detailed his view that "Negro youth have a moral obligation not to lend themselves as world-wide carriers of an evil and hellish doctrine." During World War II Hitler's racism was a sufficient enough threat for "rank-and-file Negroes . . . to submit to the Jim Crow army abuses," but Randolph insisted that Negroes would no longer "take a Jim Crow draft lying down." Labeled a traitor by many in Congress, especially southern Democrats, Randolph countered that such direct action comported with "a higher law than any passed by a national legislature in an era when racism spells our doom." He contended that "the conscience of the world will be shaken as by nothing else when thousands and thousands of us second-class Americans choose imprisonment in preference to permanent military slavery."[8]

Randolph's program of civil disobedience included appeals not only to Negro youth to resist Jim Crow military service "with the power of non-violence, with the weapons of moral principles, with the goodwill weapons of the spirit," but also to "white youth in schools and colleges who are today vigorously shedding the prejudices of their parents and professors." He urged them "to demonstrate their solidarity with Negro youth by ignoring the entire registration and induction machinery." He also stressed the ready resolve of black veterans already so deeply "bitter over army Jim Crow" that they were prepared "to join this civil disobedience movement" and would greatly assist in recruiting "their younger brothers in an organized refusal to register and be drafted." Randolph assured the Armed Services Committee that even without being prompted many of these black veterans "have indicated that they will act spontaneously in this fashion regardless of any organized movement." And lastly, he resolved to appeal to black parents and African Americans generally "to lend their moral support to their sons" as "they march with heads high to federal prison as a telling demonstration to the world that Negroes have reached the limit of human endurance."[9]

Randolph felt "morally obligated to disturb and keep disturbed the conscience of Jim Crow America." He believed that moral consistency demanded that "democracy and Christianity must be boldly and courageously applied for all men regardless of race, color, creed, or country." In resisting the "insult of Jim Crow to the souls of black America," he further testified, African Americans' struggle against racial injustice ultimately worked to "save the soul of America." Randolph thought that Negroes served "their fellow man throughout the world" by "refusing to accept compulsory military segregation." In relentlessly opposing Jim Crow "without hate or revenge," African Americans fundamentally rejuvenated "moral and spiritual progress" as well as the "safety of our country, world peace, and freedom." He couched black civil disobedience as vital to preserving the country's core democratic and Christian principles and stated clearly that "Negroes are just sick and tired of being pushed around and just don't propose to take it" any longer. If Negroes could not win genuine social justice simply "by appealing to human decency," Randolph proclaimed, then "we shall command your respect and the respect of the world by our united refusal to cooperate with tyrannical injustice."[10]

Randolph and the Committee Against Jim Crow in Military Service and Training paired this appeal to democratic and Christian principles with a more basic question. In determining the "policy of the United States government in organizing its armed forces," Randolph argued that the core "question at stake" was whether it would be "a fascist or anti-fascist one." In a May 1948 press release urging African Americans "to consider laying down their guns" if Congress passed a measure for segregating military induction and training, Randolph declared that such legislation would "amount to congressional sanction of the United States Army's adopting a Ku Klux Klan pattern and training men in the adoption and perpetuation of this mentality." In the wake of World War II, a policy of Jim Crow military service and training "assuring that white men will not be forced to mingle socially with men of another race" was "a totally false concept of what is at stake." In both combat and training settings, Randolph emphasized that "soldiers of whatever race are entirely free to associate or not associate socially or to develop personal friendships with other soldiers of the same or of another race in their unit." "Abolishing segregation," Randolph pointed out, would not "abridge the freedom of men to exercise their personal preferences, or even prejudices, in their personal associations." The real issue was not how to separate whites and blacks socially, but rather how would "Congress use the U.S. Army and other military services as a means to sanction and legalize the concept of a pure Aryan race."[11]

In just about every significant way, Randolph's push to end racial discrimination in the military mirrored his fair employment campaign. Both the March on Washington Movement and the Committee Against Jim Crow in Military Service and Training set out to rally African Americans to challenge racial discrimination and generate sufficient political pressure for social change. Both initiatives, in fact, developed from Randolph's earlier experience with the Brotherhood of Sleeping Car Porters and the aborted 1928 porters' strike. Though the porters' strike failed, it showed Randolph the potential of mass action and pressure politics for improving African Americans' lives. As African Americans' political clout improved greatly with black migration to northern cities and the emergence of Roosevelt's New Deal coalition, Randolph was able to put his evolving ideas about mass action and pressure politics to good use. In launching his campaign of civil disobedience to protest segregation in the military, Randolph and his Committee Against Jim Crow in Military Service and Training simply extended ideas that he had been developing since the early years of the Brotherhood.

Also, the remedy Randolph sought in both instances, an executive order signed by the president, reflected his basic understanding of interest group politics. In seeking to address the concerns of Pullman porters through the mid- and late 1930s, he found that Congress routinely ignored or overlooked the needs of African Americans in drafting New Deal labor legislation. Though he continued to lobby sympathetic politicians on the need to secure the economic and civil rights of African Americans through federal legislation, he quickly realized that in the war of competing interests that shaped and passed legislation in both houses of Congress, African Americans wielded insufficient political clout. He began to focus his attention on the White House instead of Capitol Hill in pursuing the fair employment issue and desegregating the armed services. Despite numerous appearances before congressional committees and continuing to meet with select congressmen, Randolph recognized that by targeting Roosevelt and later Truman he could concentrate what political leverage African Americans did possess in one branch of government instead of expending it on a disinterested Congress.[12] This strategy was all the more effective in the post–New Deal and postwar political climate where increasing numbers of southern Democrats left the Democratic Party, and African American political strength outside the South grew. Thus, in forming the March on Washington Movement and the Committee against Jim Crow in Military Training and Service and initiating broad mass action and civil disobedience campaigns around these organizations, Randolph acted directly on his growing understanding of how minority groups could effectively maneuver within the context of American interest group politics.

Randolph also saw a direct connection between the FEPC and desegregating the armed services. "When we discriminate against Negroes here at home in defense jobs," he contended, "we discriminate against soldiers and sailors upon the far-flung battlefields of the world and the seven seas." In a February 1943 editorial titled "The Negro in the American Democracy," explaining how "the violent and ceaseless struggle of the white South to keep the Negro down has caused the South to become the nation's number one problem," Randolph wrote that each opportunity denied Negroes to build ships, tanks, ammunition, and aircraft contributed to "withholding" some vital "instruments of war from the armed forces or prevents them from reaching our boys in time." As such, "the fight for democracy on the home front," became a significant "part of the fight for democracy on the foreign front."[13]

As early as 1943, Randolph and the March on Washington Movement were vigorously pushing the Roosevelt administration to root out racial segregation in the armed services and proposed permanent fair employment legislation. Randolph claimed that "by condoning Jim Crow in uniform," the federal government helped to spread segregation and discrimination. This complicity was made even more tragic because "Negro young men are giving their all to carry democracy across the world while their mothers and fathers are denied it at home."[14] In April 1943 the MOWM adopted a "resolution on democracy in the army" that called on the administration to do more to combat segregated military service. Insisting that the practice of segregation in the armed forces "violates the most basic principle of democracy and cannot but have serious postwar consequences," Randolph resolved to take the initiative "in securing the cooperation of Negro and white citizens and organizations" to pressure Roosevelt to change the policy of the U.S. Army. Every citizen "who is called upon to shed his blood in the war," Randolph reasoned, "should at least have the democratic right to fight in an unsegregated, non-Jim Crowed unit."[15]

This link between fair employment and desegregating the military also alludes to broader connections between economic, civil, and social rights at the core of Randolph's conception of social justice.[16] A long-time proponent of the view that every person regardless of race, color, or national origin deserved fair access to society's economic, social, and civil privileges, Randolph clearly viewed military service free from the taint of racial discrimination as part of that bundle of civil and social rights belonging to every American citizen. Just as the porters' fight against Pullman and the March on Washington Movement's protest against discrimination in national defense set the tone for expanding economic opportunity for African Americans in the war years and beyond, Randolph's postwar push to challenge segregation in the military set out to apply mass action tactics and pressure politics to expanding the civil rights of black soldiers. And just as the porters' victory over Pullman presaged the expansion of economic opportunity for African Americans in the form of the FEPC, Randolph assumed that successfully challenging Jim Crow in public accommodations and in voting booths in the South for black soldiers would lead to a similar expansion of civil and social rights for African Americans in general. Indeed, it is fair to speculate that at least part of the impulse behind his broad-based appeal for African Americans to take up this campaign of civil disobedience was tied to this assumption.[17]

In an April 1945 conference "to formulate a program of action to end race segregation and discrimination by the armed services," Randolph outlined many of the central principles around which he later organized the Committee Against Jim Crow in Military Service and Training. Operating on the premise "that segregation in the armed forces . . . was particularly intolerable in an army which is fighting a war against the philosophy of racial supremacy," he presented to conference participants a broad analysis of American interest-group politics. He pointed out that "pressure power determines the action of the state." He encouraged his audience to pursue a publicity campaign through the leading daily newspapers to show clearly "what segregation means to the American system and what it is doing to the spirit of the country." He also advised them to establish the machinery to coordinate lobbying efforts in Washington, D.C., to ensure that the president was fully "aware of the fact that there is a force in America which is fighting segregation." And, lastly, he insisted that "since the reaction of the American system to an issue is conditioned by the world attitude," it was crucial to develop strategies for focusing world opinion on the link between segregation and the "great world question of imperialism" that demonstrated how it hindered "the program of world peace." In the context of American interest-group politics, Randolph concluded, these collective measures would have significant "moral and spiritual value . . . and would give added ammunition for the continuation of the fight against discrimination in other phases of life."[18]

Similarly, in a wartime skit with Socialist Party leader Norman Thomas, Randolph sketched the contours of his opposition to racial discrimination in the armed services and other facets of American life. Describing his plan as "constitutional obedience," he reasoned that "the very thought of a Jim Crow army fighting to break down Nazi race theories is an anachronism of policy." It would be "humorous," he proclaimed, if it was "not so tragically dangerous and destructive." He pledged to "ponder and weigh" new strategies of "non-violent goodwill action" to attack not only segregation in the military but all aspects of racial discrimination against African Americans. Rather than just seeking "to break down American civil government," he explained the primary intent of his program of nonviolent goodwill direct action was "to challenge the social forces" of racism and discrimination without riots, violence, or bloodshed. He hoped to encourage and guide a mass campaign to meet the problems of race in instances where there did not already exist "some organized program seeking to achieve the democratic rights for the Negro people." Not only did Negroes "believe in their right of equality, economic, political, racial, and social," Randolph noted, but "they are determined to struggle to achieve it." With proper discipline and training, he concluded, nonviolent goodwill direct action would create "morally and spiritually" resilient demonstrators "prepared to press the cause for civil and democratic rights" without resorting to the "violent language or violent action" characteristic of segregationists.[19]

For Randolph, the concept of nonviolent civil disobedience followed a very specific model of protest. In addition to repeated references to Gandhi, who, in Randolph's view, initiated "the greatest resistance the British Empire ever experienced," Randolph fell back on his religious upbringing to explain that "freedom is borne of struggle which strikes at oppression rather than at oppressors." Despite his having seemingly shed the religious upbringing of his childhood, Randolph nonetheless punctuated his statements on noncompliance with the military draft with encouragements to "never forget that the greatest resistance Rome ever felt was in the quiet suffering of a man who never forsook principles and whose cross is still a symbol of victory." Randolph hoped that such references to the life, suffering, and ultimate victory of Christ over his enemies would give his program for protesting segregation an unassailable moral credibility. He counseled young African Americans who approached him about registering for the draft or entering the armed services to consider the incongruity of Jim Crow in the military. He warned that "men cannot struggle for the freedom of others in the same battle in which they fasten semi-slavery more securely upon themselves." In a statement advising noncompliance following the passage of draft legislation in 1948, Randolph maintained that while critics may distinguish between segregation and slavery, "second-class citizenship is a form of slavery." He wondered "how it is possible for a slave to fight for freedom." Randolph believed that men of conscience should not enter the army because "no segregated institution is capable of achieving freedom."[20]

Following his testimony before the Armed Services Committee in March 1948, Randolph moved to implement his program of civil disobedience by counseling, aiding, and abetting "youth both white and Negro to quarantine any Jim Crow conscription system whether it bear the label of universal military training or selective service." In a pledge devised to recruit those prepared to demonstrate against segregation in the military, he observed that "civil disobedience is not new" nor was it "a strange thing to America." Randolph cited historical examples such as the Boston Tea Party that preceded the Revolutionary War and the Underground Railroad that smuggled slaves out of the South in "direct violation of the fugitive slave law," in framing his pledge of civil disobedience. He argued that "a Jim Crow draft would violate the American ideals of equality and justice to such a degree that it is the duty of the people to maintain those ideals in spite of the law by refusing to register under a Jim Crow draft until racial segregation and discrimination are outlawed by congressional action or executive order." Though proponents of segregation might respond with intimidation and mass arrests, Randolph resolved that if the masses "act together now and make it known that they will not submit to a Jim Crow draft, the government will be forced to listen." If the nation was to be "spared the shame and humiliation of army segregation," Randolph's pledge concluded, African Americans especially "must be prepared to act with dignity and without violence" and to "stir the conscience of America" by not participating in any Jim Crow military service or training.[21]

Organizing his protest campaign into the League for Non-Violent Civil Disobedience Against Military Segregation, Randolph and the Committee Against Jim Crow in Military Service and Training explained the need for such a campaign by arguing that "no subject people have ever become free except through suffering." They contended that to overturn racial segregation in military service and training, freedom-loving citizens had to be willing "to accept punishment, prison, and even death for the cause without bitterness and contention." Because "freedom does not fall like rain from heaven nor is it served up on a platter like fried chicken," Randolph asserted, it must be "purchased at the high price of long suffering and sacrifices." Responding to charges that encouraging such resistance to military service amounted to treason, Randolph countered that the actual "aim and result" of the campaign was to demand unequivocally that the government "live up to its ideals and professions" of freedom and justice for all. "Unalterably opposed" to segregation in all facets of American life, Randolph pointed to clear "tactical and strategic reasons" for concentrating on segregated military service "as a means to eradicate Jim Crow widely." First, African Americans were understandably "more emotionally aroused" about segregation in the army "than by any other single issue." Every black family had been "crushed" by the impact of military segregation "through the intense humiliation of their husbands, sons, brothers, and sisters in the armed forces."[22]

Though not everyone shared Randolph's "faith in the efficacy of a civil disobedience campaign," the underlying intention of Randolph's program seemed to strike a chord with a great many African Americans. Walter White voiced his support in a commentary on Randolph's statement before the Armed Services Committee. He wrote that while most African Americans accepted the proposition that "Negro Americans must willingly share the burdens as well as the benefits of citizenship," they "emphatically" believed "that the disproportion between the burdens and benefits of democracy to the Negro has too long endured." Because of such racial practices as military segregation, White continued, the "United States is tobogganing downward at a perilous rate." White felt that "Mr. Randolph's blunt threat to lead a non-violent campaign of civil disobedience . . . points up in dramatic fashion the necessity for the United States to muster courage enough to face and solve this problem."[23] White's viewpoints also reflected the broad support Randolph's campaign had garnered among African Americans. According to a NAACP survey of approximately 2,200 African American college students from twenty-six campuses, draft-age African Americans widely supported Randolph's campaign of civil disobedience. When asked whether they would be willing to serve in the military "in case of a real war emergency," slightly more than half of those surveyed said they would serve "only if segregation is abolished."[24]

Despite the clear connection between the mass action component of the March on Washington Movement and the campaign led by the Committee Against Jim Crow in Military Service and Training, Randolph's conception of civil disobedience marked a significant development in his position on civil rights protest. Never a proponent of "planned violence as a method of social change," Randolph's theme of nonviolence figured much more prominently in the articulation of his program of noncompliance with the draft than it ever did with respect to mass action and the threatened 1941 March on Washington.[25] In fact, Randolph understood quite clearly that the very success of the proposed 1941 protest march was related to the potential eruption of racial violence in the nation's capital. Though he "sternly" counseled potential marchers "against violence and ill-considered and intemperate action," he nonetheless called upon African Americans to organize and coordinate "their mass power" to "shake up official Washington" and force Roosevelt to issue an executive order against racial discrimination. He argued that "if American democracy will not insure equality of opportunity, freedom, and justice to its citizens, black and white, it is a hollow mockery and belies the principles for which it is supposed to stand."[26] Though he continued to hammer this same theme in challenging segregation in the armed forces, Randolph's postwar civil disobedience campaign placed equal emphasis on the notion that "freedom is borne of struggle which strikes at oppression rather than at oppressors."[27]

When the opportunity arose in March 1948 for Randolph to meet with President Truman to discuss the desegregation issue, he came prepared to recount his experience in traveling around the country "discussing the question of discrimination against Negroes in the armed services." Reflecting back on the details of this meeting, Randolph recalled that he told the president "that black Americans today are in no mood to shoulder a gun again in defense of this country so long as they are not full-fledged citizens of the country and recognized as such in the armed services." Though he assured the president that this assertion was not intended as "a threat," Randolph stressed that his comment "was a definite statement . . . on the mood of Negroes throughout the nation with respect to the manner in which they were treated in the armed forces." Well aware of the fact "that they have fought and died in every war of this nation," Randolph continued, African Americans wanted "to fight as free men in a free army in a free country." Negroes, Randolph forthrightly asserted, "are insisting upon the total abolition of discrimination in the armed forces."[28]

Truman's response to Randolph's presentation was disturbing because, as Randolph recalled, the president "sort of drew himself up quickly" and stated somewhat ominously that he wished that Randolph "hadn't made that statement." Randolph described that Charles H. Houston, lead council for the NAACP in the 1930s, sensed the president's rising ire and stepped in to encourage him to finish listening to what Randolph had to say. As Randolph put it, Houston persuaded the president to hear him out by arguing that Truman "ought to be happy" to meet with someone like Randolph, who had the "courage" to come to the White House and speak truthfully about the situation. "You can never tell what might take place in the hearts and minds of people oppressed such as Negroes are," Houston said, "when they know that they have fought in every war for their country and are still Jim Crowed in the United States Army." The president, Randolph recollected, "was visibly affected by this statement by Mr. Houston" and bade Randolph to continue. This invitation opened the way for him to recount further examples in which racial discrimination in the military undermined American democratic principles and, with Houston's support, to convince Truman to issue an executive order abolishing discrimination in the armed forces. Though it would take years and another threatened protest demonstration to secure the practical implementation of Truman's directive, Randolph's Committee Against Jim Crow in Military Service and Training and his civil disobedience campaign succeeded in overturning the racial status quo in the military.

This brief case history of the Committee Against Jim Crow in Military Service and Training and Randolph's civil disobedience campaign provides a basis for examining the more general antidiscrimination position that Randolph continued to develop in the 1950s and beyond. Specifically he came to the view that all citizens regardless of color were entitled to certain basic rights that the government could act to protect but not nullify.[29] Throughout the 1950s and 1960s, Randolph steadfastly maintained that "while the state cannot bestow civil rights upon the individual, the state or organized society must, through law, legislation, executive orders, ordinances and court decisions, give recognition to the civil rights of an individual in order that they may have force and factuality." "Civil rights," Randolph maintained, are as much the "original property and inevitable attribute of the individual as is life." Without the sure guarantee of such rights, "recognized and sanctioned by the state," life for the individual became immensely "uncertain and insecure."[30] As the modern civil rights movement began to take on more distinct shape in these years, Randolph's discussion of the nature and meaning of real democracy and civil rights took on a broader perspective.

In a 1951 essay titled "Problems of Peace and Democracy" exploring the "three great world movements that shake and challenge our old equilibrium and system of ideas," Randolph elaborated on his view of the "meaning, purpose, and practice of democracy." Arguing that it is "a body of common purposes which transcend narrow interests of class, creed, color, or country," he defined democracy's key characteristics as valuing individual worth, equality, freedom, and the rule of law. Contending that "every human being is precious in his own right," Randolph insisted that the "purpose and measure" of the institutions, relationships, and doctrines intrinsic to democracy were determined by the degree to which they provided for the "protection and full development" of individuals. Moreover, he pointed out that since "all men, though differing in talents, should be equal before the law and in moral order," genuine democracy recognized "no races, castes, or orders commissioned by God or qualified by their own attributes to exploit, govern, or enslave their fellow human beings." Randolph believed that the essential nature of democracy involved protecting individuals' "God-given" right to pursue without interference, proscription, or oppression from the state or other elements of society the full desires of their hearts.

In terms of the interests of minority groups, Randolph argued that such injunctions should apply with equal force. "Within the framework of democratic principles," he claimed, "cultural and political minorities should be accepted, regarded, and valued as creative forces of history." All men, regardless of race, creed, color, or national origin, should be able to "participate actively in selecting leaders, in shaping the laws, and in discharging the responsibilities of government." This is what Randolph understood as the very essence of open, participatory democracy. The rule of law, he maintained, was "the indispensable guardian of freedom." All individuals, particularly racial and ethnic minorities, "should be protected in their rights and liberties" against the passion of mobs, the tyranny of police, and the arbitrary invasions of government. He asserted that when Americans "blithely" countenanced the "denial" of justice, freedom, and political, economic, and social equality to any citizen, the nation appeared as nothing more than "a sounding brass and tinkling cymbal to the world."[31]

This conception of democracy fit neatly with the understanding of social justice that Randolph and Frank Crosswaith first articulated in the 1930s. By the 1940s, Randolph was arguing even more forcefully that genuine social justice required fair and unequivocal access to society's social, political, and economic benefits for all. And, his outline of democracy's obligations to safeguard every individual's fundamental human rights and to afford each individual a reasonable opportunity to develop to his or her full potential certainly complemented this notion. His ideas about social justice were just as influential in shaping his critique of American democracy as they were in defining philosophically his quest for fair employment and desegregating the military. As he explained in a 1950s high school commencement address in

Huntington, West Virginia, titled "The Spirit of Human Rights," all citizens "must realize and act upon the social fact that America does not belong to any particular race," but rather it belongs to all "who fought to take it from British parents, worked to build it, bled and died to save it from enemies within and without." To preserve American democracy, therefore, every citizen "must fight for equality, social equality, economic equality, political equality, racial equality." All "policies and programs and practices that reflect racism in the light of the aforementioned philosophy of democracy," he proclaimed, "are incompatible and at variance with the democratic creed."[32]

In the years following the U.S. Supreme Court's 1954 *Brown* decision, years in which civil rights proponents began to implement the nonviolent direct action tactics that he helped to pioneer, Randolph refined his critique of racial discrimination in the context of American democracy. In an essay titled "Challenge to Complete an Uncompleted Revolution for Full Freedom," he wrote that "the Negro is the basic test of our democracy." He explained that "the manner in which the United States measures up to its responsibility of bringing the Negro and other minorities into the orbit of full citizenship equality is the test of the qualitative character, worth, and value of our democratic system." This assessment took on even greater significance for Randolph as Cold War tensions rose with the Soviet Union. Unless and until the problem of full citizenship for racial and ethnic minorities "is courageously faced and solved," he argued, "the United States cannot be recognized as a real and valid democracy"; it cannot "assume the moral leadership of the democratic forces of the world." He claimed that any candid assessment of the treatment of Negroes in America must recognize that "the manner in which the Negro fares as a man, as a citizen, as a worker, as a consumer, within the framework of our democratic society" will substantially determine the outcome of "the great contest" between freedom and totalitarianism for "the hearts and minds of men" in the developing world. He concluded that the influence of this "precept and example" would be without a doubt "the most decisive factor" in shaping international impressions of the United States.[33]

In a similar fashion, Randolph's effort to define the nature of civil rights and civil liberties drew additional attention to his contention that equal justice for African Americans was central to the health of American democracy. In a mid-1950s essay titled "Crisis of Struggle for Civil Rights and Civil Liberties" and a 1955 Philadelphia address commemorating Civil Rights Day, he warned that "better race relations will never possess reality and integrity" until they were firmly rooted "in the soil of the brotherhood of man." Such a condition was "unattainable" without a fundamental recognition and acceptance of "the principle of human and racial equality." Without equality that embraced all regardless of race, color, or country, "there can be no human freedom and without human freedom there can be no human justice and progress." Racial discrimination fundamentally undercut freedom and justice by denying "the concept of the worth and sacredness of the human personality first given expression, meaning, and validity by the Judeo-Christian ethic." Only when African Americans experienced full equality, Randolph concluded, will the nation "truly have a democracy."[34]

Though Randolph's 1950s examination of American democracy was not inherently different from much of his *Messenger* commentary of the 1920s on the shortcomings of American racial policies, when coupled with his fully formed ideas about social justice it becomes an important framework for understanding the civil rights expectations of the next generation of civil rights activists.[35] Just as the 1963 March on Washington revived core ideas from Randolph's 1941 March on Washington Movement and the Committee Against Jim Crow in Military Service and Training, subsequent demands for civil and social rights were rooted in notions of genuine social justice and democracy put forward by Randolph in the 1940s and 1950s. Certainly the basic goals of Martin Luther King's 1968 Poor People's Campaign, which set out to confront economic problems not addressed by civil rights reform, recalled Randolph's long-standing demand for economic as well as social justice. Not only did Randolph's mass action protest tactics become the principal model for later civil rights initiatives, but his central beliefs about the inseparability of economic, civil, and social justice also helped to shape a good bit of the philosophical foundation of the civil rights agenda of the 1960s.

Considering his understanding of the requirements of genuine social justice, the connection between issues of race and class, American interest group politics, and the political potential of nonviolent direct action, Randolph's contribution to the development of the modern civil rights movements is unmatched. Despite other avenues of protest like the NAACP's legal efforts to overturn the doctrine of separate but equal and numerous individual initiatives conducted locally across the country, the specific ways in which Randolph conceived of these basic beliefs and their fundamental intersection with each other shaped both the philosophical foundation for subsequent civil rights demonstrations and African Americans' expectations for a better future. Certainly the specific combination of ideas that first came together in initiating the fair employment fight and were further refined with the campaign to desegregate the armed forces directly determined the course of black civil rights protests in the mid-1950s and beyond. Hence, Bayard Rustin's 1969 reflections on the impact of Randolph's life and career are indeed correct in explaining Randolph's ultimate historical legacy. In recapping A. Philip Randolph's life and career, Rustin praised his long-time mentor for effectively and consistently challenging Americans "to build, through means that are democratic and non-violent, a just society in which all men need not fear poverty and in which men of all races, graced with the dignity that comes from a full life, need not fear each other." As Rustin explained, in no other way can America "at last become a nation that is at peace with itself."[36]

Notes

Introduction

1. Sitkoff, *Struggle for Black Equality,* pp. 147–50; "No Easy Walk," *Eyes on the Prize: America's Civil Rights Movement,* DVD, Blackside Productions (1987; Boston: PBS Home Video, 1990).

2. Fairclough, *To Redeem the Soul,* pp. 150–53; Podair, *Bayard Rustin,* pp. 52–53, Sitkoff, *Struggle for Black Equality,* p. 147.

3. A. Philip Randolph, Address by A. Philip Randolph on Civil Rights and the Negro at Orchestra Hall, Chicago, 17 May 1956, "Speeches 1955–58," box 2, A. Philip Randolph Collection, Schomburg Center for Research in Black Culture, New York (hereafter Randolph Collection, Schomburg).

4. Hall, "Long Civil Rights Movement," pp. 1245–46.

5. Sitkoff, *Struggle for Black Equality,* pp. 147–48.

Chapter 1: A. Philip Randolph,
Racial Identity, and Family Relations

1. Mason, *African-American Life,* p. 19.

2. A. Philip Randolph, "Vita," Vita, box 41, A. Philip Randolph Collection, Library of Congress, Washington, D.C. (hereafter Randolph Collection, LC); A. Philip Randolph, Outline—Autobiography, 4, box 42, Randolph Collection, LC; Crooks, *Jacksonville after the Fire,* pp. 13–14.

3. Randolph, Vita; Randolph, Outline—Autobiography.

4. A. Philip Randolph, Interview with John Slawson, 20 April 1970, 2, box 42, Randolph Collection, LC; Randolph, Vita.

5. Randolph, Vita.

6. Tolnay and Beck, *Festival of Violence,* pp. 17, 29; Beck and Tolnay, "When Race Didn't Matter," p. 133; Litwack, *Trouble in Mind,* pp. 218–19; Perman, *Struggle for Mastery,* pp. 245–47, 268–69.

7. Randolph, Vita; Randolph, Outline—Autobiography.

8. Mark Schultz, *Rural Face of White Supremacy,* pp. 5–7; Litwack, *Trouble in Mind,* pp. xiv, 7; Brown and Webb, *Race in the American South,* pp. 180–81.

9. Interview with A. Philip Randolph, reel 1, 5, box 43, Randolph Collection, LC; Randolph, Vita; A. Philip Randolph (untitled), 6, box 42, Randolph Collection, LC.

10. Moses, *Creative Conflict in African American Thought.*

11. Interview with Randolph, reel 1; Randolph, Vita.

12. Randolph, Vita; A. Philip Randolph: Agitator, 2, box 42, Randolph Collection, LC.

13. Randolph, Vita.

14. Ibid.; Randolph, Outline—Autobiography.

15. Randolph, Vita.

16. Ibid.

17. Little, *Disciples of Liberty,* p. 3; Rivers and Brown, *Laborers in the Vineyard,* p. 34.

18. Williams, *Christian Recorder,* pp. 12–16; Washburn, *African American Newspaper,* pp. 74–75.

19. Interview with Randolph, reel 1; Randolph, Vita.

20. Randolph, Vita; Randolph: Agitator.

21. Ann Douglas concisely describes the evolution of a "new breed of race ideologues" in the 1890s that shaped a "newly empowered, vigilant, and aggressive white nativism," which "had a crucial and complex effect on America's black population" (*Terrible Honesty,* pp. 305–6).

22. Tolnay and Beck, *Festival of Violence,* pp. 75–76; Litwack, *Trouble in Mind,* pp. 72–73; Brown and Webb, *Race in the American South,* pp. 173–74.

23. Randolph, Vita; Randolph: Agitator.

24. A. Philip Randolph (untitled), 6, box 42, Randolph Collection, LC.

25. Ibid.

26. Randolph, Vita; Randolph, Outline—Autobiography; Anderson, *A. Philip Randolph,* p. 29; Kersten, *A. Philip Randolph,* p. 1.

27. Randolph, Vita.

28. Godshalk, *Veiled Visions,* pp. 25–26, 30–31; Mixon, *Atlanta Riot,* pp. 41, 85–87; Senechal, *Sociogenesis of a Race Riot,* p. 125.

29. Randolph, Vita.

30. Crooks, *Jacksonville after the Fire,* pp. 85–92.

31. Interview with Randolph, reel 1; Randolph, Vita.

32. Interview with Randolph, reel 1; A. Philip Randolph to Paula Pfeffer, 29 September 1972, 5, box 42, Randolph Collection, LC.

33. Randolph, Vita.

34. Interview with Randolph, reel 1; Randolph, Vita.

35. Interview with Randolph, reel 1; Randolph, Vita.

36. Interview with Randolph, reel 1; Randolph, Vita.

37. Interview with Randolph, reel 1; Randolph, Vita.

38. Godshalk, *Veiled Visions,* p. 19; Mixon, *Atlanta Riot,* p. 39; Senechal, *Sociogenesis of a Race Riot,* p. 62.

39. Interview with Randolph, reel 1; Randolph, Vita.

40. Litwack, *Trouble in Mind,* p. 115.

41. Randolph, Vita.

42. Randolph: Agitator; Interview with Randolph, reel 1; Randolph, Vita.

43. Interview with Randolph, reel 1; Randolph, Vita.

44. Randolph, Vita.

45. Ibid.; Randolph, Outline—Autobiography.

46. Randolph, Vita.

47. Ibid.

48. Ibid.

49. Ibid.

50. Hunter, "'Work That Body,'" p. 74.

51. A. Philip Randolph (untitled), 2, box 42, Randolph Collection, LC; Randolph, Vita.

52. Randolph to Pfeffer; Randolph, Vita.

53. Randolph, Vita.

54. Randolph, Interview with John Slawson; Randolph, Vita.

55. Randolph, Outline—Autobiography; Randolph, Vita.

56. Randolph, Vita.

57. Interview with Randolph, reel 1.

58. Leon F. Litwack succinctly examines the role that African American churches played in facilitating black education in the South following Reconstruction (*Trouble in Mind,* pp. 62–63); Crooks, *Jacksonville after the Fire,* pp. 91–92.

59. Randolph, Outline—Autobiography; A. Philip Randolph to Carl Hermann Voss, 18 April 1974, 3, box 42, Randolph Collection, LC; Interview with Randolph, reel 1.

60. Arnesen, *Brotherhoods of Color,* pp. 7–13.

61. Interview with Randolph, reel 1.

62. Randolph, Outline—Autobiography; Interview with Randolph, reel 1.

Chapter 2: Religious Faith and Black Empowerment

1. Anderson, *A. Philip Randolph,* pp. 39–41.

2. Angell, *Bishop Henry McNeal Turner,* pp. 25–26; Taylor, *A. Philip Randolph,* p. 7.

3. Randolph, Vita.

4. Paris, *Social Teachings of the Black Churches,* pp. 10–11; Little, *Disciples of Liberty,* pp. xii, 64.

5. Randolph, Vita.

6. Walker, *Rock in a Weary Land,* pp. 7–9; George, *Segregated Sabbaths,* p. 50.

7. Angell, *Bishop Henry McNeal Turner,* p. 26.

8. Du Bois, *Philadelphia Negro,* p. 20; Campbell, *Songs of Zion,* pp. 9–10.

9. Hershberg, "Free Blacks in Antebellum Philadelphia," p. 135.

10. Gregg, *Sparks from the Anvil,* p. 2.

11. Anderson, *A. Philip Randolph,* pp. 39–41.

12. Paris, *Social Teachings of the Black Churches,* p. 9.

13. Elisha Weaver, "Suffrage for Our Oppressed Race," *Christian Recorder,* 1 July 1865, Wisconsin Historical Society, Madison (hereafter WHS).

14. Elisha Weaver, "The True Remedy for the Oppressed," *Christian Recorder,* 8 July 1865, WHS.

15. Campbell, *Songs of Zion,* pp. 86–87; Little, *Disciples of Liberty,* pp. 39–42; Williams, *Christian Recorder,* pp. 12–16.

16. Frazier, *Negro Church in America;* Mays, *Negro's God as Reflected;* Woodson, *History of the Negro Church;* Little, *Disciples of Liberty,* p. 64; George, *Segregated Sabbaths,* pp. 170–71.

17. Paris, *Social Teachings of the Black Churches,* pp. 10–11.

18. Benjamin Tucker Tanner, "The Democratic Platform," *Christian Recorder,* 12 July 1876, WHS.

19. Benjamin Tucker Tanner, "Our Opportunity," *Christian Recorder,* 6 September 1877, WHS.

20. Angell and Pinn, *Social Protest Thought,* pp. xv, 1–2.

21. Benjamin Tucker Tanner, "Our Hope! What?" *Christian Recorder,* 12 October 1876, WHS.

22. Sernett, *Black Religion and American Evangelicalism,* p. 74; Paris, *Social Teachings of the Black Churches,* p. 6; Angell and Pinn, *Social Protest Thought,* pp. 131–32.

23. Benjamin Tucker Tanner, "The Present and Future," *Christian Recorder,* 4 January 1877, WHS.

24. A. Philip Randolph (untitled), 6, box 42, Randolph Collection, LC.

25. Randolph, Vita.

26. Taylor, *A. Philip Randolph,* p. 36.

27. Benjamin Tucker Tanner, "Americans: Not Negroes," *Christian Recorder,* 14 March 1878, WHS.

28. A. Philip Randolph (untitled), 6, box 42, Randolph Collection, LC; Randolph: Agitator.

29. Little, *Disciples of Liberty,* pp. 63–65; Pinn, *Moral Evil and Redemptive Suffering,* pp. 12–17.

30. Tanner, "Present and Future."

31. Benjamin Tucker Tanner, "Where Responsibility Comes In," *Christian Recorder,* 5 October 1876, WHS.

32. Cyrus J. Marshall, "What We Must Do," *Christian Recorder,* 2 August 1877, WHS.

33. Benjamin Tucker Tanner, "No Aid to the Enemy," *Christian Recorder,* 21 February 1878, WHS.

34. Randolph, Vita.

35. Richard Allen Hildebrand to A. Philip Randolph, 13 January 1958, 1, box 4, Randolph Collection, LC.

36. Fry and Kurz, *Washington Gladden as a Preacher,* pp. 14–16.

37. Hopkins, *Rise of the Social Gospel,* p. 19.

38. May, *Protestant Churches and Industrial America,* p. 85.

39. Visser 't Hooft, *Background of the Social Gospel,* p. 16.

40. Zunz, *Why the American Century?* pp. 26–45.

41. Little, *Disciples of Liberty,* p. 13; Angell and Pinn, *Social Protest Thought,* pp. 310–12.

42. Rader, *Academic Mind and Reform,* p. 35; Curtis, *Consuming Faith,* pp. 16, 44–46.

43. Hopkins, *Rise of the Social Gospel,* p. 33.

44. Curtis, *Consuming Faith,* p. 46.

45. Taylor, *A. Philip Randolph,* p. 50; Anderson, *A. Philip Randolph,* p. 73.

46. Frank R. Crosswaith, "The Negro at the Crossroads," 5, box 2, Frank R. Crosswaith Papers, Schomburg Center (hereafter Crosswaith Collection, Schomburg).

47. Linden Lewis, "Richard B. Moore," pp. 592–93.

48. W. A. Domingo, "Socialism: The Negroes' Hope," *Messenger,* July 1919, Alderman Library, University of Virginia (hereafter Ald-UVa).

49. Paris, *Social Teachings of the Black Churches,* pp. 10–11; Williams, *Christian Recorder,* pp. 12–16.

50. Foner, *American Socialism and Black Americans,* pp. 84–86.

51. Taylor, *A. Philip Randolph,* p. 50.

52. Ransom, *Pilgrimage of Harriet Ransom's Son,* p. 33; Wills, "Reverdy C. Ransom," pp. 187–88; Goddard, "Black Social Gospel in Chicago," p. 232.

53. Morris, *Reverdy C. Ransom,* p. 33.

54. Elizabeth Lasch-Quinn explains that "the black church has historically combined functions as diverse as daycare, welfare, employment counseling, education, entertainment, and social activism" (*Black Neighbors,* p. 47); in effect the black church was a settlement house before the settlement house movement ever existed. Ransom's application of the social gospel in founding Institutional Church and Social Settlement expanded the purpose of the church's traditional program. He saw the social gospel and social science as important tools for improving African American lives, and he believed that by using them effectively African Americans could also demonstrate their ability to adapt to modern industrial society.

55. Reverdy C. Ransom, "Social Settlements," *Christian Recorder,* 19 July 1900, WHS.

56. Reverdy C. Ransom, "The Institutional Church and Social Settlement," *Christian Recorder,* 29 November 1900, WHS.

57. Spear, *Black Chicago,* pp. 95–96; Luker, "Missions, Institutional Churches, and Settlement Houses," pp. 102–4.

58. Benjamin Tucker Tanner, "Cooperative Association," *Christian Recorder,* 2 April 1877, WHS; Du Bois, *Philadelphia Negro,* pp. 392–93.

59. Randolph, Vita.

60. Judith Weisenfeld focuses on African American women's role in transforming the Harlem YWCA into a "venue for religious work and for community activism that defied narrow definitions of 'religious' and 'secular' and yet upheld the black church tradition of religiously grounded social engagement" ("Harlem YWCA," p. 63). Her discussion, however, also sheds light on the philosophical and organizational contributions Ransom and his wife, Emma, made to this effort.

61. Randolph, Vita; Randolph, Outline—Autobiography; Anderson, *A. Philip Randolph,* pp. 57–60.

62. U.S. Department of Commerce, *Negroes in the United States, 1920–32,* p. 543.

63. Walker, *Rock in a Weary Land,* pp. 64–65.

64. Rivers and Brown, *Laborers in the Vineyard of the Lord,* pp. 45–49.

65. Sernett, *Black Religion and American Evangelicalism,* pp. 48–51.

66. Walker, *Rock in a Weary Land,* pp. 75–77.

67. U.S. Department of Commerce, *Negroes in the United States, 1920–32,* p. 543.

68. A. Philip Randolph (untitled), 6, box 42, Randolph Collection, LC.

Chapter 3: Black Radicalism in Harlem

1. Randolph, Outline—Autobiography; Randolph, Vita.

2. Lowry, *Her Dream of Dreams,* pp. 429–30; Watson, *Harlem Renaissance,* pp. 4–5; David Levering Lewis, *When Harlem Was in Vogue,* pp. 105, 166.

3. Sacks, *Before Harlem,* pp. 187–92.

4. Foner, *American Socialism and Black Americans,* pp. 211–14; Perry, *Hubert Harrison Reader,* p. 52.

5. Randolph, Vita.

6. Marable, *W. E. B. Du Bois,* pp. 89–91.

7. Randolph, Outline—Autobiography; Randolph, Vita.

8. Gaines, *Uplifting the Race,* pp. 236–37; Trotter, *Black Milwaukee,* pp. 44–45.

9. Interview with Randolph, reel 1.

10. Ibid.; Ernest Boynton, "Elder Statesman of Civil Rights," *City College Alumnus* 65, no. 5 (March 1970), City College of the City University of New York; "Negroes' Leader a Man of Dignity," *New York Times,* 29 August 1963, A. Philip Randolph File,

Ex. 19, Morris Raphael Cohen Library, City College of the City University of New York (hereafter CL-CUNY).

11. Earl Lewis, "Expectations, Economic Opportunities, and Life," pp. 24–25.

12. Randolph, Outline—Autobiography; Randolph, Vita.

13. Randolph, Vita.

14. Randolph, Outline—Autobiography; Anderson, *A. Philip Randolph*, pp. 56–57; Kersten, *A. Philip Randolph*, pp. 12–13; Calvin Craig Miller, *A. Philip Randolph*, pp. 31–32.

15. James N. Gregory, *Southern Diaspora*, pp. 23–24; Lowry, *Her Dream of Dreams*, p. 369.

16. Philpott, *Slum and the Ghetto*, p. 119; Trotter, *Black Milwaukee*, pp. 9–13.

17. Kusmer, *Ghetto Takes Shape*; Osofsky, *Harlem*; Spear, *Black Chicago*; Trotter, *Black Milwaukee*.

18. Anderson, *This Was Harlem*, pp. 49–50; James N. Gregory, *Southern Diaspora*, pp. 125–26; Watson, *Harlem Renaissance*, pp. 11–13; Kornweibel, *No Crystal Stair*, pp. 43–44.

19. Douglas, *Terrible Honesty*, pp. 303–4.

20. Meier and Rudwick, *From Plantation to Ghetto*, p. 243.

21. Steven Gregory, *Black Corona*, pp. 24–25.

22. Osofsky, *Harlem*, pp. 78, 88–90; Douglas, *Terrible Honesty*, pp. 310–12.

23. Jones, *Conquering Gotham*, p. 89.

24. Steven Gregory, *Black Corona*, pp. 24–25.

25. Anderson, *This Was Harlem*, pp. 43–45.

26. James N. Gregory, *Southern Diaspora*, pp. 119–20.

27. Boynton, "Elder Statesman of Civil Rights."

28. Gaines, *Uplifting the Race*, pp. 236–37.

29. Cohen, *Making a New Deal*, pp. 261–67; Baldwin, *Chicago's New Negroes*, p. 16; A. Philip Randolph to Henry Williams, 31 October 1972, 3, box 42, Randolph Collection, LC; Turner, *Caribbean Crusaders*, p. 27; Foner, *American Socialism and Black Americans*, pp. 265–66.

30. Foner, *American Socialism and Black Americans*, pp. 207–10; Richard B. Moore, "Afro-Americans and Radical Politics," 7, box 9, Richard B. Moore Collection, Schomburg Center (hereafter Moore Collection, Schomburg); Turner, *Caribbean Crusaders*, pp. 15–17.

31. Henry, "Black Political Tradition," p. 456; Linden Lewis, "Richard B. Moore," pp. 593–94.

32. Gaines, *Uplifting the Race*, pp. 241–42.

33. Kusmer, *Ghetto Takes Shape*, p. 248; Sacks, *Before Harlem*, pp. 194–96; Turner, *Caribbean Crusaders*, pp. 124–25.

34. A. Philip Randolph, "A New Crowd—A New Negro," *Messenger*, May–June 1919, Ald-UVa.

35. Frank R. Crosswaith, "To the Negro Members of the I.L.G.W.U.," 2, box 2, Crosswaith Collection, Schomburg.

36. Frank R. Crosswaith, "The Negro Press," 2, box 2, Crosswaith Collection, Schomburg.

37. Perry, *Hubert Harrison Reader,* p. 52; Foner, *American Socialism and Black Americans,* p. 210.

38. Frank R. Crosswaith, "The Negro at the Crossroads," 5, box 2, Crosswaith Collection, Schomburg.

39. Ibid.

40. A. Philip Randolph, Text of Address Given by A. Philip Randolph, International President of the Brotherhood of Sleeping Car Porters, at the Union United Church, "Speeches 1955–58," box 2, Randolph Collection, Schomburg.

41. A. Philip Randolph, Statement to Educational Political Conference in Chicago, at the International House, "Speeches ND," box 2, Randolph Collection, Schomburg.

42. Foner, *American Socialism and Black Americans,* p. 210.

43. Ibid., pp. 265–66.

44. Randolph to Williams.

45. Ferguson, *Sage of Sugar Hill,* p. 68.

46. Interview with Randolph, reel 1; Anderson, *A. Philip Randolph,* p. 56; Kersten, *A. Philip Randolph,* p. 10.

47. Marcy S. Sacks describes the important role of social outreach programs sponsored by African American churches in Harlem during the migration years (*Before Harlem,* pp. 182–85).

48. Randolph, Vita.

49. Randolph, Outline—Autobiography; Anderson, *A. Philip Randolph,* pp. 57–60; David Levering Lewis, *When Harlem Was in Vogue,* pp. 75–78.

50. Who's Who in Labor, 6, box 42, Randolph Collection, LC; Randolph, Outline—Autobiography; Randolph, Interview with John Slawson; Press Release from the Brotherhood of Sleeping Car Porters, 13 April 1962, 8, box 1, Randolph Collection, LC; Anderson, *A. Philip Randolph,* pp. 69–73; David Levering Lewis, *When Harlem Was in Vogue,* pp. 110–11.

51. Ferguson, *Sage of Sugar Hill,* p. 139.

52. A. Philip Randolph to Melvin Yoken, 11 June 1971, 3, box 42, Randolph Collection, LC; Randolph, Outline—Autobiography; Anderson, *A. Philip Randolph,* pp. 73–75.

53. Gomez-Jefferson, *Sage of Tawawa,* pp. 56–57, 66–68; Foner, *American Socialism and Black Americans,* p. 85.

54. Reverdy C. Ransom, "The Negro and Socialism," *A.M.E. Church Review,* October 1896, rpt. in Pinn, *Making the Gospel Plain;* Weisenfeld, "Harlem YWCA," p. 63.

55. Henry, "Black Political Tradition," pp. 456–58; Perry, *Hubert Harrison Reader,* pp. 4–5; Foner, *American Socialism and Black Americans,* pp. 208, 266.

56. African-American Labor History Center Oral History Program, Interview with A. Philip Randolph, 6 June 1973, 3, box 42, Randolph Collection, Schomburg.

57. Foner, *American Socialism and Black Americans,* pp. 266–68; Moore, "Afro-Americans and Radical Politics."

58. Cary D. Wintz explains that Garvey was "overwhelmed by what he encountered in the United States." For Garvey, "the wealth of the country, the size and relative wealth of the African American community, the social and political turbulence (especially in the black community) unleashed by World War I and the accompanying black migration, and the divisions within African American leadership seemed a fertile ground for political organization" (*African American Political Thought,* p. 11).

59. African-American Labor History Center Oral History Program, Interview with A. Philip Randolph; Anderson, *A. Philip Randolph,* pp. 86–88; Ferguson, *Sage of Sugar Hill,* p. 38.

Chapter 4: Crossing the Color Line

1. Foner discusses the origins and evolution of the Intercollegiate Socialist Society and its impact on college students on both white and black college campuses (*American Socialism and Black Americans,* pp. 255–56); Weinstein, *Decline of Socialism,* pp. 75–76.

2. Melvyn Dubofsky succinctly outlines William Haywood's evolution from "hard-rock miner" to radical syndicalist in the years surrounding the beginning of the twentieth century (*Hard Work,* pp. 84, 89–90); Chace, *1912,* pp. 169–70.

3. Paul Delaney, "A. Philip Randolph, Rights Leader, Dies; President Leads Tribute," *New York Times,* 18 May 1979, A. Philip Randolph File, Ex. 19, CL-CUNY; Anderson, *A. Philip Randolph,* pp. 72–73.

4. Henry, "Black Political Tradition," pp. 456–58; Foner, *American Socialism and Black Americans,* p. 266.

5. Turner, *Caribbean Crusaders,* pp. 52–53; Perry, *Hubert Harrison Reader,* p. 52.

6. Delaney, "A. Philip Randolph."

7. Ibid.; Boynton, "Elder Statesman of Civil Rights."

8. Westmeyer, *History of American Higher Education,* p. 78.

9. Gorelick, *City College,* p. 63; Rudy, *College of the City of New York,* p. 33; Gettleman, *Elusive Presence,* pp. 149–50.

10. Gettleman, *Elusive Presence,* pp. 156–57.

11. Thomas and Vanderhoof, "Charles Eliot of Harvard," pp. 83–84; Hawkins, *Between Harvard and America,* pp. 89–91; Westmeyer, *History of American Higher Education,* pp. 114–16.

12. Gorelick, *City College,* p. 82.

13. Gettleman, *Elusive Presence,* p. 172.

14. Rudy, *College of the City of New York,* pp. 225–27.

15. Ibid., p. 235.

16. Friedman-Kasaba, *Memories of Migration*, p. 13; Gettleman, *Elusive Presence*, p. 162.

17. Rudy, *College of the City of New York*, p. 292.

18. Pritchett, *Brownville, Brooklyn*, pp. 18, 34–35.

19. Hollinger, *Morris R. Cohen*, pp. 77–79, 102–7.

20. Boynton, "Elder Statesman of Civil Rights."

21. Anderson, *A. Philip Randolph*, p. 65.

22. Randolph, Outline—Autobiography.

23. Harris, *Keeping the Faith*, p. 29; Howe, *Socialism and America*, pp. 42–44.

24. Interview with Randolph, reel 1.

25. Anderson, *A. Philip Randolph*, pp. 127–28.

26. Wintz, *African American Political Thought*, p. 15; Stein, *World of Marcus Garvey*, pp. 161–62; Foner, *American Socialism and Black Americans*, p. 329.

27. Marable, *W. E. B. Du Bois*, pp. 101–2; Stein, *World of Marcus Garvey*, pp. 50–51; Wintz, *African American Political Thought*, pp. 11–12.

28. Stein, *World of Marcus Garvey*, pp. 48–50; Wintz, *African American Political Thought*, pp. 11–13.

29. Randolph, Outline—Autobiography.

30. Interview with Randolph, reel 1; A. Philip Randolph (untitled), 5, box 42, Randolph Collection, LC.

31. Foner, *American Socialism and Black Americans*, pp. 270–71.

32. Interview with Randolph, reel 1.

33. Shannon, *Socialist Party of America*, pp. 21–25; Sally M. Miller, *Victor Berger*, pp. 10–13. Norma Fain Pratt details Hillquit's particular disdain for the Industrial Workers of the World (*Morris Hillquit*, pp. 99–100).

34. Shannon, *Socialist Party of America*, p. 3; Sally M. Miller, *Victor Berger*, p. 10.

35. A. Philip Randolph, Address by A. Philip Randolph at Reunion of Old Timers, 29 October 1955, "Speeches 1955," box 35, Randolph Collection, LC.

36. Pratt, *Morris Hillquit*, pp. 50–53; Sally M. Miller, *Victor Berger*, pp. 25–27.

37. Pratt, *Morris Hillquit*, pp. 55–57; Sally M. Miller, *Victor Berger*, pp. 30–31.

38. Moore, "Afro-Americans and Radical Politics"; Trotter, *Black Milwaukee*, p. 55.

39. "Negroes Organizing in Socialist Party," *Messenger*, July 1918, Ald-UVa; Randolph, Outline—Autobiography.

40. Salvatore, *Eugene V. Debs*, pp. 68–72; Tripp, *I. W. W. and the Paterson Silk Strike*, pp. 8–12; Weinstein, *Decline of Socialism*, pp. 10–12.

41. Weinstein, *Decline of Socialism*, pp. 93–103.

42. Randolph to Yoken; Randolph, Interview with John Slawson.

43. Du Bois, *Souls of Black Folk*, pp. 8–9, 151–54, 42–45.

44. Salvatore, *Eugene V. Debs*, pp. 68–79.

45. Eugene V. Debs, "Appeal to Negro Workers," 20, box 2, Moore Collection, Schomburg.

46. Ibid.

47. Ibid.

48. A. Philip Randolph and Chandler Owen, Letter to Lela Faye Secor, in "People's Council Invites Chandler Owen and A. Philip Randolph to Present Problem of Negroes at Convention," *Messenger*, November 1917, Ald-UVa.

49. Robin D. G. Kelley's description of the process by which black Alabamans found a "framework for understanding the roots of poverty and racism" but engaged communism largely on their own terms is also useful for understanding communism's appeal for West Indian radicals in Harlem (*Hammer and Hoe*, pp. 92–93). Though far more versed in Marxist ideology and much closer to the center of power in the American Communist Party than the subjects of Kelley's work, Briggs, Domingo, and Moore were as captivated by communism's apparent regard for the interests of ethnic and racial minorities as any black mill worker in Alabama.

50. Stephens, *Black Empire*, pp. 40–46; for a discussion of race, masculinity, and civil rights see Estes, *I Am a Man!* and Van Deburg, *New Day in Babylon*.

51. Interview with Randolph, reel 1.

52. Perry, *Hubert Harrison Reader*, p. 52; Kornweibel, *No Crystal Stair*, pp. 46–48.

53. Moore, "Afro-Americans and Radical Politics."

54. African-American Labor History Center Oral History Program, Interview with A. Philip Randolph.

55. Richard B. Moore, "Outline on the Negro Question," 4, box 6, Moore Collection, Schomburg.

56. Richard B. Moore, "History of Negro Liberation," 3, box 6, Moore Collection, Schomburg.

57. Naison, *Communists in Harlem*, p. 39.

58. Stein, *World of Marcus Garvey*, pp. 161–62.

59. Moore, "Outline on the Negro Question."

60. "Marcus Garvey!" *Messenger*, July 1922, Ald-UVa.

61. Marcus Garvey, "A Warning to the Enemy," *Negro World*, 5 August 1922, Humanities, Social Sciences, and Education Library Microfilm, Purdue University (hereafter HSSE).

62. Anderson, *A. Philip Randolph*, pp. 130–33.

63. Moore, "Afro-Americans and Radical Politics"; Turner, *Caribbean Crusader*, pp. 52–53.

64. Randolph, Outline—Autobiography.

65. Moore, "Afro-Americans and Radical Politics"; "Institute for Social Study," 2, box 8, Moore Collection, Schomburg.

66. "Institute for Social Study"; Turner, *Caribbean Crusader*, pp. 52–53.

67. A. Philip Randolph and Richard Parrish, Interview with John Seabrook, 1 May 1975, 3, box 42, Randolph Collection, LC.

68. "Negroes Organizing in Socialist Party," *Messenger*, July 1918, Ald-UVa.

69. "Negro Workers: The A.F. of L. or I.W.W.," *Messenger*, July 1919, Ald-UVa.

70. "Workmen's Council," *Messenger,* November 1917, Ald-UVa.

71. Turner, *Caribbean Crusaders,* pp. 51–52; Kornweibel, *No Crystal Stair,* p. 26.

72. Anderson, *A. Philip Randolph,* pp. 115–16.

73. "The Negro and the New Social Order," *Messenger,* March 1919, Ald-UVa.

74. "Negroes Organizing in Socialist Party."

75. "Negro Workers."

76. Weinstein, *Decline of Socialism,* pp. 114–15.

77. "Reasons Why White and Black Workers Should Combine in Labor Unions," *Messenger,* July 1919, Ald-UVa.

78. "Negro Workers."

79. Stein, *World of Marcus Garvey,* pp. 47–48.

80. David Levering Lewis, *When Harlem Was in Vogue,* pp. 35–39.

81. Wintz, *African American Political Thought,* p. 15.

82. "Negro Workers."

83. "The Negro Worker—A Menace to Radicalism," *Messenger,* May–June 1919, Ald-UVa.

Chapter 5: A New Crowd, A New Negro

1. Kornweibel, *No Crystal Stair,* pp. 274–75.

2. African-American Labor History Center Oral History Program, Interview with A. Philip Randolph.

3. Randolph and Parrish, Interview with Seabrook, Randolph Collection, LC.

4. Kornweibel, *No Crystal Stair,* p. 46.

5. Ibid., pp. 50–51.

6. "Making the World Safe for Democracy," *Messenger,* November 1917, Ald-UVa.

7. Randolph and Owen, Letter to Lela Faye Secor.

8. "The Hanging of the Negro Soldiers," *Messenger,* January 1918, Ald-UVa.

9. "Americanism," *Messenger,* September 1920, Ald-UVa.

10. "The Hun in America," *Messenger,* July 1919, Ald-UVa.

11. Frank R. Crosswaith, "The Negro at the Crossroads"; Randolph, "Statement to Educational Political Conference in Chicago, Illinois, at the International House," "Speeches ND," box 2, Randolph Collection, Schomburg.

12. Foner, *American Socialism and Black Americans,* pp. 281–82.

13. Randolph and Owen, Letter to Lela Faye Secor.

14. Ferguson, *Sage of Sugar Hill,* p. 68.

15. Wintz, *African American Political Thought,* p. 15.

16. Randolph to Yoken; Randolph, Outline—Autobiography; Anderson, *A. Philip Randolph,* pp. 73–75.

17. William N. Colson, "An Analysis of Negro Patriotism," *Messenger,* August 1919, Ald-UVa.

18. "How Germans Treated Negro Soldiers," *Messenger*, May–June 1919, Ald-UVa.

19. W. E. B. Du Bois, "Close Ranks," *Crisis*, July 1918, HSSE.

20. "American Lawlessness," *Messenger*, July 1918, Ald-UVa.

21. "Lynching: A Domestic Question," *Messenger*, July 1919, Ald-UVa.

22. "Pro-Germanism among Negroes," *Messenger*, July 1918, Ald-UVa.

23. "An Open Letter to the Union League Club of New York," *Messenger*, May–June 1919, Ald-UVa.

24. "Prof. Harry H. Jones—The Crisis in Negro Leadership," *Messenger*, April–May 1920, Ald-UVa.

25. "The Crisis of the Crisis," *Messenger*, July 1919, Ald-UVa.

26. "New Leadership for the Negro," *Messenger*, May–June 1919, Ald-UVa.

27. "The Negro in Public Utilities," *Messenger*, May–June 1919, Ald-UVa.

28. "A Reply to Congressman James F. Byrnes of South Carolina," *Messenger*, October 1919, Ald-UVa.

29. "Constitution Day—September 17th," *Messenger*, September 1919, Ald-UVa.

30. "Our Reason for Being," *Messenger*, August 1919, Ald-UVa.

31. Kornweibel, *No Crystal Stair*, p. 46.

32. Crosswaith, "To the Negro Members of the I.L.G.W.U."

33. "Aftermath of Exodus," *Messenger*, November 1923, Ald-UVa.

34. "Chas. W. Anderson," *Messenger*, April 1923, Ald-UVa.

35. "If We Must Die," *Messenger*, September 1919, Ald-UVa.

36. "Young Negro Dies like Man," *Messenger*, December 1919, Ald-UVa.

37. "The Hun in America," *Messenger*, July 1919, Ald-UVa.

38. "Thanksgiving," *Messenger*, December 1919, Ald-UVa.

39. A. Philip Randolph, "A New Crowd—A New Negro," *Messenger*, May–June 1919, Ald-UVa.

40. "How to Stop Lynching," *Messenger*, August 1919, Ald-UVa.

41. Stephens, *Black Empire*, p. 37.

42. "A Reply to Congressman James F. Byrnes of South Carolina."

43. "The Ku Klux Klan—How to Fight It," *Messenger*, November 1921, Ald-UVa.

44. "If We Must Die."

45. "Jacksonville Negroes Boycott Big White Insurance Company," *Messenger*, March 1920, Ald-UVa.

46. Randolph, "Statement to Educational Political Conference in Chicago, Illinois, at the International House"; Frank R. Crosswaith, Editorial, 20, box 3, Crosswaith Collection, Schomburg.

47. Randolph, "A New Crowd—A New Negro."

48. A. Philip Randolph, Socialism, 4, box 2, Randolph Collection, Schomburg.

49. "The New Negro Woman," *Messenger*, July 1923, Ald-UVa.

50. "The New Negro—What Is He?" *Messenger*, August 1920, Ald-UVa.

51. Gregory, *Southern Diaspora*, pp. 120–21.

52. Kusmer, *Ghetto Takes Shape*, p. 248.

53. Randolph, "A New Crowd—A New Negro."

54. A. Philip Randolph to Virginia D. Randolph, 1 March 1956, "Correspondence," box 1, Randolph Collection, LC.

55. "Legalized Lynching," *Messenger*, February 1920, Ald-UVa.

56. "Tar and Feathers," *Messenger*, December 1919, Ald-UVa.

57. "Labor and Lynching," *Messenger*, February 1920, Ald-UVa.

58. "Tar and Feathers."

Chapter 6: Black and White Unite

1. Randolph, Statement to Educational Political Conference in Chicago, at the International House, "Speeches ND," box 2, Randolph Collection, Schomburg.

2. "Organized Labor and Negro Workers," *Messenger*, March 1920, Ald-UVa.

3. "When Labor Is Awakened," *Messenger*, April–May 1920, Ald-UVa.

4. "Organized Labor and Negro Workers"; "Break Up the A.F. of L.," *Messenger*, May–June 1919, Ald-UVa.

5. "The Reasons Why White and Black Workers Should Combine in Labor Unions," *Messenger*, July 1919, Ald-UVa; "Our Reason for Being," *Messenger*, August 1919, Ald-UVa.

6. "Reasons Why White and Black Workers Should Combine."

7. "Our Reason for Being."

8. In a reflections piece titled "Working for Workers," published in *Community* in 1957, Frank Crosswaith explained that the short-lived National Association for the Promotion of Labor Unionism among Negroes "helped to establish a climate favorable" to interracial trade unionism. Subsequent efforts like the Negro Labor Committee organized in 1935 benefited from the successes and failures of previous efforts to ensure that the "assets and potential contributions" of Negroes were not wasted by the "regulation of Negroes to the lowest levels of occupations" (Negro Labor Committee, box 23, Brotherhood of Sleeping Car Porters Collection, Library of Congress, Washington, DC [hereafter Brotherhood, LC]).

9. "The Deportation of Agitators," *Messenger*, March 1919, Ald-UVa.

10. "The Passing of the Republican Party," *Messenger*, July 1918, Ald-UVa.

11. "Should Black Workers Join White Unions?" *Messenger*, September 1920, Ald-UVa.

12. "Why the President's Industrial Conference Failed," *Messenger*, December 1919, Ald-UVa.

13. "The Task of Local 8—The Marine Transport Workers of Philadelphia," *Messenger*, October 1921, Ald-UVa.

14. Harris, *Keeping the Faith*, p. 39.

15. Arnesen, *Brotherhoods of Color*, pp. 28–29.

16. A. Philip Randolph, "Black Unionism," "Speeches," box 2, Randolph Collection, Schomburg.

17. "The Fight of the Negro Workers," *Messenger*, August 1920, Ald-UVa.

18. A. Philip Randolph, "Lynching: Capitalism Its Cause; Socialism Its Cure," *Messenger*, March 1919, Ald-UVa.

19. "Negro Workers: The A.F. of L. or I.W.W."

20. Cohen, *Making a New Deal*, pp. 34–35.

21. "Labor's Race Relations Commissions," *Messenger*, July 1921, Ald-UVa.

22. "Propaganda," *Messenger*, February 1920, Ald-UVa.

23. Randolph and Owen, Letter to Lela Faye Secor.

24. "The Negro—A Republican," *Messenger*, September 1919, Ald-UVa.

25. "Organized Labor and the Negro," *Messenger*, March 1920, Ald-UVa.

26. Randolph, Statement to Educational Political Conference in Chicago.

27. "The General Strike," *Messenger*, August 1919, Ald-UVa.

28. Bates, "New Crowd Challenges the Agenda," p. 360.

29. "Strike," *Messenger*, September 1919, Ald-UVa.

30. "White Labor Unions Foiled," *Messenger*, May 1923, Ald-UVa.

31. "The March of Industrial Unionism," *Messenger*, September 1919, Ald-UVa.

32. Pratt, *Morris Hillquit*, p. 84; Howe, *Socialism and America*, pp. 8–9.

33. "Still the Panic," *Messenger*, March 1921, Ald-UVa; "The National Brotherhood Association," *Messenger*, August 1919, Ald-UVa; "Negroes to Organize Tenants and Consumers' Co-Operative League," *Messenger*, January 1918, Ald-UVa.

34. "Organizing the Negro Actor," *Messenger*, November 1917, Ald-UVa.

35. "Wage Reductions," *Messenger*, August 1922, Ald-UVa; Rick Halpern describes the challenges to interracial industrial unionism and consequences for both black and white unskilled labor (*Down on the Killing Floor*, pp. 30–33, 65–72).

36. "Break Up the A.F. of L."

37. "Wage Reductions."

38. "The March of Industrial Unionism," *Messenger*, September 1919, Ald-UVa.

39. Arnesen, *Brotherhoods of Color*, pp. 28–29.

40. "Break Up the A.F. of L."

41. "Why Negroes Should Join the I.W.W.," *Messenger*, July 1919, Ald-UVa.

42. "Break Up the A.F. of L."

43. Howe, *Socialism and America*, pp. 13–15.

44. "The Cause of and Remedy for Race Riots," *Messenger*, September 1919, Ald-UVa.

45. "Why Negroes Should be Socialists," *Messenger*, December 1919, Ald-UVa.

46. Naison, *Communists in Harlem*, pp. 13–14, 310.

47. Anderson, *A. Philip Randolph*, pp. 132–36.

48. "A Supreme Negro Jamaican Jackass," *Messenger*, January 1923, Ald-UVa.

Chapter 7: Ridin' the Rails

1. President Randolph's Third National Report to the Brotherhood of Sleeping Car Porters Convention, 3, box 10, Randolph Collection, LC.

2. Turner, *Caribbean Crusaders,* pp. 54–55; Frank R. Crosswaith, "A Message to Harlem Theater Patrons from the Harlem Labor Committee," 7, box 4, Crosswaith Collection, Schomburg.

3. Eric Arnesen addresses the question of whether or not "a consciousness of race" undermined or overwhelmed a "consciousness of class" among southern railroad brotherhoods by explaining that for white trade unionists who viewed themselves as "embattled" as both workers and citizens, "class, race, and national identity were inextricably linked" ("'Like Banquo's Ghost,'" pp. 1603, 1633).

4. Arnesen, *Brotherhoods of Color,* pp. 59–61; Harris, *Keeping the Faith,* pp. 17–18.

5. A. Philip Randolph, "Story of Rail Porters to Organize," "Speeches 1953," box 34, Randolph Collection, LC.

6. Dubofsky, *State and Labor,* p. 74.

7. Randolph, "Story of Rail Porters to Organize."

8. Dubofsky, *State and Labor,* pp. xiv, 192; Cohen explains that in the aftermath of wartime regulation of American industry, businessmen came to view "the corporation as the most responsible institution in society" and thus devised a conception of welfare capitalism "that aimed to make workers dependent on employers instead of their own communities or the state" (*Making a New Deal,* pp. 180–82).

9. A. Philip Randolph, "The Story of the Brotherhood of Sleeping Car Porters," "BSCP History Undated," box 10, Randolph Collection, LC; Randolph, "Story of Rail Porters to Organize."

10. Ibid.

11. Randolph, "Story of Rail Porters to Organize."

12. Brotherhood of Sleeping Car Porters, "The Pullman Porter," 06/01/04, box 17, 490 Pullman Company Archives, Newberry Library, Chicago (hereafter Pullman Archives, Newberry).

13. President Randolph's Third National Report.

14. Brotherhood of Sleeping Car Porters, "Pullman Porter."

15. Randolph, "Story of the Brotherhood."

16. Harris, *Keeping the Faith,* pp. 26–27.

17. Brotherhood of Sleeping Car Porters, "Pullman Porter."

18. In documenting the contributions of porter wives, Melinda Chateauvert helps to spotlight the issue of union autonomy in pushing forward the Brotherhood's cause (*Marching Together).*

19. A. Philip Randolph, Brotherhood of Sleeping Car Porters Outline, "BSCP History Undated," box 10, Randolph Collection, LC; Theodore S. Brown, The Brother-

hood of Sleeping Car Porters in the City of New York, "BSCP History Undated," box 10, Randolph Collection, LC; Turner, *Caribbean Crusaders,* p. 53.

20. Harris, *Keeping the Faith,* p. 34; Randolph, "Story of Rail Porters."

21. Randolph, "Story of the Brotherhood."

22. Interview with A. Philip Randolph, reel 2.

23. Arnesen, *Brotherhoods of Color,* pp. 58–60.

24. Harris, *Keeping the Faith,* pp. 33–34.

25. Ibid., pp. 31, 110–11.

26. A. Philip Randolph, "A Declaration of Conscience," "Articles by A. Philip Randolph," box 1, Randolph Collection, Schomburg.

27. Bates, *Pullman Porters,* p. 152.

28. Randolph, "Black Unionism."

29. A. Philip Randolph to William Hough, 19 January 1949, "Correspondence," box 1, Randolph Collection, LC.

30. Boston Citizens' Committee, "High Points of Deep Interest in the Pullman Porters' Struggle: The Story of a Race's Exploitation," 06/01/01, box 1, 4, Pullman Archives, Newberry.

31. A. Philip Randolph to Robert-Ellen Arnold, 8 August 1952, "Correspondence," box 1, Randolph Collection, LC.

32. William Green to A. Philip Randolph, 11 December 1940, "General Correspondence, 1940–1966, ND," box 14, Brotherhood Collection, LC.

33. A. Philip Randolph to Virginia D. Randolph.

34. Randolph, "Black Unionism."

35. Nelson, *Divided We Stand,* pp. xxvi–xxxi; Arnesen, "'Like Banquo's Ghost,'" p. 1617; Roediger, *Wages of Whiteness,* pp. 148–50.

36. "Skeleton Brief of the Case in Support of the Brotherhood of Sleeping Car Porters," "BSCP Legal Papers, Briefs," box 12, Randolph Collection, LC.

37. Ibid.

38. Ibid.

39. Ibid.

40. Dubofsky, *State and Labor,* pp. 100–101.

41. Korstad and Lichtenstein, "Opportunities Found and Lost," pp. 787–88.

42. President Randolph's Third National Report.

43. Harris, *Keeping the Faith,* p. 107; Arnesen, *Brotherhoods of Color,* pp. 93–94.

44. Brotherhood of Sleeping Car Porters vs. Pullman Company, 15 October 1930, 06/01/01, box 1, 15, Pullman Archives, Newberry.

45. F. L. Simmons to G. A. Kelly, In Re: Brotherhood of Sleeping Car Porters v. the Pullman Company, 21 March 1933, 06/01/01, box 1, 14, Pullman Archives, Newberry.

46. Brotherhood of Sleeping Car Porters v. Pullman Company No. 100084, 10 January 1934, 06/01/01 box 1, 15, Pullman Archives, Newberry.

47. Brotherhood of Sleeping Car Porters vs. Pullman Company, 15 October 1930.

48. President Randolph's Third National Report.

49. Randolph, "Story of the Brotherhood."

50. Dubofsky, *State and Labor*, pp. 111–12.

51. A. Philip Randolph to Oscar DePriest, 15 May 1934, file 3, box 42, Randolph Collection, LC.

52. Randolph, "Story of the Brotherhood."

53. Randolph to DePriest.

54. President Randolph's Third National Report; Brotherhood of Sleeping Car Porters; Dubofsky, *State and Labor*, pp. 111–24.

55. "The Negro Worker—A Menace to Radicalism."

Chapter 8: Where Class Consciousness Falls Short

1. Bates, *Pullman Porters*, pp. 98–100; Chateauvert, *Marching Together*, pp. 52–56; Dubofsky, *State and Labor*, pp. 100–101.

2. Randolph, "Story of the Rail Porters."

3. A. Philip Randolph to William Green, 25 April 1940, 2, box 14, Brotherhood Collection, LC.

4. Randolph, Interview with John Slawson.

5. Randolph, "Story of the Rail Porters."

6. Chateauvert, *Marching Together*, p. 60.

7. President Randolph's Third National Report; Harris, *Keeping the Faith*, p. 155.

8. President Randolph's Third National Report.

9. A. Philip Randolph to William Green, 12 December 1941, 2, box 14, Brotherhood Collection, LC.

10. Randolph, Interview with John Slawson.

11. A. Philip Randolph, Speech Given at AFL Convention—Boston 1943, "Speeches 1943," box 34, Randolph Collection, LC.

12. William Green to A. Philip Randolph, 21 November 1939, 2, box 14, Brotherhood Collection, LC.

13. Resolution Submitted to the Seventy-second Convention of the American Federation of Labor in St. Louis, September 1953 by the Delegates of the Brotherhood of Sleeping Car Porters—A. Philip Randolph, M. P. Webster, and T. D. McNeal, A.F.L. Civil Rights Information Center, 1, box 1, Brotherhood Collection, LC; Resolution Submitted to the Seventy-third Convention of the American Federation of Labor in Los Angeles, California, September 1954 by the Delegates of the Brotherhood of Sleeping Car Porters—A. Philip Randolph, M. P. Webster, and C. L. Dellums, United States Supreme Court Decision Against Segregated Public Schools, 1, box 1, Brotherhood Collection, LC; Resolution Submitted to the Seventy-third Convention of the American Federation of Labor in Los Angeles, California, September 1954 by the Delegates of the Brotherhood of Sleeping Car Porters—A. Philip Randolph, M. P.

Webster, and C. L. Dellums, Abolishing Jim Crow Housing, 1, box 1, Brotherhood Collection, LC; Resolution Submitted to the Seventy-fourth Convention of the American Federation of Labor in New York, New York, December 1955 by the delegates of the Brotherhood of Sleeping Car Porters—A. Philip Randolph, M. P. Webster, and C. L. Dellums, Civil Rights, 1, box 1, Brotherhood Collection, LC.

14. Interview with A. Philip Randolph, reel 2.

15. Randolph, "Story of Rail Porters."

16. Randolph, "Story of the Brotherhood"; Randolph, "Story of Rail Porters."

17. President Randolph's Third National Report.

18. A. Philip Randolph to Oscar Joseph, 3 February 1971, 3, box 42, Randolph Collection, LC.

19. Resolutions Adopted by the Third Negro Labor Conference of Washington, D.C., 1, box 10, Randolph Collection, LC; Bates emphasizes the "dual agenda" of the Brotherhood as both "a labor union and a social movement, in embryo, for all black Americans" (*Pullman Porters,* p. 98).

20. President Randolph's Third National Report.

21. Crosswaith (untitled), 13, box 2, Crosswaith Collection, Schomburg.

22. A. Philip Randolph to Harry W. Laidler, 18 December 1930, "Correspondence," box 1, Randolph Collection, LC.

23. Resolutions Adopted by the Third Negro Labor Conference of Washington, D.C.

24. John P. Davis, Introduction, in The Official Proceedings of the National Negro Congress, "National Negro Congress 1936–51," box 29, Randolph Collection, LC.

25. The Keynote Address of President A. Philip Randolph, printed in The Official Proceedings of the National Negro Congress, "National Negro Congress 1936–51," box 29, Randolph Collection, LC.

26. A. Philip Randolph, A Message from the National President, National Negro Congress News, 7 October 1937, "National Negro Congress 1936–51," box 29, Randolph Collection, LC.

27. Frank R. Crosswaith, Report of Activities of the Negro Labor Committee, January 1 to December 31, 1938, 2, box 5, Crosswaith Collection, Schomburg.

28. 1st Anniversary of the Negro Labor Committee, 2, box 5, Crosswaith Collection, Schomburg.

29. A. Philip Randolph, To the Brotherhood Men, 8, box 4, Crosswaith Collection, Schomburg.

30. Drake and Cayton, *Black Metropolis,* pp. 197–98.

31. Crosswaith, "Message to Harlem Theater Patrons."

32. Frank R. Crosswaith, Editorial, 20, box 3, Crosswaith Collection, Schomburg.

33. Brodsky, *Great Mayor,* pp. 319–20.

34. Mayor's Commission on Conditions in Harlem, "The Negro in Harlem: A

Report on Social and Economic Conditions Responsible for the Outbreak of March 19, 1935," "The Negro in Harlem: A Report," box 30, Randolph Collection, LC.

35. Ibid.

36. Roberta Senechal's examination of the 1908 Springfield, Illinois, race riot contradicts the view of the "typical" rioter as "riffraff, criminals—the scum of the community (*Sociogenesis of a Race Riot*, p. 8). Her examination shows that riot participants came from all segments of the community. These findings corroborate the commission's determination that criminal activity and random mayhem were not important factors in the Harlem riot.

37. Brown, "Brotherhood of Sleeping Car Porters in the City of New York."

38. Mayor's Commission, "Negro in Harlem."

39. Ibid.

40. Crosswaith, "A Message to Harlem Theater Patrons from the Harlem Labor Committee."

41. Mayor's Commission, "Negro in Harlem."

42. Ibid.

43. Ibid.

44. Randolph, To the Brotherhood Men.

45. Mayor's Commission, "Negro in Harlem."

46. "The Menace of Negro Communists," *Messenger,* August 1923, Ald-UVa.

47. A. Philip Randolph, "Are Communists a Threat to Democratic Organizations?" "Speeches ND," box 2, Randolph Collection, Schomburg.

48. Ibid.

49. A. Philip Randolph, "Should Negroes Help the USA Win the Cold War against the USSR?" 25, box 2, Randolph Collection, Schomburg.

50. A. Philip Randolph to Dr. Catherine Lealtad, 7 January 1952, "Correspondence," box 1, Randolph Collection, LC.

51. Randolph, "Story of Rail Porters."

52. "Randolph Says Negroes Would Fight for the USA against Soviet Russia," "Speeches ND," box 2, Randolph Collection, Schomburg.

53. Proceedings of the First Negro Labor Conference, 5, box 3, Crosswaith Collection, Schomburg.

54. Proceedings of the First Negro Labor Conference.

55. Ibid.

56. Randolph, "The Crisis of the Negro and the Constitution," 7, box 6, Moore Collection, Schomburg.

57. Randolph, Message from the National President.

58. Randolph, "Crisis of the Negro and the Constitution."

59. Randolph, Message from the National President.

Chapter 9: Marching Toward Fair Employment

1. Bayard Rustin, A. Philip Randolph, "Biographical Materials," box 1, Randolph Collection, Schomburg.

2. A. Philip Randolph, Keynote Address to the Policy Conference of the March on Washington Movement, Detroit, *March on Washington Movement: Proceedings of Conference Held in Detroit, September 26–27, 1942,* "March on Washington Movement 1943," box 1, Randolph Collection, Schomburg.

3. Robert Korstad explains how a civil rights agenda and workplace justice came together in mobilizing black Reynolds workers in Winston-Salem, N.C. (*Civil Rights Unionism*).

4. A. Philip Randolph, Statement on Presentation of Plaque to William Green from the Brotherhood of Sleeping Car Porters, "Speeches ND," box 2, Randolph Collection, Schomburg.

5. A. Philip Randolph, "Randolph Defies Boss Crump," "Speeches ND," box 2, Randolph Collection, Schomburg.

6. Nelson, *Divided We Stand,* p. xxvi.

7. Theodore E. Brown, A. Philip Randolph and the Brotherhood of Sleeping Car Porters: A Few Observations, "Biographical Material," box 1, Randolph Collection, Schomburg.

8. A. Philip Randolph, "Negroes and Race Riots," "Speeches ND," box 2, Randolph Collection, Schomburg.

9. A. Philip Randolph, "The Economics of Black America," "Speeches ND," box 2, Randolph Collection, Schomburg.

10. Randolph, "The Negro and the Next Five Years," "Articles by A. Philip Randolph," box 1, Randolph Collection, Schomburg.

11. Randolph, "The Role of the Negro Worker in the American Trade Union Movement and the Problem of Racial Discrimination," "Speeches 1958–60," box 2, Randolph Collection, Schomburg.

12. A. Philip Randolph, "The Negro, the War, and the Future of Democracy," "Speeches ND," box 2, Randolph Collection, Schomburg.

13. A. Philip Randolph, Speech Given at AFL Convention—Boston 1943.

14. Ibid.

15. A. Philip Randolph, Randolph Tells of Fight against Racial Discrimination at the A.F.L.-CIO Convention in San Francisco, "Speeches 1955–58," box 2, Randolph Collection, Schomburg.

16. A. Philip Randolph, "Racially Segregated Unions," 22, box 2, Randolph Collection, Schomburg.

17. A. Philip Randolph, Statement of A. Philip Randolph regarding S.692: A Bill to Prohibit Discrimination in Employment because of Race, Color, Religion, National Origin, or Ancestry, before the Subcommittee on Civil Rights of the Committee on

Labor and Public Welfare of the Senate of the 83rd Congress, "Speeches 1955–58," box 2, Randolph Collection, Schomburg.

18. Randolph, "Negroes and Race Riots."

19. Garfinkel, *When Negroes March*, pp. 34–35; Merl E. Reed, *Seedtime for the Modern Civil Rights Movement*, p. 13.

20. Cohen, *Making a New Deal*, pp. 270–71; Meier and Bracey, "NAACP as a Reform Movement," pp. 15–16; Touré F. Reed, *Not Alms but Opportunity*, p. 108.

21. Weiss, *Farewell to the Party*, pp. 274–78.

22. Bates, "New Crowd Challenges the Agenda," pp. 340–41.

23. Randolph, Interview with John Slawson.

24. Bates explains that Randolph turned the March on Washington Committee into the March on Washington Movement "shortly after the executive order was issued" to oversee "enactment of 8802" and "put teeth into FEPC investigations" (*Pullman Porters*, p. 161); Kirby, *Black Americans in the Roosevelt Era*, pp. 170–71.

25. Garfinkel, *When Negroes March*, pp. 38–41; Bates, *Pullman Porters*, pp. 151–53; Touré F. Reed, *Not Alms but Opportunity*, pp. 102–4.

26. For a more detailed historiographical examination of the origins and impact of the FEPC, see Garfinkel, *When Negroes March*; Bennett, *Confrontation*; Meier, "Civil Rights Strategies"; Merl E. Reed, *Seedtime for the Modern Civil Rights Movement*.

27. Pfeffer, *A. Philip Randolph*, pp. 55–58.

28. Garfinkel, *When Negroes March*, p. 41.

29. Merl E. Reed, *Seedtime for the Modern Civil Rights Movement*, pp. 353–57.

30. Randolph, Keynote Address to the Policy Conference of the March on Washington Movement.

31. A. Philip Randolph, Address by A. Philip Randolph, National Director, March on Washington Movement, in the Chicago Coliseum, June 26, 1942, 1, box 34, Randolph Collection, LC; Kirby, *Black Americans*, pp. 172–73.

32. Randolph, To the Brotherhood Men.

33. A. Philip Randolph, "Weeping for the Poor White Folks," "Speeches 1943," box 34, Randolph Collection, LC.

34. Ibid.

35. Randolph, Interview with John Slawson.

36. Kirby, *Black Americans*, p. 173.

37. A. Philip Randolph, "Why and How the March Was Postponed," *Black Worker*, August 1941, Ald-UVa.

38. Weiss explains that while the New Deal "transformed" the NAACP and National Urban League, African Americans "remained far behind other groups in the political power that they could muster" (*Farewell to the Party*, pp. 62–63).

39. A. Philip Randolph, The Crisis of the Negro and the Constitution, 6, box 7, Moore Collection, Schomburg.

40. A. Philip Randolph, "Call to Negro America to March on Washington for Jobs and Equal Participation in National Defense," *Black Worker*, May 1941, Ald-UVa.

41. Ibid.

42. A. Philip Randolph, "The March on Washington," *Black Worker*, July 1941, Ald-UVa.

43. A. Philip Randolph, "President Roosevelt's Statement on Racial Barriers," *Black Worker*, June 1941, Ald-UVa.

44. Sugrue, "Affirmative Action from Below," pp. 152–53.

45. A. Philip Randolph, Employment in Defense Industries, 1, box 34, Randolph Collection, LC.

46. Brodsky, *Great Mayor*, p. 453.

47. Interview with A. Philip Randolph, reel 2; Randolph, Employment in Defense Industries.

48. Randolph, Employment in Defense Industries; Randolph, Interview with John Slawson; George T. McJimsey discusses Eleanor Roosevelt's role in this conference and how her "leadership provided a context for other New Dealers to advance civil rights" (*Presidency of Franklin Delano Roosevelt*, pp. 163–64); Kirby, *Black Americans*, pp. 80–81.

49. A. Philip Randolph, "Call to Negro America to March on Washington for Jobs and Equal Participation in National Defense."

50. Randolph, Interview with John Slawson; Randolph, Employment in Defense Industries.

51. Randolph, Employment in Defense Industries; Interview with A. Philip Randolph, reel 2.

52. Randolph, Employment in Defense Industries.

53. Randolph, Interview with John Slawson.

54. Both Richard M. Flanagan (*Mayors and the Challenges*, pp. 150–51), and Lawrence Elliot (*Little Flower*, pp. 226–27) detail La Guardia's extraordinary political acumen.

55. Randolph, Interview with John Slawson.

56. Randolph, Employment in Defense Industries.

57. A. Philip Randolph to Anna Rosenberg, 11 July 1941, "Fair Employment Practices Committee Correspondence," box 18, Randolph Collection, LC.

58. Ibid.; Merl E. Reed, *Seedtime for the Modern Civil Rights Movement*, pp. 21–23.

59. Draft of Letter to the President to be signed by A. Philip Randolph or by Randolph and White on Behalf of March on Washington Committee, 11 July 1941, "Fair Employment Practices Committee Correspondence," box 18, Randolph Collection, LC.

60. Franklin D. Roosevelt to Francis Biddle, 5 November 1943, "Fair Employment Practices Committee Correspondence," box 18, Randolph Collection, LC.

61. Ibid.

62. Randolph to Rosenberg, 11 July 1941.

63. A. Philip Randolph to Mr. Mark Ethridge, Chairman, Committee on Fair Em-

ployment Practices, 7 August 1941, "Fair Employment Practices Committee Correspondence," box 18, Randolph Collection, LC.

64. Randolph, Employment in Defense Industries.

65. A. Philip Randolph, Memorial, "Fair Employment Practices Committee Correspondence," box 18, Randolph Collection, LC.

66. *Philadelphia Inquirer,* 7 March 1944; *Washington Post,* 7 March 1944; *Pittsburgh Post-Gazette,* 20 March 1944.

67. Sugrue, "Affirmative Action from Below," p. 148.

68. A. Philip Randolph, Editorial Comment on FEPC, 1944, "Speeches 1944," box 34, Randolph Collection, LC; *Bismarck Tribune,* 16 October 1944.

69. A. Philip Randolph to Franklin D. Roosevelt, 6 April 1943, "Fair Employment Practices Committee Correspondence," box 19, Randolph Collection, LC.

70. Transcript of Conference on Scope and Powers of Committee on Fair Employment Practices, 19 February 1943, "Fair Employment Practices Committee Correspondence, 1943–52," box 17, Randolph Collection, LC.

71. Ibid.

72. Ibid.

73. Ibid.

74. Ibid.

75. Ibid.; Kevin M. Schultz, "FEPC and the Legacy," pp. 75–76.

76. Outline of Principles: The National Council for a Permanent FEPC, "Fair Employment Practice Committee Constitution, Principles, and Prospectus, 1945 + undated," box 18, Randolph Collection, LC.

77. General Statement by the Conference in Support of a Bill for a Permanent FEPC, "FEPC 1949–51," box 1, Randolph Collection, Schomburg.

78. Ibid.

79. A. Philip Randolph, Radio Address of A. Philip Randolph, Co-Chairman of the National Council for a Permanent Fair Employment Practice Committee, "Speeches 1948," box 34, Randolph Collection, LC.

Epilogue

1. Kevin M. Schultz, "FEPC and the Legacy," pp. 71–72.

2. Rustin, A. Philip Randolph.

. 3. A. Philip Randolph, "Are Negroes American Citizens?" "Articles by A. Philip Randolph," box 1, Randolph Collection, Schomburg.

4. Grant Reynolds and A. Philip Randolph, Committee Against Jim Crow in Military Service and Training, "Committee to End Jim Crow in the Armed Services 1943–47," box 15, Randolph Collection, LC.

5. A. Philip Randolph, Testimony before the Senate Armed Services Committee, 31 March 1948, 2, box 15, Randolph Collection, LC.

6. A. Philip Randolph, "Randolph to Urge Negroes in Army to Drop Guns if Russell Segregation Amendment Passes," 2, box 15, Randolph Collection, LC.

7. Grant Reynolds and A. Philip Randolph to the Editor of the *New York Times,* 10 December 1947, "Committee to End Jim Crow in the Armed Services 1943–47," box 15, Randolph Collection, LC.

8. Randolph, Testimony before the Senate Armed Services Committee.

9. Ibid.

10. Ibid.

11. Randolph, "Randolph to Urge Negroes in Army to Drop Guns."

12. Bates, *Pullman Porters,* pp. 148–50.

13. A. Philip Randolph, "The Negro in the American Democracy," "Articles by A. Philip Randolph," box 1, Randolph Collection, Schomburg.

14. Randolph, "Randolph Defies Boss Crump," "Speeches ND," box 2, Randolph Collection, Schomburg.

15. Resolution on Democracy in the Army, "Committee to End Jim Crow in the Armed Services 1943–47," box 15, Randolph Collection, LC.

16. Nelson Lichtenstein echoes this point, asserting that the modern civil rights movement took shape out of "proletarianization and unionization" of black workers (*Most Dangerous Man in Detroit,* p. 207); Heather Ann Thompson argues that African Americans and progressive whites in Detroit began to unite against racial injustice and political conservativism in the 1950s and left a "legacy of possibility, not merely polarization, for the Detroiters of the 1960s to reckon with" (*Whose Detroit?* pp. 11–12); Meier and Rudwick, *Black Detroit,* pp. 175–76.

17. Bates places Randolph's demand for an executive order banning discrimination in war industry jobs in the context of laying claim to basic rights guaranteed in the U.S. Constitution (*Pullman Porters,* pp. 154–55). Randolph's determination to pursue genuine social justice for African Americans fits into this examination of citizenship and its application to all Americans regardless of race or class.

18. Bertha Gruner, Minutes of Proceedings of Conference Called by A. Philip Randolph, President Brotherhood of Sleeping Car Porters, AFL; Willard S. Townsend, President United Transport Service Employees, CIO; Morris Milgrim, National Secretary Workers Defense League; and Wilfred H. Kerr, Co-Chairman Lynn Committee to Abolish Segregation in the Armed Forces in Order to Formulate a Program of Action to End Race Segregation and Discrimination by the Armed Services, "Committee to End Jim Crow in the Armed Services 1943–47," box 15, Randolph Collection, LC.

19. Race Discrimination in America: A Discussion by Norman Thomas and A. Philip Randolph, "Committee to End Jim Crow in the Armed Services 1943–47," box 15, Randolph Collection, LC.

20. A. Philip Randolph, Statement Counseling Non-registration to be made by A. Philip Randolph, 4, box 15, Randolph Collection, LC; A. Philip Randolph, Statement Counseling Non-Registration to be made by A. Philip Randolph When Asked by

Negro and White Youth of Draft Age if They Should Register and Submit to Induction under the 1949 Draft Act, 3, box 15, Randolph Collection, LC.

21. If We Must Die, 4, box 15, Randolph Collection, LC.

22. Questions on Civil Disobedience, 2, box 15, Randolph Collection, LC.

23. Walter White, "Mr. Randolph's Statement," 4, box 15, Randolph Collection, LC.

24. Questions on Civil Disobedience.

25. Interview with A. Philip Randolph, reel 3, 5, box 42, Randolph Collection, LC.

26. A. Philip Randolph, "Call to Negro America to March on Washington for Jobs and Equal Participation in National Defense."

27. Randolph, Statement Counseling Non-Registration to be made by A. Philip Randolph.

28. Randolph, Interview with John Slawson.

29. Randolph, Randolph to Urge Negroes in Army to Drop Guns.

30. A. Philip Randolph, "Crisis of Struggle for Civil Rights and Civil Liberties," "Speeches ND," box 2, Randolph Collection, Schomburg.

31. A. Philip Randolph, "Problems of Peace and Democracy," "Speeches ND," box 2, Randolph Collection, Schomburg; Randolph, "Crisis of Struggle for Civil Rights and Civil Liberties."

32. A. Philip Randolph, "The Spirit of Human Rights," "Speeches ND," box 2, Randolph Collection, Schomburg.

33. A. Philip Randolph, "Challenge to Complete an Uncompleted Revolution for Full Freedom," "Speeches ND," box 2, Randolph Collection, Schomburg.

34. A. Philip Randolph, Civil Rights Day, "Speeches 1955–58," box 2, Randolph Collection, Schomburg; Randolph, "Crisis of Struggle for Civil Rights and Civil Liberties."

35. Kevin M. Schultz, "FEPC and the Legacy," p. 72.

36. Rustin, A. Philip Randolph.

Bibliography

Manuscript Collections

A. Philip Randolph Collection. Library of Congress, Washington, D.C.

A. Philip Randolph Collection. Schomburg Center for Research in Black Culture, New York.

Brotherhood of Sleeping Car Porters Collection. Library of Congress, Washington, D.C.

Frank R. Crosswaith Collection. Schomburg Center for Research in Black Culture, New York.

Norman Thomas Collection. New York Public Library, New York.

Pullman Company Archives. Newberry Library, Chicago.

Richard B. Moore Collection. Schomburg Center for Research in Black Culture, New York.

Richard Parrish Collection. Schomburg Center for Research in Black Culture, New York.

Newspapers and Journals

A.M.E. Review, Wisconsin Historical Society, University of Wisconsin—Madison.

Bismarck Tribune, Chester Fritz Library, University of North Dakota, Grand Forks.

Black Worker, Alderman Library, University of Virginia, Charlottesville.

Christian Recorder, Wisconsin Historical Society, University of Wisconsin-Madison.

Crisis, Humanities, Social Sciences, and Education Library, Purdue University, West Lafayette, Ind.

Messenger, Alderman Library, University of Virginia, Charlottesville.

Negro World, Humanities, Social Sciences, and Education Library, Purdue University, West Lafayette, Ind.

New York Times, Alderman Library, University of Virginia, Charlottesville.

Philadelphia Inquirer, Paterno Library, Pennsylvania State University, University Park.

Pittsburgh Post-Gazette, Center for Research Libraries, Chicago.

Washington Post, Hicks Undergraduate Library, Purdue University, West Lafayette, Ind.

Books and Articles

Anderson, Jervis. *A. Philip Randolph: A Biographical Portrait.* New York: Harcourt, 1973.

———. *This Was Harlem: A Cultural Portrait, 1900–1950.* New York: Farrar, Straus and Giroux, 1982.

Angell, Stephen W. *Bishop Henry McNeal Turner and African-American Religion in the South.* Knoxville: University of Tennessee Press, 1992.

Angell, Stephen W., and Anthony B. Pinn, eds. *Social Protest Thought in the African Methodist Episcopal Church, 1862–1939.* Knoxville: University of Tennessee Press, 2000.

Arnesen, Eric. *Brotherhoods of Color: Black Railroad Workers and the Struggle for Equality.* Cambridge, Mass.: Harvard University Press, 2001.

———. "'Like Banquo's Ghost, It Will Not Down': The Race Question and the American Railroad Brotherhoods, 1880–1920." *American Historical Review* 99, no. 5 (December 1994): 1601–33.

Baldwin, Davarian L. *Chicago's New Negroes: Modernity, the Great Migration, and Black Urban Life.* Chapel Hill: University of North Carolina Press, 2007.

Bates, Beth Thompson. "A New Crowd Challenges the Agenda of the Old Guard in the NAACP, 1933–1941." *American Historical Review* 102, no. 2 (April 1996): 340–77.

———. *Pullman Porters and the Rise of Protest Politics in Black America, 1925–1945.* Chapel Hill: University of North Carolina Press, 2001.

Beck, E. M., and Stewart E. Tolnay. "When Race Didn't Matter: Black and White Violence against Their Own Color." In *Under Sentence of Death: Lynching in the South,* ed. W. Fitzhugh Brundage. Chapel Hill: University of North Carolina Press, 1997.

Bennett, Lerone, Jr. *Confrontation: Black and White.* Chicago: Johnson, 1965.

Brodsky, Alyn. *The Great Mayor: Fiorello La Guardia and the Making of the City of New York.* New York: St. Martin's Press, 2003.

Brown, David, and Clive Webb. *Race in the American South: From Slavery to Civil Rights.* Gainesville: University Press of Florida, 2007.

Bynum, Cornelius L. "The Arrival of the New Crowd: The New Negro and Class-Consciousness during the Harlem Renaissance, 1917–1937." *Journal of the Gilded Age and Progressive Era* 10, no. 1 (January 2011).

Campbell, James T. *Songs of Zion: The African Methodist Episcopal Church in the United States and South Africa*. Chapel Hill: University of North Carolina Press, 1998.

Chace, James. *1912: Wilson, Roosevelt, Taft & Debs—The Election That Changed the Country*. New York: Simon and Schuster, 2004.

Chateauvert, Melinda. *Marching Together: Women of the Brotherhood of Sleeping Car Porters*. Urbana: University of Illinois Press, 1998.

Cohen, Lizabeth. *A Consumers' Republic: The Politics of Mass Consumption in Postwar America*. New York: Vintage Books, 2003.

———. *Making a New Deal: Industrial Workers in Chicago, 1919–1939*. New York: Cambridge University Press, 1990.

Crooks, James B. *Jacksonville after the Fire, 1901–1919: A New South City*. Jacksonville: University of North Florida Press, 1991.

Curtis, Susan. *A Consuming Faith: The Social Gospel and Modern American Culture*. Baltimore: Johns Hopkins University Press, 1991.

Dickerson, Dennis C. *Out of the Crucible: Black Steelworkers in Western Pennsylvania, 1875–1980*. Albany: State University of New York Press, 1986.

Douglas, Ann. *Terrible Honesty: Mongrel Manhattan in the 1920s*. New York: Farrar, Straus and Giroux, 1995.

Drake, St. Clair, and Horace R. Cayton. *Black Metropolis: A Study of Negro Life in a Northern City*. Chicago: University of Chicago Press, 1993.

Dubofsky, Melvyn. *Hard Work: The Making of Labor History*. Urbana: University of Illinois Press, 2000.

———. *The State and Labor in Modern America*. Chapel Hill: University of North Carolina Press, 1994.

Du Bois, W. E. B. *The Philadelphia Negro: A Social Study*. New York: Schocken Books, 1967.

———. *The Souls of Black Folk*. Boston: Bedford Books, 1997.

Elliot, Lawrence. *Little Flower: The Life and Times of Fiorello La Guardia*. New York: William Morrow, 1983.

Estes, Steve. *I Am a Man! Race, Manhood, and the Civil Rights Movement*. Chapel Hill: University of North Carolina Press, 2005.

Fairclough, Adam. *To Redeem the Soul of America: The Southern Christian Leadership Conference and Martin Luther King, Jr.* Athens: University of Georgia Press, 1987.

Ferguson, Jeffrey B. *The Sage of Sugar Hill: George S. Schuyler and the Harlem Renaissance*. New Haven, Conn.: Yale University Press, 2005.

Flanagan, Richard M. *Mayors and the Challenge of Urban Leadership*. Lanham, Md.: University Press of America, 2004.

Foner, Philip S. *American Socialism and Black Americans: From the Age of Jackson to World War II*. Westport, Conn.: Greenwood Press, 1977.

Frazier, E. Franklin. *The Negro Church in America*. New York: Schocken Books, 1964.

Friedman-Kasaba, Kathie. *Memories of Migration: Gender, Ethnicity, and Work in the Lives of Jewish and Italian Women in New York, 1870–1924.* Albany: State University of New York Press, 1996.

Fry, C. George, and Joel R. Kurz. *Washington Gladden as a Preacher of the Social Gospel, 1882–1918.* Lewiston, N.Y.: Edwin Mellon Press, 2003.

Gaines, Kevin K. *Uplifting the Race: Black Leadership, Politics, and Culture in the Twentieth Century.* Chapel Hill: University of North Carolina Press, 1996.

Garfinkel, Herbert. *When Negroes March: The March on Washington Movement in the Organizational Politics for FEPC.* New York: Atheneum, 1969.

George, Carol V. R. *Segregated Sabbaths: Richard Allen and the Emergence of Independent Black Churches, 1760–1840.* New York: Oxford University Press, 1973.

Gettleman, Marvin E. *An Elusive Presence: The Discovery of John H. Finley and His America.* Chicago: Nelson-Hall, 1979.

Goddard, Terrell Dale. "The Black Social Gospel in Chicago, 1896–1906: The Ministries of Reverdy C. Ransom and Richard R. Wright, Jr." *Journal of Negro History* 84, no. 3 (Summer 1999): 227–46.

Godshalk, David Fort. *Veiled Visions: The 1906 Atlanta Race Riot and the Reshaping of American Race Relations.* Chapel Hill: University of North Carolina Press, 2005.

Gomez-Jefferson, Annetta L. *The Sage of Tawawa: Reverdy Cassius Ransom, 1861–1959.* Kent, Ohio: Kent State University Press, 2002.

Gorelick, Sherry. *City College and the Jewish Poor: Education in New York, 1880–1924.* New Brunswick, N.J.: Rutgers University Press, 1981.

Grant, Colin. *Negro with a Hat: The Rise and Fall of Marcus Garvey.* New York: Oxford University Press, 2008.

Greenberg, Cheryl. *Or Does It Explode? Black Harlem in the Great Depression.* New York: Oxford University Press, 1991.

Gregg, Robert. *Sparks from the Anvil of Oppression: Philadelphia's African Methodists and Southern Migrants, 1890–1940.* Philadelphia: Temple University Press, 1993.

Gregory, James N. *The Southern Diaspora: How the Great Migrations of Black and White Southerners Transformed America.* Chapel Hill: University of North Carolina Press, 2005.

Gregory, Steven. *Black Corona: Race and the Politics of Place in an Urban Community.* Princeton, N.J.: Princeton University Press, 1998.

Hall, Jacquelyn Dowd. "The Long Civil Rights Movement and the Political Uses of the Past." *Journal of American History* 91, no. 4 (March 2005): 1233–63.

Halpern, Rick. *Down on the Killing Floor: Black and White Workers in Chicago's Packinghouses, 1904–54.* Urbana: University of Illinois Press, 1997.

Harris, William H. *The Harder We Run: Black Workers since the Civil War.* New York: Oxford University Press, 1982.

———. *Keeping the Faith: A. Philip Randolph, Milton P. Webster, and the Brotherhood of Sleeping Car Porters, 1925–37.* Urbana: University of Illinois Press, 1977.

Hawkins, Hugh. *Between Harvard and America: The Educational Leadership of Charles W. Eliot.* New York: Oxford University Press, 1972.

Henry, Keith S. "The Black Political Tradition in New York: A Conjunction of Political Cultures." *Journal of Black Studies* 7, no. 4 (June 1977): 455–84.

Hershberg, Theodore. "Free Blacks in Antebellum Philadelphia: A Study of Ex-Slaves, Freeborns, and Socioeconomic Decline." In *African Americans in Pennsylvania: A Shifting Historical Perspective,* ed. Joe Trotter Jr. and Eric Ledell Smith. University Park: Penn State University Press, 1997.

Hollinger, David A. *Morris R. Cohen and the Scientific Ideal.* Cambridge, Mass.: MIT Press, 1975.

Honey, Michael K. *Southern Labor and Black Civil Rights: Organizing Memphis Workers.* Urbana: University of Illinois Press, 1993.

Hopkins, Charles Howard. *The Rise of the Social Gospel in American Protestantism, 1865–1915.* New Haven, Conn.: Yale University Press, 1967.

Howe, Irving. *Socialism and America.* New York: Harcourt, Brace, Jovanovich, 1985.

Hunter, Tera W. "'Work That Body': African American Women, Work, and Leisure in Atlanta and the New South." In *The Black Worker: Race, Labor, and Civil Rights since Emancipation,* ed. Eric Arnesen. Urbana: University of Illinois Press, 2007.

Jackson, Kenneth. *The Ku Klux Klan in the City, 1915–1930.* New York: Oxford University Press, 1967.

Jacobs, Meg. *Pocketbook Politics: Economic Citizenship in Twentieth-Century America.* Princeton, N.J.: Princeton University Press, 2005.

Jones, Jill. *Conquering Gotham: The Construction of Penn Station and Its Tunnels.* New York: Viking, 2007.

Kelley, Robin D. G. *Hammer and Hoe: Alabama Communists during the Great Depression.* Chapel Hill: University of North Carolina Press, 1990.

Kersten, Andrew E. *A. Philip Randolph: A Life in the Vanguard.* New York: Rowman and Littlefield, 2007.

———. *Race, Jobs, and the War: The FEPC in the Midwest, 1941–46.* Urbana: University of Illinois Press, 2000.

Kirby, John B. *Black Americans in the Roosevelt Era: Liberalism and Race.* Knoxville: University of Tennessee Press, 1980.

Kornweibel, Theodore, Jr. *No Crystal Stair: Black Life and the Messenger, 1917–1928.* Westport, Conn.: Greenwood Press, 1975.

Korstad, Robert Rodgers. *Civil Rights Unionism: Tobacco Workers and the Struggle for Democracy in the Mid-Twentieth-Century South.* Chapel Hill: University of North Carolina Press, 2003.

Korstad, Robert, and Nelson Lichtenstein, "Opportunities Found and Lost: Labor, Radicals, and the Early Civil Rights Movement." *Journal of American History* 75, no. 3 (December 1988): 786–811.

Kusmer, Kenneth L. *A Ghetto Takes Shape: Black Cleveland, 1870–1930.* Urbana: University of Illinois Press, 1976.

Lasch-Quinn, Elizabeth. *Black Neighbors: Race and the Limits of Reform in the American Settlement House Movement, 1890–1945.* Chapel Hill: University of North Carolina Press, 1993.

Lewis, David Levering. *When Harlem Was in Vogue.* New York: Penguin Books, 1997.

Lewis, Earl. "Expectations, Economic Opportunities, and Life in the Industrial Age: Black Migration to Norfolk, Virginia, 1910–1915." In *The Great Migration in Historical Perspective: New Dimensions of Race, Class, and Gender,* ed. Joe William Trotter Jr. Bloomington: Indiana University Press, 1991.

Lewis, Linden. "Richard B. Moore: The Making of a Caribbean Organic Intellectual: A Review Essay." *Journal of Black Studies* 25, no. 5 (May 1995): 589–609.

Lewis, Rupert. *Marcus Garvey: Anti-Colonial Champion.* Trenton, N.J.: Africa World Press, 1988.

Lichtenstein, Nelson. *The Most Dangerous Man in Detroit: Walter Reuther and the Fate of American Labor.* New York: Basic Books, 1995.

Little, Lawrence S. *Disciples of Liberty: The African Methodist Episcopal Church in the Age of Imperialism, 1884–1916.* Knoxville: University of Tennessee Press, 2000.

Litwack, Leon F. *Trouble in Mind: Black Southerners in the Age of Jim Crow.* New York: Alfred A. Knopf, 1998.

Lowry, Beverly. *Her Dream of Dreams: The Rise and Triumph of Madam C. J. Walker.* New York: Alfred A. Knopf, 2003.

Luker, Ralph E. "Missions, Institutional Churches, and Settlement Houses: The Black Experience, 1885–1910." *Journal of Negro History* 69, no. 3/4 (Summer 1984): 101–13.

MacLean, Nancy. *Freedom Is Not Enough: The Opening of the American Workplace.* Cambridge, Mass.: Harvard University Press, 2008.

Marable, Manning. *W.E.B. Du Bois: Black Radical Democrat.* Boston, Mass.: G.K. Hall, 1986.

Martin, Tony. *Literary Garveyism: Garvey, Black Arts, and the Harlem Renaissance.* Dover, Mass.: Majority Press, 1983.

———. *Marcus Garvey, Hero: A First Biography.* Dover, Mass.: Majority Press, 1983.

Mason, Herman. *African-American Life in Jacksonville, Florida.* Dover, N.H.: Arcadia, 1997.

May, Henry R. *Protestant Churches and Industrial America.* New York: Octagon Press, 1977.

Mays, Benjamin E. *The Negro's God as Reflected in His Literature.* New York: Russell and Russell, 1968.

McJimsey, George T. *The Presidency of Franklin Delano Roosevelt.* Lawrence: University Press of Kansas, 2000.

Meier, August. "Civil Rights Strategies for Negro Employment." In *Race, Employment, and Poverty,* ed. Arthur M. Ross and Herbert Hill. New York: Harcourt, Brace, and World, 1967.

Meier, August, and John H. Bracey. "The NAACP as a Reform Movement, 1909–1965: "To Reach the Conscience of America." *Journal of Southern History* 59, no. 1 (February 1996): 3–30.

Meier, August, and Elliot Rudwick. *Black Detroit and the Rise of the UAW.* New York: Oxford University Press, 1979.

———. *From Plantation to Ghetto*. New York: Hill and Wang, 1976.

Miller, Calvin Craig. *A. Philip Randolph and the African-American Labor Movement*. Greensboro, N.C.: Morgan Reynolds, 2005.

Miller, Sally M. *Victor Berger and the Promise of Constructive Socialism, 1910–1920*. Westport, Conn.: Greenwood Press, 1973.

Mixon, Gregory. *The Atlanta Riot: Race, Class, and Violence in a New South City*. Gainesville: University of Florida Press, 2005.

Morris, Calvin S. *Reverdy C. Ransom: Black Advocate of the Social Gospel*. Lanham, Md.: University Press of America, 1990.

Moses, Wilson Jeremiah. *Creative Conflict in African American Thought: Frederick Douglass, Alexander Crummell, Booker T. Washington, W. E. B. Du Bois, and Marcus Garvey*. New York: Cambridge University Press, 2004.

Naison, Mark. *Communists in Harlem during the Depression*. New York: Grove Press, 1983.

Nelson, Bruce. *Divided We Stand: American Workers and the Struggle for Black Equality*. Princeton, N.J.: Princeton University Press, 2001.

Osofsky, Gilbert. *Harlem: The Making of a Ghetto*. New York: Harper & Row, 1971.

Paris, Peter J. *The Social Teachings of the Black Churches*. Philadelphia: Fortress Press, 1985.

Perman, Michael. *Struggle for Mastery: Disfranchisement in the South, 1888–1908*. Chapel Hill: University of North Carolina Press, 2001.

Perry, Jeffrey B. *Hubert Harrison: The Voice of Harlem Radicalism, 1883–1918*. New York: Columbia University Press, 2008.

———, ed. *A Hubert Harrison Reader*. Middletown, Conn.: Wesleyan University Press, 2001.

Pfeffer, Paula F. *A. Philip Randolph, Pioneer of the Civil Rights Movement*. Baton Rouge: Louisiana State University Press, 1990.

Philpott, Thomas Lee. *The Slum and the Ghetto: Immigrants, Blacks, and Reformers in Chicago, 1880–1930*. Belmont, Calif.: Wadsworth, 1991.

Pinn, Anthony B., ed. *Making the Gospel Plain: The Writing of Bishop Reverdy C. Ransom*. Harrisburg, Pa.: Trinity International Press, 1999.

———. *Moral Evil and Redemptive Suffering: A History of Theodicy in African American Religious Thought*. Gainesville: University of Florida Press, 2002.

Podair, Jerald. *Bayard Rustin: American Dreamer*. Lanham, Md: Rowan & Littlefield, 2009.

Pratt, Norma Fain. *Morris Hillquit: A Political History of an American Jewish Socialist*. Westport, Conn.: Greenwood Press, 1979.

Pritchett, Wendell E. *Brownville, Brooklyn: Blacks, Jews, and the Changing Face of the Ghetto*. Chicago: University of Chicago Press, 2002.

Rader, Benjamin G. *The Academic Mind and Reform: The Influence of Richard T. Ely in American Life*. Lexington: University of Kentucky Press, 1966.

Ransom, Reverdy C. *Pilgrimage of Harriet Ransom's Son*. Nashville, Tenn.: Sunday School Union, 1949.

Reed, Merl E. *Seedtime for the Modern Civil Rights Movement: The President's Committee on Fair Employment Practice, 1941–1946.* Baton Rouge: Louisiana State University Press, 1991.

Reed, Touré F. *Not Alms but Opportunity: The Urban League and the Politics of Racial Uplift, 1910–1950.* Chapel Hill: University of North Carolina Press, 2008.

Rivers, Larry, and Canter Brown Jr. *Laborers in the Vineyard of the Lord: The Beginnings of the AME Church in Florida, 1865–1895.* Gainesville: University of Florida Press, 2001.

Roediger, David R. *The Wages of Whiteness: Race and the Making of the American Working Class.* Rev. ed. New York: Verso Press, 1991.

Rudy, Willis S. *The College of the City of New York: A History, 1847–1947.* New York: City College Press, 1949.

Sacks, Marcy S. *Before Harlem: The Black Experience in New York City before World War I.* Philadelphia: University of Pennsylvania Press, 2006.

Salvatore, Nick. *Eugene V. Debs: Citizen and Socialist.* Urbana: University of Illinois Press, 1982.

Schultz, Kevin M. "The FEPC and the Legacy of the Labor-Based Civil Rights Movement of the 1940s." *Labor History* 49, no. 1 (February 2008): 71–92.

Schultz, Mark. *The Rural Face of White Supremacy: Beyond Jim Crow.* Urbana: University of Illinois Press, 2005.

Senechal, Roberta. *The Sociogenesis of a Race Riot: Springfield, Illinois, in 1908.* Urbana: University of Illinois Press, 1990.

Sernett, Milton C. *Black Religion and American Evangelicalism: White Protestants, Plantation Missions, and the Flowering of Negro Christianity, 1787–1865.* Metuchen, N.J.: Scarecrow Press, 1975.

Sewell, Tony. *Garvey's Children: The Legacy of Marcus Garvey.* Trenton, N.J.: Africa World Press, 1990.

Shannon, David A. *The Socialist Party of America.* New York: Macmillan, 1955.

Sitkoff, Harvard. *The Struggle for Black Equality.* Rev ed. New York: Hill and Wang, 1993.

Spear, Allan H. *Black Chicago: The Making of a Negro Ghetto, 1890–1920.* Chicago: University of Chicago Press, 1967.

Stein, Judith. *The World of Marcus Garvey: Race and Class in Modern Society.* Baton Rouge: Louisiana State University Press, 1986.

Stephens, Michelle Ann. *Black Empire: The Masculine Global Imaginary of Caribbean Intellectuals in the United States, 1914–1962.* Durham, N.C.: Duke University Press, 2005.

Sugrue, Thomas J. "Affirmative Action from below: Civil Rights, the Building Trades, and the Politics of Racial Equality in the Urban North, 1945–1969." *Journal of American History* 91, no. 1 (June 2004): 145–73.

———. *Sweet Land of Liberty: The Forgotten Struggle for Civil Rights in the North.* New York: Random House, 2008.

Taylor, Cynthia. *A. Philip Randolph: The Religious Journey of an African American Labor Leader.* New York: New York University Press, 2006.

Thomas, Cornell, and William Vanderhoof. "Charles Eliot of Harvard, 'The Elective System.'" In *Watersheds in Higher Education,* ed. James J. Van Patten. Lewiston, N.Y.: Edwin Mellen Press, 1997.

Thompson, Heather Ann. *Whose Detroit? Politics, Labor, and Race in a Modern American City.* Ithaca, N.Y.: Cornell University Press, 2001.

Tolnay, Stewart Emory, and E. M. Beck. *A Festival of Violence: An Analysis of Southern Lynchings, 1882–1930.* Urbana: University of Illinois Press, 1995.

Tripp, Anne Huber. *The I. W. W. and the Paterson Silk Strike of 1913.* Urbana: University of Illinois Press, 1987.

Trotter, Joe William, Jr. *Black Milwaukee: The Making of an Industrial Proletariat, 1915–45.* Urbana: University of Illinois Press, 1985.

Turner, Joyce Moore. *Caribbean Crusaders and the Harlem Renaissance.* Urbana: University of Illinois Press, 2005.

Van Deburg, William L. *A New Day in Babylon: The Black Power Movement and American Culture, 1965–1975.* Chicago: University of Chicago Press, 1993.

Visser 't Hooft, Willem A. *The Background of the Social Gospel in America.* St. Louis, Mo.: Bethany Press, 1963.

Walker, Clarence E. *A Rock in a Weary Land: The African Methodist Episcopal Church during the Civil War and Reconstruction.* Baton Rouge: Louisiana State University Press, 1982.

Washburn, Patrick S. *The African American Newspaper: Voice of Freedom.* Evanston, Ill.: Northwestern University Press, 2006.

Watson, Steven. *The Harlem Renaissance: Hub of African-American Culture, 1920–1930.* New York: Pantheon Books, 1995.

Weinstein, James. *The Decline of Socialism in America, 1912–1925.* New York: Monthly Review Press, 1967.

Weisenfeld, Judith. "The Harlem YWCA and the Secular City, 1904–1945." *Journal of Women's History* 6, no. 3 (Fall 1994): 62–79.

Weiss, Nancy J. *Farewell to the Party of Lincoln: Black Politics in the Age of FDR.* Princeton, N.J.: Princeton University Press, 1983.

Westmeyer, Paul. *A History of American Higher Education.* Springfield, Ill.: Charles C. Thomas, 1985.

Williams, Gilbert Anthony. *The Christian Recorder, Newspaper of the African Methodist Episcopal Church: History of a Forum for Ideas, 1854–1902.* Jefferson, N.C.: McFarland, 1996.

Wills, David. "Reverdy C. Ransom: The Making of an A.M.E. Bishop." In *Black Apostles: Afro-American Clergy Confront the Twentieth Century,* ed. Randall K. Burkett and Richard Newman. Boston: G. K. Hall, 1978.

Wintz, Cary D., ed. *African American Political Thought, 1890–1930: Washington, Du Bois, Garvey, and Randolph.* Armonk, N.Y.: M.E. Sharpe, 1996.

Woodson, Carter G. *The History of the Negro Church.* Washington, D.C.: Associated Publishers, 1921.

Zieger, Robert H. *The CIO, 1935–1955.* Chapel Hill: University of North Carolina Press, 1995.

Zunz, Olivier. *Why the American Century?* Chicago: University of Chicago Press, 1998.

Miscellaneous Documents

United States Department of Commerce, Bureau of the Census. *Negroes in the United States, 1920–32.* Washington, D.C.: U.S. Government Printing Office, 1935.

Index

Addams, Jane, 35, 39

AFL (American Federation of Labor): and Brotherhood of Sleeping Car Porters, 125, 136–39, 159; class obligations of, 100; condemnation of racial wage differential, 139; discriminatory practices of, 79, 105, 113, 128–29, 138–39, 158–63; endorsement of anti-lynching legislation, 139; and FEPC, 174; versus IWW, 112; and socialism, 70–71

African Americans: and the AFL, 79, 100, 105, 113, 128–29, 138–39, 158–63; anger and disillusionment of, 94, 145–49, 164–65, 195; in the armed services, xv, 87–91, 94, 164, 172–73, 185–96, *illus.*; black unionism, 139, 225n16; class solidarity, 152–54; and communism, 151–52, 211n49; and the Democratic Party, xv, 177, 190; discrimination in war industry jobs, 163–65, 169–70, 174; exclusion from higher-paying jobs, 146–48; FEPC representation, 175; and the Great Depression, 72, 119, 146; in Harlem, 47–54; history, importance of, 5–8, 75–76; and industrial unionism, 113; and labor law, xv, 135; middle-class and professional, 40; northern migration, xv, 39–40, 49–53; paperboys, 20; political leverage, xiv–xv, 168–69, 171, 177, 190, 222n38; postwar expectations, 92–93; racial pride, 4–8, 10, 22, 31, 51, 143; and racial self-sufficiency, 80–81, 99, 127–28, 141, 154–55, 166–67; Randolph's plan for future, 191–92; and the Republican Party, 98–99; social, economic and political justice as goals of, xii–xiii, 54–58, 98–100, 126–39, 157, 161, 197–200; and the Socialist Party, 70–73, 78–80; and union membership, 68, 111. *See also* black unionism; Jim Crow; New Negroes

African Blood Brotherhood, 54, 78

African heritage, pride in, 31

African Methodist Episcopal Church. *See* AME Church

African Methodist Episcopal Zion Church, 42–43

"Afro-Americans and Radical Politics" (Moore), 74

Allen, Richard, 7, 25–26

Allen Christian Endeavor Society of Bethel AME Church (NYC), 59, 62

A.M.E. Church Review (AME Church journal), 4, 6

AME Church, xvi, 9–12, 15, 17, 28–38, 43–44. *See also specific churches*

American Communist Party, 114, 150

American Federation of Labor. *See* AFL

"Americanism" (*Messenger*), 87

"American Lawlessness" (*Messenger*), 90

American Negro Labor Congress, 114

"Analysis of Negro Patriotism, An" (Colson), 89–90

Anderson, Charles W., 94

anti-West Indian sentiment, 114
"Appeal to Negro Workers" (Debs), 73
"Are Communists a Threat to Democratic Organizations?" (Randolph), 150
"Are Negroes American Citizens?" (Randolph), 186
armed services: discrimination in, xv, 87–91, 94, 164, 185–96, *illus.;* racial equality in, 172–73
Armed Services Committee, 187–88, 193
association, freedom of, 158

Baptist Young People's Union of Mount Olivet Baptist Church (NYC), 59
Beecher, Henry Ward, 33–34
Berger, Victor, 69–70
Bethel AME Church (Chicago, Ill.), 39
Bethel AME Church (NYC), 60–61
Bethel Methodist Church (Philadelphia, Pa.), 26
Biddle, Francis, 176, 180
Bismarck Tribune, 180
black church, 205n54. *See also* AME Church
black nationalism, 74
black radicalism, 53
black unionism, 105–6, 126, 128–29, 135, 139, 225n16
Black World, xviii
Boston Citizens' Committee, 127
boycotts, 97, 143–47
Briggs, Cyril, xi, 54, 74, 78, 81, 114
Brotherhood of Labor, 59
Brotherhood of Locomotive Firemen and Engineers, 181
Brotherhood of Sleeping Car Porters: AFL affiliation, 125, 136–39, 159; appeals to Federal agencies, 124–26, 129–35, 136; background information, 119–24; as black union, 105; challenges in organizing, 114–15; and communism, 151–52; and economic justice, 100; educational meetings, 123–24; integration of unions, 128–29; and interracial class cooperation, 55; lessons learned, xiv-xv, 168, 171, 189; Negro Labor Conference sponsorship, 140–41; ongoing struggles, 143; photographs of, *illus.;* and race versus class consciousness, 126–29; recognition of, 125–26, 134
Brotherhood of Sleeping Car Porters' Protective Union, 120

Brown, Theodore E., 159
Bunch, Ralph, 141
Bushnell, Horace, 33–34
Byrnes, James F., 92

"Call to Negro America to March on Washington . . ." (Randolph), 168
Calvinism, 33
capitalism. *See* industrial capitalism; welfare capitalism
"Challenge to Complete an Uncompleted Revolution for Full Freedom" (Randolph), 198
Chicago Commons, 39
childhood lessons of courage 7, 10, 18–19, 21–22
Christian principles, appeals to, 188
Christian Recorder, 4, 6, 27–28, 32
CIO (Congress of Industrial Organizations), 175
City College of New York, 53, 62–67
civil disobedience, xv, xvi, 110, 186–96, 192. *See also* nonviolence
civil rights movement, x, 185, 198–200, 225n16
Clarke, Edward Young, 76
class consciousness: and colonialism in Africa, 68; and interracial class cooperation, 55, 73, 152–54; and the New Negroes, 54–55; and organized labor, 111–14; and racial consciousness, xiii-xiv, 40, 156–63, 185, 216n3; and racial discrimination, 72, 126–29, 139–42; and racial justice, 99–100; Randolph's awareness of, 48
class solidarity, 55, 73, 101–9, 152–54. *See also* unions
CME (Colored Methodist Episcopal) Church, 42
Cohen, Morris R., 66–67
Cold War, 198
collective action: against businesses that discriminated, 143–47; collective bargaining, xv, 131, 134, 157; and New Negroes, 97; and nonviolence, 31; to pressure government, xv-xvi; as response to racial violence, 10, 22–23; roots of Randolph's beliefs, 110; to support FEPC, 186. *See also* civil disobedience; class solidarity; March on Washington Movement (MOWM)
colonialism in Africa, 68, 74

Colored Methodist Episcopal (CME) Church, 42

Colson, William, 89–90

Committee Against Jim Crow in Military Service and Training, 186, 188–91, 193, 196

communism, xiii, 53, 114, 149–52, 211n49

community study/discussion groups, 60–61, 77, 89

conductors, Pullman, 129–31

Congress of Industrial Organizations (CIO), 175

Cox, Courtland, x

"Crisis of Struggle for Civil Rights and Civil Liberties" (Randolph), 198

Crosswaith, Frank R., 54–56, 75, 93, 140–47, 214n8, illus.

Crusader (Briggs's journal), 54, 93

Cullen, Frederick, 59

Davis, John P., 141

Debs, Eugene, 53, 60, 63, 71–74

defense contracting, 163–65, 169–70, 174

democracy: and civil disobedience, 188; and civil rights, 161, 196–200; democratic socialism, 57–58, 97–100; industrial, 142, 144, 152; at odds with racial discrimination, 87–92, 169, 179; participatory, xii–xiii, 57, 150–52, 197

Democratic Party, xv, 28, 104, 167, 177–78, 190

democratic socialism, 57–58, 97–100

"Deportation of Agitators, The" (Messenger), 103

DePriest, Oscar, 133–34

discrimination. See government-sanctioned discrimination; racial discrimination

disfranchisement, 88, 91–92

Domingo, W. A., 37–38, 60–62

draft, military, 187–88, 190–96

dual unionism, 70–71

Du Bois, W. E. B.: on African Americans in the armed services, 90; community study/discussion groups, 77; criticism of middle-class and professional African Americans, 40; and Debs, 72–73; influence on Randolph, 4, 48–49, 53; on racial discrimination, 72; "Returning Soldiers," 94; Souls of Black Folk, The, 28, 72; split with Socialist Party, 81

Eastman, Joseph, 133

Eastman, Max, 78

economic justice, xiv, 101, 146–49, 157–61, 179–85

"Economics and Sociology of the Negro Problem, The" (Randolph and Owen), 78

"Economics of Black America, The" (Randolph), 160

economic theory, classical, 35–37

editorial cartoons, 108–9

education, importance of, 4–6, 20–21, 32, 38, 142

Ely, Richard T., 36, 65

Emancipator, 61

Emergency Transportation Act (1933), 133–34

Employee Representation Plan (of Pullman Company), 120–23, 125, 130–33

Episcopal Church, 26

Epworth League of Salem Methodist Episcopal Church (NYC), 59

Espionage Act (1917), 67

executive orders banning discrimination: in the armed forces, x, 195–96; in war industry jobs, x, 169–74, 176–77, 180, 222n24, 225n17

Fair Employment Practice Commission (FEPC), xiv, xvii, 157, 174–84, 185–86, 190, illus.

fascism, 161

Fifteenth Amendment, 93

Fifteenth Regiment of New York National Guard, 47

"Fight of the Negro Worker, The" (Messenger), 106

Finley, John Huston, 65

First African Church of St. Thomas (Philadelphia, Pa.), 26

Four Freedoms, 173, 184

Fourteenth Amendment, 93

Free African Society, 25–26

Freeman, Joseph, 77

Friends of Negro Freedom, 77

Gaines, William, 42

Gandhi, Mahatma, 192

Garvey, Marcus: campaign against imperialism, 62; and Clarke, 76; in Harlem, 47, 75; on independent African state, 76; on political potential of African Americans, 209n58; race-first appeal, 68; and racial self-sufficiency, 80–81; Randolph's opposition to, 76–77, 81, 114

"Garvey Must Go" campaign, 68, 76–77, 81

ghettoes, 99

Gladden, Washington, 33–34, 36–37, 39

God, question of existence of, 5, 15, 19

Goldstein, Israel, 182

Gompers, Samuel, 128

government-sanctioned discrimination: in the armed services, xv, 164, 186–96, *illus.*; and war industry jobs, 163–66, 169–70, 181–83

Granger, Lester, 165, 180–82

Great Depression, 72, 119, 146

Green, Lucille E., 59–60

Green, William, 136–37

Hall, James, 42

Harlem, N.Y., 47–54, 60–62, 144–49

Harlem Labor Committee, 55, 93, 147

Harlem Renaissance, 51, 58, 143

Harlem street corner lectures, 61, 75

Harrison, Hubert, xi, 54, 61, 75, 77, 81

Haywood, William "Big Bill," 63, 70, 79

Headwaiters and Sidewaiters Society of Greater New York, 78, 86

Hebrew Trades, 154

"High Points of Deep Interest in the Pullman Porters' Struggle" (Boston Citizens' Committee), 127

Hill, T. Arnold, 164

Hillman, Sidney, 172, 174

Hillquit, Morris, 53, 68–70, 79

"History of Negro Liberation" (Moore), 75

Hood, James, 43

Hotel Messenger, 86. See also *Messenger, The*

Houston, Charles H., 195–96

"How to Stop Lynching" (*Messenger*), 95

Hull House, 39

"Hun in America, The" (*Messenger*), 87–91

Hylan, John F., 68

ICSS (Institutional Church and Social Settlement), 40–41, 205n54

"If We Must Die" (McKay), 94

"If We Must Die" (*Messenger*), 94

Independent Political Council, 89

industrial capitalism: and civil rights, 158–63; class solidarity as answer to, 101–9; as enemy of social, economic and political justice, 56, 58; exploitation of racial tensions, 73, 80, 103–5, 106–9, 158–59; and labor organization, 57; profit motive of, 107; Randolph's criticism of, xii, 54, 56–57, 85–86; and the social gospel, 35–37; socialism as answer to, 69–70

industrial democracy, 142, 144, 152

Industrial Relations Commission, 129

industrial sabotage, 70, 79, 113

Industrial Workers of the World (IWW), 63, 70–71, 79

Institute for Social Study, 77

Institutional Church and Social Settlement (ICSS), 40–41, 205n54

Intercollegiate Socialist Society, 63

interracial class cooperation, 55, 73, 152–54. *See also* class solidarity

Interstate Commerce Commission, 124, 133

IWW (Industrial Workers of the World), 63, 70–71, 79

"Jacksonville Negroes Boycott Big White Insurance Company" (*Messenger*), 97

Jewish workers, 111

Jim Crow: in the armed services, xv, 74, 87–91, 94, 164, 185–96, *illus.*; in the South, 4, 7, 18, 22, 51; unions as means to eliminate, 159. *See also* disfranchisement

Johnson, J. Rosamond, 47

Johnson, James Weldon, 47, 49, 53

Joint Committee on National Recovery, 141

Jones, Absalom, 25–26

journalists, radical, 87

Kelly, G. A., 132

Kennedy, John F., ix

King, Martin Luther, Jr., 199

Knox, Frank, 172–73

"Ku Klux Klan—How to Fight It, The" (*Messenger*), 96

"Labor and Lynching" (*Messenger*), 100

labor law and African American workers, xv, 135–36

labor relations, industrial, 36, 52. *See also* industrial capitalism

labor unrest, 39
La Guardia, Fiorello, 144, 170, 172–73, *illus.*
Laidler, Harry W., 140
Lancaster, Roy, 122
League for Non-Violent Civil Disobedience Against Military Segregation, 193
League of Darker Races, 68, 89
Lewis, John, ix–x
liberation theology, xvi, 27–33
Liberty League, 61
Lilienthal, David E., 132
lobbying campaigns, xv, 191
L'Ouverture, Toussaint, 7
Lovestone, Jay, 62
loyalty, 91–92
Lyceum of Saint Mark's Methodist Church (NYC), 59
Lynch, James, 42
Lynch, Walter F., 132
"Lynching: Capitalism Its Cause, Socialism Its Cure" (*Messenger*), 106
lynchings, 8–10, 91, 95, 107

maids, Pullman, 121–22. *See also* Brotherhood of Sleeping Car Porters
"Making the World Safe for Democracy" (*Messenger*), 87
manhood, concept of, xi, 73–74
"March of Industrial Unionism, The" (*Messenger*), 111
March on Washington (1963), ix–x, 165
March on Washington Committee (MOWC), 165, 167, 175–76
March on Washington Movement (MOWM), xv, 157, 163–74, 190
Marrow, Edwin P., *illus.*
Marxism, 75–76
material wealth, 14, 17
Mayor's Commission on Conditions in Harlem, 144–49
Mays, Robert L., 124
McKay, Claude, 94
McNutt, Paul V., 178–82
Meany, George, 139
Messenger, The: on African Americans and the Socialist Party, 78; anti-Pullman propaganda campaign, 123; on class solidarity, 101–9; on common goals of black and white workers, 80; on communism, 150;

editorial cartoons, 108–9; founding of, 37, 54, 60, 85–87; on New Negroes, 94–100; photographs of, *illus.*; as platform for Randolph's message, xvii-xviii; on postwar expectations of African Americans, 92–93; on treatment of African American soldiers, 87; on the U.S. Constitution, 93. *See also specific articles*
Methodist Church, 26, 43
Milgrim, Morris, 182
military draft, 187–88, 190–96
Moore, Fred R., 123
Moore, Richard B., xi, 54, 60–61, 74–78, 81, 114
MOWC (March on Washington Committee), 165, 167, 175–76
MOWM (March on Washington Movement), xiv, 157, 163–74, 190

National Association for the Promotion of Labor Unionism among Negroes, 93, 103, 214n8
National Council for a Permanent FEPC, 183–84
National Independent Political Council, 60–61
National Industrial Recovery Act (1933), 133–34
National Negro Congress (NNC), 141–42, 155, *illus.*
National Negro Congress News, 141
National Railroad Administration, 120
National Urban League, 181–82
Nearing, Scott, 78, 89
Negro, use of term, 31
"Negro, The War, and the Future of Democracy, The" (Randolph), 161
"Negro and the Next Five Years, The" (Randolph), 160
"Negroes and Race Riots" (Randolph), 158–63
"Negro in Public Utilities, The" (*Messenger*), 92
"Negro in the American Democracy, The" (Randolph), 190
Negro Labor Committee (NLC), 142, 214n8
Negro Labor Conference (1931), 140–41
Negro Labor Conference (1935), 152–54
Negro Voice, 93

"Negro Workers: The A.F. of L. or I.W.W."
(*Messenger*), 106–7
Negro World, 76
"New Crowd—A New Negro, A" (Randolph), 55, 97, 99
New Crowd Negroes, 97–100
New Deal, xv, 164, 222n38
New Hope AME Church (Jacksonville, FL), 9
New Negroes, 51, 54–55, 58, 74, 80–81, 93–100
"New Negro—What is He, The?" (*Messenger*), 98
New York Times, 187
Niagara Movement, 40
NLC (Negro Labor Committee), 142, 214n8
NNC (National Negro Congress), 141–42, 155, *illus.*
nonviolence, 31, 96. *See also* civil disobedience

Office of Production Management, 174
"Open Letter to the Union League Club of New York, An" (*Messenger*), 91
Order of Sleeping Car Conductors, 130, 137–38
organized labor. *See* unions
"Our Reason for Being" (*Messenger*), 93, 103
"Outline on the Negro Questions" (Moore), 76
Owen, Chandler, 54, 60, 67, 78, 86. See also *Messenger, The*

Paris Peace Conference, 68, 74
Parliament of Religions (1893), 39
participatory democracy, xii–xiii, 57, 150–52, 197
People's Council of America for Peace and Democracy, 88
People's Educational Forum, 77
personal tenacity, 14, 18, 20
Philadelphia Inquirer, 179
Pittsburgh Post-Gazette, 179
political forums, 89. *See also* community study/discussion groups
political leverage of African Americans, xiv–xv, 168–69, 171, 177, 190, 222n38
political militancy and religious faith, 27–33, 29
Poor People's Campaign, 199

porters, Pullman, 121–22. *See also* Brotherhood of Sleeping Car Porters
poverty and racism, 39
"Problems of Peace and Democracy" (Randolph), 196
"Problems of Race and Imperialism" (Freeman), 77
"Prof. Harry H. Jones - The Crisis in Negro Leadership" (*Messenger*), 92
profit motive, 107
"Pro-Germanism among Negroes" (*Messenger*), 91
Protestantism and the social gospel, 33–34
publicity campaigns, 191
Pullman Company, 105, 120–23, 128–31, 132. *See also* Brotherhood of Sleeping Car Porters
Pullman Strike (1894), 128
purchasing power, 109–10

race and class consciousness, xiii–xiv, 40, 156–63, 185, 216n3
racial discrimination: by the AFL, 79, 105, 113, 128–29, 138–39, 158–63; African American anger and disillusionment, 94, 145–49, 164–65, 195; in the armed services, xv, 87–91, 94, 164, 172–73, 185–96, *illus.*; and class consciousness, 72, 126–29, 139–42; in the Democratic Party, 167; in the draft system, 187–88, 190–96; government-sanctioned, xv, 163–66, 169–70, 181–83, 186–96, *illus.*; and Harlem riot, 145–48; and labor unrest, 39; moral and religious falsity of, 28; at odds with democracy, 87–92, 169, 179; Randolph's continuing plan to fight, 191–92; and social justice, 86; in unions, 102–3, 158–63; whites excluded from MOWM, 167. *See also* executive orders
"Racially Segregated Unions" (Randolph), 163
racial militancy and unionization, 58
racial prejudice and class solidarity, 103
racial pride, 4–8, 10, 22, 31, 51, 143. *See also* New Negroes
racial self-sufficiency, 80–81, 99, 127–28, 154–55, 166–67
racial violence: between black and white workers, 52; collective action as response to, 10, 22–23; Harlem riot, 144–49; and

labor organization, 98; and militancy of New Negroes, 95–97; race riots (1919), 107–8; self-defense against, 95–97; Springfield, Ill. riot (1908), 220n36; at turn of the century, 8–10

racism, 39, 75

railroads, discrimination hearings, 178, 180–83

Railway Labor Act (1926), 124–26, 129–34

Railway Men's International Benevolent Industrial Association, 120

Ramsey, John, 60

Randolph, A. Philip: childhood, xvi, 3–8, 21–25; early jobs of, 21, 50; education of, 62–64, 66–67; family influence on, 3–21; in Harlem, 47–54, 75; influence on civil rights movement, x, 185, 198–200; performing arts interests, 49, 58–59, 64; photographs of, *illus.*; political campaigns of, 71; political education of, 63–64; radicalization of, 53–62; treason accusations, 187, 194; union organizing in Virginia, 68. See also *Messenger, The; specific articles and speeches*

Randolph, Elizabeth, 9, 12, 14–18, 31

Randolph, James, Jr., 18–21

Randolph, James, Sr., 3–15, 17, 31

Randolph, Lucille E. (née Green), 59–60, *illus.*

Randolph, Virginia D., 100

Rand School of Social Science, 78

Ransom, Reverdy C., 38–41, 59, 60–61

Rauschenbusch, Walter, 33–34

"Reasons Why White and Black Workers Should Combine in Labor Unions" (*Messenger*), 102

Reconstruction, 6–7, 43

religious faith, xiii, 4–5, 27–33, 36, 188, 192. *See also* AME church

Republican Party, 98–99, 104

"Returning Soldiers" (Du Bois), 94

Revels, Willis, 42

Reynolds, Grant, 187

riots, 107–8, 144–49, 220n36

"Role of the Negro Worker in the American Trade Union Movement" (Randolph), 161

Roosevelt, Eleanor, 170, 223n48, *illus.*

Roosevelt, Franklin D., 169, 171–74, 176–78

Rosenberg, Anna, 175

Russian Revolution, 96, 114

Rustin, Bayard, ix–x, 185, 200

sabotage, industrial, 70, 79, 113

scabs, 102–3, 108

self-defense against racial violence, 95–97

self-esteem, 4–8, 10, 17–18, 22, 24–28, 31

self-improvement, 32

self-reliance, 80–81, 99, 127–28, 141, 154–55, 166–67

settlement house movement, 35, 39–40

Shakespeare, William, 58, 64

sharecropping system, 13

"Should Black Workers Join White Unions" (*Messenger*), 104

Simmons, F.L., 132

"Skeleton Brief of the Case in Support of the Demands of the Brotherhood of Sleeping Car Porters," 129, 131

Slawson, John, 164

social gospel, 33–37, 39–40, 205n54

socialism: and AFL, 70–71; as answer to industrial capitalism, 69–70; as answer to poverty and discrimination, 113–14; at City College of New York, 63; democratic, 57–58, 97–100; influence on Randolph, 37; in New York City, 53; and World War I, 74

Socialist Party of America, 69–81

social justice: African American demands for, xii–xiii, 54–58, 126–39, 157, 161; and African Americans in the armed services, xv, 87–91, 94, 164, 185–96, *illus.*; as aim of New Negroes, 98–100; and the AME Church, 29; Crosswaith on, 142–43; and economic justice, xii–xiiv, 101, 149, 157, 185, 197–200; and industrial capitalism, 56, 58; and industrial democracy, 142, 144, 152; and race and class issues, 40, 86; and Randolph's childhood influences, 22; and universal human rights, 85

Souls of Black Folk, The (Du Bois), 28, 72

Southern Carriers Committee, 181

Southern Democrats, xv, 28, 177–78, 190

Southern Tenant Farmers Union, 153

speech, freedom of, 158

"Spirit of Human Rights, The" (Randolph), 198

St. George's Methodist Episcopal Church (Philadelphia, Pa.), 25

"Story of the Brotherhood of Sleeping Car Porters, The" (Randolph), 134

street corner lectures, Harlem, 61, 75

strikebreakers, 102–3, 108

strikes, 63, 110, 128, 131
syndicalism, 113

"talented tenth," 48, 53
Tanner, Benjamin Tucker, 28–32
"Task of Local 8, The" (*Messenger*), 105
Taylor, Graham, 35, 39
Terms of Peace and the Darker Races (Randolph and Owen), 86
textile strikes, 63
"Thanksgiving" (*Messenger*), 95
Thomas, Norman, 78, 89, 192
Thomas, William, 49–50
Thurman, Wallace, *illus.*
tipping, 133
totalitarian governments, 63, 161
Totten, Ashley, 122–23
Trade Union Committee for Organizing Negro Workers (TUC), 55, 140–41
Transportation Act (1920), 120
Truman, Harry S., 195–96
Truth, Sojourner, 7
Truth about Lynching, The (Randolph and Owen), 86
TUC (Trade Union Committee for Organizing Negro Workers), 55, 140–41
Turner, Henry McNeal, 30–31, 42–44

UNIA (Universal Negro Improvement Association), 76, 80–81, 143
unions: African American membership in, 55, 68, 111; black unionism, 100, 105–6, 126, 128–29, 135, 139, 225n16; and class solidarity, 101–9; corruption within, 86; discriminatory practices of, 102–3, 158–63; dual unionism, 70–71; economic, racial and social justice through, 161; effectiveness of, 110–14; and industrial capitalism, 57, 86; industrial unionism, 112–13; interracial, 100, 103–4, 128–29, 214n8; and Jim crow elimination, 159; racial tensions, 158–59; radicalism of, 98. *See also specific unions*
United Hebrew Trades, 111
Universal Negro Improvement Association. *See* UNIA
U.S. Congress, 134–35

U.S. Constitution, 93
U.S. Mediation Board, 129

Vesey, Denmark, 43

wage scale, 109–10, 112, 129–30, 133
Walker, A'Lelia, 47, 59
Walker, C. J., 59
Ware, Walter, 94–95
War Manpower Commission, 177–82
Washington, Booker T., 4
Washington, March on. *See* March on Washington Movement (MOWM)
Washington Post, 179
Weaver, Elisha, 27
Webster, Milton P., 133
"Weeping for the Poor White Folks" (Randolph), 166
Welcome, Ernest T., 59
welfare capitalism, 120–23, 216n8
West Indian radicals, 114
"When Labor is Awakened" (*Messenger*), 102
"When They Get Together They'll Dump Us Off" (*Messenger*), 109
White, Walter, 164–65, 170–72, 180, 182, 194
White House meetings, 164
white supremacy, 4–8, 27
women, 98, 206n60
women's suffrage movement, 57
Women's Trade Union League, 154
"Working for Workers" (Crosswaith), 214n8
Works Progress Administration, 142
world opinion on discrimination, 191
"World Problems of Race" (Harrison), 77
World War I, 67–68, 74
World War II, 159. *see also* government-sanctioned discrimination
Wright, R. R., Jr., 38

Ye Friends of Shakespeare, 58–59
Young Communist League, 149
Young Liberators, 149
"Young Negro Dies Like Man" (*Messenger*), 94–95
YWCA (of Harlem), 206n60

THE NEW BLACK STUDIES SERIES

Beyond Bondage: Free Women of Color in the Americas—*Edited by David Barry Gaspar and Darlene Clark Hine*

The Early Black History Movement, Carter G. Woodson, and Lorenzo Johnston Greene—*Pero Gaglo Dagbovie*

"Baad Bitches" and Sassy Supermamas: Black Power Action Films—*Stephane Dunn*

Black Maverick: T. R. M. Howard's Fight for Civil Rights and Economic Power —*David T. Beito and Linda Royster Beito*

Beyond the Black Lady: Sexuality and the New African American Middle Class —*Lisa B. Thompson*

Extending the Diaspora: New Histories of Black People—*Dawne Y. Curry, Eric D. Duke, and Marshanda A. Smith*

Activist Sentiments: Reading Black Women in the Nineteenth Century —*P. Gabrielle Foreman*

Black Europe and the African Diaspora—*Edited by Darlene Clark Hine, Trica Danielle Keaton, and Stephen Small*

Freeing Charles: The Struggle to Free a Slave on the Eve of the Civil War —*Scott Christianson*

African American History Reconsidered—*Pero Gaglo Dagbovie*

Freud Upside Down: African American Literature and Psychoanalytic Culture —*Badia Sahar Ahad*

A. Philip Randolph and the Struggle for Civil Rights—*Cornelius L. Bynum*

CORNELIUS L. BYNUM is an assistant professor
of history at Purdue University.

The University of Illinois Press
is a founding member of the
Association of American University Presses.

———————————————————

Composed in 10.5/13 Adobe Minion Pro
with Frutiger display
by Jim Proefrock
at the University of Illinois Press
Manufactured by Sheridan Books, Inc.

University of Illinois Press
1325 South Oak Street
Champaign, IL 61820-6903
www.press.uillinois.edu